TRIBES WITHOUT RULERS

TRIBES WITHOUT RULERS
Studies in African Segmentary Systems

LAURA BOHANNAN   JEAN BUXTON
GODFREY LIENHARDT   EDWARD WINTER
DAVID TAIT   JOHN MIDDLETON

Edited by
John Middleton and David Tait

Preface by E. E. Evans-Pritchard

LONDON
ROUTLEDGE & KEGAN PAUL LTD

First published 1958
© *by Routledge & Kegan Paul Ltd*
Broadway House, 68–74 Carter Lane
London, E.C.4
Printed in Great Britain
by Lowe & Brydone (Printers) Ltd
London
Second impression 1964
Third impression 1967

CONTENTS

v

FOREWORD

THIS book was planned as a successor to Fortes' and Evans-Pritchard's *African Political Systems*. That volume, Evans-Pritchard's *The Nuer*, Fortes' *The Dynamics of Clanship among the Tallensi*, Forde's papers on the Yakö and a few other short essays provided a basis for the study of the politics of African peoples, and subsequent work in this field has been an elaboration and refinement of that of the authors of those books. However, it seemed clear that the simple classification of political systems made in *African Political Systems*, which we took for our starting point, had become out of date. We decided to make a more refined terminology and classification, and also in an introduction to attempt to consider some of the basic assumptions and findings of the research done in Africa since 1940. This volume consists of six essays on the political systems of African peoples, and an introduction based largely upon these essays.

The book is limited to consideration of what have been called segmentary lineage systems as found in six politically uncentralized societies in Africa. The choice was made from the work being done at the time: we realize that the geographical spread of the six societies is hardly very wide, and we have no example of matrilineal systems. We wished to study only those societies without centralized political authority and with segmentary lineage structures, and to include enough variants of this type to permit the distinction of a number of sub-types. There is, of course, comparative material for societies in other parts of the world, such as Firth's *We, the Tikopia*. But we decided not to consider material from outside Negro Africa.

The production of this book has taken a long time. It was planned in 1953. David Tait was killed in Accra in March, 1955,

vii

after all the contributions had been received and the main part of the Introduction prepared. Since then I have completed the editing in the way we had originally planned. His death is a great loss, and I wish to pay tribute to him as a friend as well as collaborator.

Professor I. Schapera has guided the book's production from the beginning; Professor Evans-Pritchard has also kept an eye on its general progress and has kindly written a Preface. Among those others who have read the Introduction and given advice and encouragement in many ways are Dr. J. H. M. Beattie, Dr. Paul Bohannan, Dr. Mary Douglas, Dr. L. A. Fallers, Professor Daryll Forde, Professor M. Fortes, Mr. R. Horton, Dr. Phyllis Kaberry, Dr. R. G. Lienhardt and Dr. E. H. Winter.

London, 1957   JOHN MIDDLETON

PREFACE

By E. E. Evans-Pritchard

A BOOK of this kind serves several useful purposes, as Professor Fortes and I found when we edited a somewhat similar book, *African Political Systems*, in 1940. Perhaps its chief value is that a number of anthropologists give us concise accounts of the main political and other institutions of the peoples they have studied within a reasonable term of years after their researches have been completed. We only too often have to wait many years to learn about the chief institutions of a people when these are presented in a series of monographs. However detailed may be an author's account of some particular topic, we cannot entirely assess its significance until other features of the society are known, especially its main structural features; and these may not be known till, years later, other volumes appear. My own case is a sad warning. I began my study of Zande social life in 1927 and published a book on one aspect of it, on witchcraft, oracles and magic, in 1937. It is now 1957, and I have not yet published an account of their political institutions, their family and kin activities, their modes of livelihood, etc. In this case it is a mitigating circumstance that others have treated these subjects in their writings; but this circumstance is often lacking. Then death may intervene, and we never get a rounded account. The late Professor Malinowski gave us some brilliant reports on certain activities of the Trobriand Islanders, but we are still in the dark about many features of, for example, their chieftainship and their kinship system.

This collection of essays will also prove to be a valuable textbook for students in anthropological departments in this country and elsewhere, especially in America, where interest in African ethnography is rapidly growing. They have here in a single volume an outline of the social structures of six African societies; and if this book is taken together with *African Political Systems*, fourteen African societies. The student can by reading these two books get a very good idea of what African societies are like, those described being representative of most types of African society and, since they are widely distributed throughout the continent, representative of most distinctive forms of African culture. The layman, or someone working in a cognate discipline, who can hardly be expected to read numerous and lengthy anthropological monographs on African peoples, can by reading a book of this kind skim the cream of recent research and get an idea also of its methods, for these essays also illustrate the advance anthropology has made in recent years in method and theory.

This advance in a new generation of anthropologists might be taken for granted, but I think it is excellently brought to notice by a book in which a number of the younger anthropologists who have recently completed field studies treat a single topic within the general structural framework, and the editors then point to what conclusions, if any, can be drawn from the material organized by each essayist on much the same lines, and therefore easily comparable. The subject treated here may be said to be chiefly the reciprocal relations between descent groups and local and political groups, between lineages and clans and local and political communities. This is a subject which has, of course, long interested students of the simpler societies. Some excellent descriptions, for example, of lineage systems, though not so named, are to be found in Maine's *Ancient Law* (1861), Fustel de Coulanges' *La Cité Antique* (1864), Robertson Smith's *Kinship and Marriage in Early Arabia* (1885), and Pedersen's *History of Israel* (1920), to mention only a few classics; but I think that one of the first systematic field studies of a lineage system was my own study of the Nuer of the Anglo-Egyptian Sudan, which began in 1929. A more prolonged and detailed study was Professor Fortes' investigation of the Tallensi of the Gold Coast, begun in 1934. Since the results of these researches have been published, a fair number of societies with clans and lineages have been studied, and the tentative typology Professor Fortes and I put forward, and which was intended to be no more than a convenient start towards a more detailed classification of types of African society, in which the absence or presence of forms of descent groups and of state institutions were two criteria, has been expanded and refined. We now know far more than we did twenty years ago about the great variety of types of African society, and this book is another step forward towards a systematic classification based not only on the morphology but also on the functions of African institutions.

It remains for me to express the great loss felt by his colleagues at the death, in a motor-car accident in Ghana, of one of the editors, Mr. David Tait. This book has to serve a final purpose: to be a memorial to a young anthropologist of great promise.

INTRODUCTION

John Middleton and David Tait

THE six essays that compose this book deal with the maintenance of social order within certain societies in Africa that have no centralized political authority. They are the Dinka, Mandari, Amba and Lugbara of East Africa and the Tiv and Konkomba of West Africa. They represent certain types of uncentralized African societies only. Although they differ considerably as to ecology, size, density of population, genealogical depth of lineages and degree of specialization of political role, in all of them a system of unilineal descent groups is of importance. We consider them as indigenous systems, unaffected by European contact.

Political relations are those in which persons and groups exercise power or authority for the maintenance of social order within a territory. They are twofold. There are first those relations between a given unit and others, which ensure its unity *vis-à-vis* other units. These external relations may be seen as essentially antagonistic or competitive, and are likely to be those based upon power devoid of legitimate authority, or at least uncontrolled by any superior authority. They are between structurally equal units (nations, tribes, clans, lineages). And secondly there are those relations internal to the given unit, which ensure the cohesion of its constituent elements and its orderly internal administration. These relations are particularly those of legitimate authority and are usually between units arranged hierarchically (king and subject, clan head and clan member).

In the Introduction to *African Political Systems* three types of political system in Africa are distinguished. The first is exemplified by the Bushmen, where the largest political units embrace people all of whom are interrelated by kinship so that 'political relations are coterminous with kinship relations and the political structure and kinship organization are completely fused' (Fortes and Evans-Pritchard 1940: 6–7). The second type includes those with specialized political authority that is institutionalized and vested in roles attached to a state administration. They are unitary states, with a king or paramount chief at the centre who holds authority to wield supreme political power as part of his status. He may delegate it to others but their authority is subordinate and can originate only in his. Here there are typically specialized political roles and structures. Relations between component groups of the society are internal administrative relations, and political roles are hierarchically arranged in a series of superordinate and subordinate statuses.

The third type includes societies in which political authority is uncentralized. In them there is no holder of political power at the centre, and specialized roles with clearly defined political authority are less easy to find. Local groups are recruited by unilineal descent or by fiction of such descent and relations between them are characterized by their being in a state of segmentary opposition. In *African Political Systems* they are called 'segmentary lineage systems'. One problem of the study of politics in these latter societies is to discover the means by which relations of government, both external and internal to various component groups of the society, are instituted and sanctioned. Power and authority of government may be significant in relations that are many-sided and not purely political. In all societies roles that are politically significant may have vested in them legitimate authority to wield power, but in uncentralized societies this authority is usually not specialized.

In point of fact, the morphological range of political systems in Africa is by no means limited to these three types, which were distinguished merely to provide a basis for classification. The chief factors that differentiate African political organizations are the degree of specialization in roles that enter into political and administrative activities, the number of structural levels at which authority is exercised, and the principle of relationship between political functionary and subject. Each of these factors is widely variable and in consequence there are many morphological intermediates between the types described in *African Political Systems*.

Among politically uncentralized societies alone, there are several examples which do not conform to the types mentioned in that book. In much of Central Africa, for example, there are politically uncentralized societies in which there is no corporate lineage. The main political structure is provided by relations between chiefs and villages of cognatic kin, related in various ways to a headman and free to choose their village residence where they please. Political authority is here vested in chiefs and headmen (Gluckman 1950; Colson and Gluckman 1951).

Another type is that in which political relations between local groups are controlled by the holders of statuses in age-set and age-grade systems, in whom political authority is vested. They are found mainly in East Africa among the Nilo-Hamitic-speaking peoples and their neighbours (Huntingford 1953a and 1953b; Gulliver 1953; Middleton 1953). Yet another includes those societies in which political authority is vested in village councils and associations, such as the Ibo and Yakö (Forde and Jones 1950; Forde 1939).

In none of these three types of uncentralized society is political authority vested in statuses attached to lineages. The holders of roles in which this authority is vested may also occupy statuses in the lineage system, but nevertheless the roles are distinct. In this book we are not concerned with these types but only with those societies with segmentary lineage systems, a somewhat arbitrarily defined category. We shall discuss them in some detail.

THE LINEAGE AND THE LINEAGE SYSTEM

The societies with which we are here concerned are composed of local groups which are recruited by unilineal descent, or by a fiction of such descent. Local groups tend to be identified with descent groups—lineages, clans and sub-clans.

A lineage is a corporate group of unilineal kin, with a formalized system of authority; it is a single group that is assumed to be permanent, to which rights and duties may be attached as to a single unit and which may usually be represented *vis-à-vis* other groups by a single person. It is generally named and within it an accepted genealogical relationship is known between all members. It includes both living and dead.[1] A lineage may be subdivided or segmented into smaller groupings each with genealogies of shallower depth and narrower span. Each segment is then a unit in a system of segments, all being corporate groups. There may well be segments which can be separated out genealogically but which are not significant in any social activity at a given time and are not corporate. We do not call these generation-segments lineages, although they are, of course, potential lineages.

The clan is to be distinguished. This term is a long-standing one in anthropological literature and is generally used to refer to a unilineal descent group, especially when it is exogamous. It consists of several lineages, which may be segmented.[2] It may be a mere category of dispersed people, not forming a corporate group and with only a vague notion of original common ancestry, as among many Central African peoples (Gluckman 1950: 5). Its use is best restricted to unilineal descent groups, or clusters of such groups, within which exact' genealogical relationships are not traced, although the clan is usually believed to have a single founding ancestor. There may be societies without specific clans, as the Tiv. Exogamy and totemism are often given as defining attributes, but this is unnecessary, even though exogamy may be a norm of clanship in a particular society.

Lineages are found in many types of society. Shallow depth lineages may be found in societies in which the political unit is a wandering band or horde composed of only a few families, as the Hottentots. But here internal subdivision on a lineage basis does not occur. The segmentation of local groups and lineages seems to be a response to pressures of which one is that of numbers; settled residence and the presence of heritable wealth may be important.[3] Lineages are also found in many centralized states, notably among the Southern Bantu and in West Africa in Ashanti, Dahomey and the Yoruba states. Here they are relevant in inheritance of status and property, and

[1] For definitions of lineage, see Gluckman 1950: 4–5; Fortes 1953: 26ff; Radcliffe-Brown 1941: 70; Evans-Pritchard 1940: 192.

[2] This is the usage of Lowie 1950: 9, and Evans-Pritchard 1940: 192.

[3] See Forde 1947.

4

local organization may be conceived in terms of them when local groups are recruited by unilineal descent and so closely associated with lineages. In political contexts, however, the hierarchical arrangement of statuses to which political authority is attached is preponderant and the lineage system loses importance as a means of controlling external relations between political groups.

In the societies with which we are dealing there is an ideology by which certain social relations are expressed in terms of kinship. Relations conceived in this idiom may be concerned with the interests either of individuals or of aggregates of unilineal kin. In the former case the relations concerned are those of personal kinship, in the latter they are those of lineage. Where membership of a local group is by unilineal descent, status within it and rights to land, livestock, women and other resources are usually vested within the descent group concerned, as a corporation. Actual residential membership of the local group may vary in size over time, due to ecological and other factors, but the lineage is persistent. Even if members move from one local group to another they still remain lineage members with their rights vested in their lineage; rights in inheritance are not affected, and the network of their personal kinship ties remains unchanged.

Relations between local groups can be conceived in terms of relations between lineages, and are then seen in terms of the kin relationships between the apical ancestors of the lineages by which the local groups define their membership. Lineage organization thus reflects the territorial organization of local groups. The lineage relationships may be seen as unchanging, and so relations between the local groups, which may vary in size and locality over time, can none the less be seen as persistent. The lineages then compose a total structure, the lineage structure. This is an abstraction, a concept used by the actors, and by ourselves in analysis, to express certain relations between aggregates of people composing local groups.

The concept of a lineage structure may be used in various situations, to express various sorts of social relationship. Some of these are those of government, in which political power and authority are exercised between groups and statuses. The social distance between them is then conceived as being that between units in a system of lineages. The concept may be used to express and to validate forms of common action, such as reciprocal help and protection, joint responsibility in bride-wealth and blood compensation, help in feud and war, regulation of intermarriage and observance of responsibility to the dead. And it may also be used in other contexts in which political power and authority are not significant. No single structure need be significant only in political situations, to the exclusion of other contexts. That is, no particular social relation need be only of political significance but may be many-sided.

When there is no centralized political authority for the whole society, external political relations of local groups are often conceived in lineage terms. The roles in which internal political authority is vested may also be attached to lineages; but they can be attached to other structures. These may be age-sets and age-classes, ritual congregations, village councils and associations, secret societies and other selective associations. All these may be found in conjunction with lineage structures.

SEGMENTARY STRUCTURES

In societies lacking ranked and specialized holders of political authority the relations of local groups to one another are seen as a balance of power, maintained by competition between them. Corporate groups may be arranged hierarchically in a series of levels; each group is significant in different circumstances and in connection with different social activities —economic, ritual and governmental. Relations at one level are competitive in one situation, but in another the formerly competitive groups merge in mutual alliance against an outside group. A group at any level has competitive relations with others to ensure the maintenance of its own identity and the rights that belong to it as a corporation, and it may have internal administrative relations that ensure cohesion of its constituent elements. The aggregates that emerge as units in one context are merged into larger aggregates in others, so that a segment that in one situation is independent finds that it and its former competitors are merged together as subordinate segments in the internal administrative organization of a wider

6

overall segment that includes them both. This wider segment is in turn in external competitive relations with other similar segments, and there may be an entire series of such segments. Co-ordinate groups that are so related are in a state of complementary opposition. The total structure is of the type called 'segmentary' by Fortes and Evans-Pritchard, and when the segments of the structure are lineages we speak of a 'segmentary lineage system'.

The term 'segmentary' has been used in reference to several types of social systems, but the essential features are the 'nesting' attribute of segmentary series[1] and the characteristic of being in a state of continual segmentation and complementary opposition. The series may be one of lineages, smaller ones nesting inside and composing larger ones, which in turn compose still larger ones, and so on; or it may be one of territorial groups (hamlets, villages, sections, tribes, nations), or of others. Subtraction or change in size of segments lead to a re-organization, although not necessarily to re-structuring, of the total system. Analysis of the process involved in this re-organization within an unchanging total structure has led to the use of the term to refer to the second characteristic. This is the process of continual segmentation of the structure. The constituent units are all of the same order and segment (and merge, the complementary process) in response to various factors, one of which is the increase of numbers in a segment so that it splits into two or more new segments each of a population nearer the optimum population within the given system. A corollary is that within the structure co-ordinate segments which have come into existence as a result of segmentation are regarded as complementary and as formally equal, even if in actuality they are not so in population, wealth or in other ways. If political power and authority are vested in the structure, then its constituent units are politically equal. These two features are, of course, intimately connected. They refer to different ways of analysing a situation, those of considering morphology and of analysing process. Segmentation should be distinguished from fission. By fission a group ceases to exist as an entity, becoming two or more new groups that are no longer in a state of complementary

---

[1] See Barnes 1954: 49.

opposition; by segmentation a group merely divides in certain contexts but retains its corporate identity in others.[1]

THE POLITICAL UNIT AND THE LINEAGE SYSTEM

In all societies considered in this book the basic unit of the political system is a joint or extended family based upon a three or four generation lineage. Its component families are generally the productive and consuming units, but the joint family is the largest purely domestic unit and is under the domestic authority of a single head, who may also represent it as a corporate unit in political and ritual situations. It has clearly defined rights over land and controls its own livestock. It may contain non-lineage members but they are closely related by cognatic ties. We refer to it as the nuclear group.[2] There is in every society an optimum size for the nuclear group, determined largely by ecological factors. This size may vary from any one part of any society to another, with edaphic and climatic variation and differences in methods of production. There is also an optimum size for the unit whose members can conveniently accept the overall domestic authority of a single head, and a maximum size in terms of the distance between its constituent homesteads, which is to a large extent determined by the carrying capacity of the land.[3]

---

[1] This usage of 'segmentary' is different from that of Durkheim (1893), in which segmentary systems are those formed by the repetition of smaller segments (clans). Durkheim applied the term to those societies lacking an elaborate division of labour, those based on mechanical solidarity. Here neither the nesting attribute nor that of a continual process of segmentation need be present. All that is necessary is an exhaustive series of equal units. In his type a unit can be subtracted from the total series without disorganization: a segment is merely lopped off. The term 'segmental' may be retained in this sense. Durkheim referred to clans; it may also be used to refer to other forms of grouping, which may be significant in many different types of social situation. These are the units that compose segmental structures of age-groups, secret societies, title and trade associations, and others, so long as the segments are exhaustive.

[2] The same seems to be found in almost all African subsistence societies. Where it does not occur, as in Ganda and Southern Kikuyu, there are specific local reasons.

[3] That there is an optimum size is an assumption, based on the fact that groups of a certain size in any of these societies segment: there is thus at least a convenient maximum. The optimum could be determined by detailed study of ecological factors but these are not available for most of the societies described in this book.

The widest political unit in these societies we call the jural community. It is composed of several nuclear groups, which may be grouped into several levels of intermediate units arranged in a segmentary organization. It is to be regarded as a cluster of nuclear groups rather than as a clear-cut unit. It may not be a territorially contiguous group at all but consist of a number of scattered units linked by certain ties, as the clusters of lineages linked by exogamy among the Amba, or by 'clanship' among the Tallensi. In any case it is the widest grouping within which there are a moral obligation and a means ultimately to settle disputes peaceably. It may vary in span from one part of the society to another and may also vary in size over time, depending on what ties and cleavages are relevant in any given situation. It is the largest autonomous grouping in political contexts.[1]

The composition of local groups varies. In some societies, such as Amba and to a less extent Konkomba and Tiv, there is little or no dispersal of lineages. In others, such as Dinka, Mandari and Lugbara, there is a considerable scatter of lineages across local groups; lineage ties are remembered for at least some generations after the movement of a lineage segment or member away from the main body of agnatically related lineages. The degree of this dispersal depends on factors such as the carrying capacity of the land, the population density, external conquest, and migration. The economic, political and ritual value of land, for example, varies widely. If there is little common lineage interest in land or property, or in political or ritual status attached to a descent line, dispersal of a lineage may occur in every generation and there may also be a wide scattering of dispersing segments. Ancestral connections may soon be forgotten because of infrequent contact. But they may be remembered if rights in property or in offices that are valued are attached to the lineage.

Lineages provide the cores of local groups and provide a permanent framework for ever-changing relations between them. Local units are thus bound together into a single system by the assumed genealogical relationships between the lineage

---

[1] It is the 'tribe' of Dinka, Lugbara, Konkomba and Nuer, the chiefdom of Mandari, the exogamous cluster in Amba; in Tiv it varies but seems usually to be a territorial group identified with a lineage of eight to ten generations in depth.

founders, who are at the points of articulation of the lineage system. The genealogy may reflect actual relationships between segment founders; or, where lineages are scattered, what were originally cognatic and quasi-cognatic ties become accepted as agnatic ties in genealogical reckoning. This latter is often found with a differentiation between authentic and accessory groups, which may be seen as dominant and subordinate in terms of power or prestige.

Nuclear units are bound together by lineage genealogies: the genealogical structure expresses lineage unity and its persistence through time. In some of these societies, such as Tiv, Konkomba and Amba, where lineages are not dispersed but form locally compact descent groups, the genealogical depth of a lineage is to a large extent conditioned by its numbers and the total depth of genealogies reflects the size of the widest groups recognized as single corporations in any situation. Among Amba and Konkomba the widest political groups and genealogical depth are both small; among the Tiv genealogical depth is great and all Tiv society is reckoned as a single unit—*tar Tiv*—in some contexts. In one respect the greater the number of generations recognized the greater is the sense of perpetuity of the group. This is one aspect of its attribute of corporateness, so that we might expect long genealogies to be found in those systems where corporate lineages provide the central political framework of the total structure, and where there is no specialized political authority outside the lineage. Where lineages are scattered and interspersed, as in Dinka, Mandari and Lugbara, the length of genealogy reflects the structural position of the lineage. The genealogies of dominant or 'authentic' groups are longer than those of accessory groups, and it is the genealogies of the former that are politically the more significant. Other factors also enter. In societies with double unilineal descent, for example, lineage genealogies tend to be short since the recognition of long genealogies would be cumbersome, as in Yakö and some Nuba tribes. And the institution of chiefship tends to inhibit the recognition of long genealogies, as we mention below.

The genealogy of which agreed details are known by a group covers the units within its field of direct social relations. This includes those other groups with which its members come into direct and frequent contact; groups beyond this range are rarely included in a group's field of genealogical knowledge. Genealogical depth is thus a function of the range of economic and social self-sufficiency. The range of exogamy, in terms of lineage span, is relevant here. It varies from one society to another, and also within any particular society, the variation being largely determined by factors such as the pattern of settlement, the degree of interspersal of agnatically related lineages and of attachment of unrelated lineages.[1]

With scatter of lineages a distinction is often found between dominant or authentic and accessory clans or lineages. Among the Lugbara, like the Nuer, each tribe has a dominant clan or lineage. The dominant clan does not extend beyond the jural community but provides an internal structure for it, thus enabling a considerable number of lineages not agnatically related to each other to recognize themselves as forming a single territorial group with a high degree of cohesion and of observance of orderly administrative relations. Chiefship may be attached to the dominant descent group, as to the Bora clan among the Mandari, a clan which provides a total structure around which the entire society is organized, although it is significant mainly in administrative relations within the chiefdom itself, the jural community.

The number of levels of lineage segmentation within the jural community is continuously variable, from a high number (Tiv) to only two or three levels significant in social action (Konkomba). Each level of segmentation is associated with a group or cluster which is differentiated from others in a particular social context. A segment that is significant as an autonomous unit in one situation is merged with others in other situations, and there occurs the interlocking of groups and statuses that are associated with different activities and their consequent rights and duties. This makes for a high degree of cohesion of units in a single system where there is no single political authority to provide a sense of common solidarity. When there is specialization of political authority then this interlocking of segments seems to be of less importance and

[1] An example is found among the Lugbara, described in this book. Another is in Ibo, where a group dependent, for ecological reasons, upon outside trade, may approve of widely dispersed out-marriages and one not so dependent become exogamous. (Information from R. Horton.)

there is less complexity of segmentation. Somewhat similar in this respect is the degree of complementary filiation recognized, which may be complex, as in Tiv, or simple, as in Lugbara. The Tiv recognize a large number of uterine lineages as being important, with multiple individuation of sibling groups and persons. This also provides an elaborate network of interlocking ties.

TYPES OF SEGMENTARY LINEAGE SYSTEM

In the classification of these uncentralized political systems certain features are especially significant. They are the way in which genealogical articulation is used to conceive and express relations between local groups; the degree of autonomy or inter-dependence of local groups in political situations; the degree of specialization of offices with purely political authority; and the way in which organized violence is used in the settlement of dispute, in particular of homicide. These factors do not vary discontinuously to any marked extent, and degree of variation in one is not necessarily nor invariably commensurate with that in another: the classification of these six societies into three groups is not intended to provide a clear-cut typology but merely to throw into relief certain of the more important points of difference between them.

There are several ways in which descent groups may be linked into a single system. In some societies, including the Tiv, Lugbara and Nuer, a single all-inclusive lineage genealogy is sufficient to explain significant political identification of lineage with territorial segmentation, and the political system is built upon a framework of agnatic lineages which are units in a single pyramidal system. This pyramidal system covers the whole jural community. It need not cover the entire society; it does so among the Tiv, but not among the Lugbara, nor the Nuer. The societies of this type, the Nuer especially, are those in which the units are in continual movement and proliferation. Tiv and Lugbara are agriculturalists but in neither is a lineage or local group tied to a particular piece of land, and there is continual migration and spatial movement of groups. This system of linking lineages would seem to be incompatible with the development of factors that fix immutable boundaries between local groups or social barriers between descent groups. Permanent settlement; indivisible rights in property, especially in land; political rights inherited within a descent group, especially one of wide span; these all tend to inhibit systems of this type.[1] We refer to them as systems of Group I.

In societies of this type jural communities are relatively economically and socially autonomous; even though inter-marriage may occur between them most seems to take place within the jural community. What ties may exist between them, or between their agnatic lineage cores where there are authentic and accessory lineages, are politically relatively unimportant. Such are clan ties, as in Lugbara and Nuer, which are not important in contexts where inter-group relations are concerned, although they may be ritually significant and may affect inter-personal relations, as in rules to do with inter-marriage. These societies have little specialization of political authority and what functionaries there are who are politically important are primarily holders of domestic or ritual roles.

We refer to the Konkomba, Amba and also the Tallensi as societies of Group II. The political units of these societies consist of small descent groups, usually of shallow genealogical depth, which are relatively interdependent. They are grouped into overlapping clusters by ritual links of various kinds (often by forming the congregations of earth cults and other cults not based on descent) and by quasi-kinship ties. The internal hierarchical administrative organization of any single major political unit is based upon a single lineage genealogy. At the political level units are not linked by a single genealogy but rather by the recognition of mutual obligations. These are usually those of exogamy and peaceful and religious alliances. They may be explained by the people as resulting from common agnatic ancestry, but they are expressed in terms of clanship, in which exact genealogical relationship is not reckoned. By this, however, the network of interlocking ties, seen essentially in ritual terms, that makes for cohesion at the level of smaller segments within which interpersonal ties of agnatic kinship are operative, is also used in the wider sphere of political relations between the larger units of the structure. Exogamy is usually a

[1] This does not mean, however, that they need be found in systems of other types.

significant criterion of clanship. Ties between groups whose members intermarry may lack solidarity due to disputes between affines; exogamy is thus an essential aspect of ties of clanship where these provide a framework of political importance. The genealogies of these interlocked clusters may be formally con-tradictory but since they are invoked on separate occasions they may never be brought to actual comparison.[1] In these societies lineages are arranged in a segmentary organization, but are concerned with inheritance, exogamy and family matters rather than with political relations proper.[2]

The third type of organization found among the societies de-scribed in this book we refer to as that of Group III. This has been described by Dr. Lienhardt in his essay as 'aggregational' or 'associated'. The Dinka tribe, the jural community, has a lineage structure, but relationships between all its territorial segments cannot usually be explained by reference to a single agnatic genealogy. It is composed of lineages from different clans—as among Nuer or Lugbara also—but the whole is con-sidered as a compound structure of lineages which cannot be placed into a single pyramidal system as can that of the other two societies. Although among the Dinka each territorial sec-tion is associated with a dominant lineage, sections that are seg-ments of a wider section do not necessarily have agnatically related lineages as cores, in the way that they do among Nuer and Lugbara. The Mandari have a somewhat similar organiza-tion, to which Dr. Buxton refers as 'polycephalous'. These systems are characterized by the lack of an all-inclusive lineage genealogy at any level of organization except that of the nuclear group itself. They also have chiefs with certain specialized functions, although the Dinka chief, the 'master of the fishing spear' is not a very powerful political figure.

We may summarize the differences between the systems of Groups I and III as being those of linkage of constituent units of the jural community and of degree of specialization of political authority. In both the lineage system provides the framework for the main political structure of the society. The basic units are relatively autonomous in political situations, this autonomy being partially reflected in the occurrence of the feud in both

[1] See Winter 1956, Ch. XI, for a description of genealogical contradiction of this kind.　　　　[2] For example, see Fortes 1945; 1949, Ch. I.

groups. Lineages may be clustered into ritual congregations, but this temporary collaboration does not lessen their autonomy in non-ritual situations nor does it inhibit the expression of hostility between them, usually by open fighting.

The political units of societies of Group II, on the other hand, are relatively interdependent. They are grouped into overlapping clusters which are significant in contexts other than temporary ritual ones only. In societies of Groups I and III the distribution of political authority is coterminous with territorial segmentation, but this is not so in those of Group II. There the statuses with political authority (where these exist) are attached to fields of clanship, there being a network of politically independent and overlapping clusters of maximal lineages. This provides a very different form of political organization from that based mainly upon a segmentary lineage structure alone.

Most of the systems that would be included in Group I seem to be more or less culturally homogeneous[1]; whereas some of Group III, such as the Mandari, are amalgamations of many diverse groups of different languages and cultures: similar societies in this respect are the Madi (Middleton 1955) and Alur (Southall 1956). These societies have specialized chiefships and 'aggregational' lineage systems. Among the Lugbara, and the Nuer, the absorption of war captives and other strangers, even in large numbers, has been by the attachment of individuals and their immediate families to those of their captors and hosts. Their descendants may in time become independent lineages but there seems to be no way in these two societies by which complete sections of some size may be attached to a host group—although a complete tribe living on the borders of Lugbara or Nuer might in time be accepted as part of the total society. In Mandari, Madi and Alur there are large groupings of several hundreds of persons which have become part of the society, the various groups forming what are federations each with many chiefs.[2] Here no clear genealogical tie is postulated

---

[1] The Nuer absorb many Dinka, but they are culturally very similar and adopt Nuer language and habits.

[2] Some of these systems may be regarded as multiple states, the constituent units being fairly large clusters each under the political authority of a single head or chief. Within each unit all relations are 'internal' administrative relations, and the only 'external' competitive political relations are between the units. Southall therefore describes the Alur as a 'segmentary state' (Southall 1956).

between original hosts and clients, unlike the situation in Lugbara and Nuer. When there is a chiefship, which provides a focus for the attachment of diverse cultural groups, this enables those groups to maintain their own identity to a greater degree, whereas the Lugbara and Nuer type system forces a common identity upon both hosts and attached strangers. The nature of the tie is reflected in the clan system. Clans in societies of Group III may not form a single common system with common mythical origin, as do those of Group I, but each clan or set of clans may have its own corpus of myth. Such myths usually explain the relationship between different clans of the society but do not give them a common origin nor even origins of the same type.

POLITICAL OFFICE AND THE LINEAGE SYSTEM

In some uncentralized societies there are no holders of political office apart from those who hold primarily domestic authority, and what political power there is recognized is distributed among them. But usually there is some form of institutionalized political leadership. The terms 'chief', 'elder', 'lineage head' and others are used to refer to political functionaries, the nature and extent of whose authority and powers of representation vary widely.

In a group that is culturally homogeneous, sharing common values, social relations can adequately be controlled by the operation of universally accepted obligations and religious sanctions; when these prove inadequate then resort may be made to self-help, and the feud or warfare are found. Lineage heads exist with internal domestic authority over kin-groups. Relations between kin-groups and territorial groups may partially be controlled by primarily ritual functionaries, such as the Nuer 'leopard-skin chief'. They may stand outside the organization of jural communities altogether so as to be impartial in lineage disputes, and also outside and above the system of lineages (although they may hold 'private' internal lineage authority as well). In their political role, that is to say, the principle of allegiance to them of their subjects is not essentially

16

one of agnatic kinship.[1] Where kin-groups in a society are culturally diverse it seems that customary and religious sanctions may not be sufficient to control conflict of interests between them. We may assume that the society would then dissolve into its component parts: cleavages in the total system will be too great for conflict of interests to be resolved within the structure. Institutionalized and formal chiefship may provide some kind of machinery for the resolution of conflicts and the enforcement of decisions deliberately given in disputes between groups. The chiefship also symbolizes the whole community—at least the jural community—a group that may not be based upon common descent but on common locality in which the symbols and values provided by the lineage structure alone are not sufficient. The chiefship is usually tied to a particular lineage of the locality, which ensures continuity by the regulation of succession and the association of the myth of chiefship with a permanent descent line. Chiefship seems particularly consistent with cultural heterogeneity.[2]

Examples of chiefship are found especially among societies of Group III. We have comparatively little historical information as to their development; these we have mentioned are indigenous developments but in most cases we do not know when they developed nor in response to what factors. Many chiefships found today are the creations of European administration, as the modern chiefs among the Lugbara. Chiefships of a very modified sort in West Africa are often part of a European administration (Kissi, Basare) or other alien administration in a heterogeneous society (Dagomba among Konkomba or Mamprusi among Tallensi, societies of Group II). But these 'chiefs' had little indigenous authority. Among the Ga there are modern chiefs who first appeared as military leaders against the Ashanti and who became chiefs under British rule (Field 1940). Among the Ibo, especially the Northern Ibo, a tendency towards chiefship was perhaps observable in that lineage seniority and seniority in the title societies were both required for political leadership (Forde and Jones 1950).

---

[1] The position of diviners and other ritual functionaries whose roles have political significance is also usually outside the lineage system.

[2] As among the Mandari. See also the most detailed account of the chiefship in Alur, in Southall 1956.

The chief often represents certain segments whose members are politically and in other ways dominant over commoners. In such a system each class or rank has certain roles attached to it which only its members can perform, and so is symbiotically related to the others.[1] Symbiotic union of a rather different kind occurs in West Africa, where there may be a distinction between 'chiefs' and earth priests, each representing groups which claim originally different ethnic origin and which are symbiotically related to one another so as to link all units into a single social system. Linkage of this sort is similar in many respects to that we have referred to as 'aggregational' when discussing societies of Group III. This process of differentiation provides a means of absorbing aliens into the society. Whole groups may be absorbed, the original settlers perhaps becoming specially associated with the earth cult while the invaders become associated more with a purely political chiefship.

The institution of the chief's non-chiefly assistant is often found. The power of the chief is curbed by the chiefly role being split between him and his assistant, who represents the subordinate part of the population, or at least stands for the commoners as against the chief's immediate supporters. An example is that of the Mandari, where the chief is intimately associated with his 'client'.

Some types of chiefship, seen in religious terms and especially in the form of prophets or messianic leaders who acquire rudimentary political power, may well develop as a response to external stresses, some of which at least are due to pressure of population and ecological factors. In this case the pressure may be external to a given jural community rather than to the entire society. It seems that when the pressure is internal to the total society then the new leaders or prophets may be closely linked to the jural communities (as in northern Lugbara, with a high population pressure and rain-chiefs and later Yakan prophets to each tribe); when there is also pressure external to the whole society then they are not so linked and may claim authority over jural communities over a wide area, providing a new basis for the overall organization of the society (as the Nuer and Dinka prophets and the 'King' of Bwamba).

[1] For example, the division of the Madi into rainmaking chiefly lineages and commoner lineages without rainmaking powers (Middleton 1955).

THE EXERCISE OF VIOLENCE

Existing accounts of political systems in Africa refer to various types of overt expression of hostility between groups as warfare, feud, blood-vengeance, fighting or vendetta. These are all forms of self-help, and it is often difficult—and often pointless—to distinguish them clearly. Self-help occurs at some level of organization in all social systems; here we are concerned with its occurrence between corporate groups or clusters of such groups, and not between individuals. It occurs in those societies that lack centralized political authority which can provide sanctions to regulate relations between constituent units, and where commonly accepted values that prohibit the use of armed force are not recognized. These sanctions may take the form of authority vested in a chief with machinery for enforcement of his decisions, or in a functionary who may invoke the force of God or the dead. This is not to say that the exercise of self-help is never found within the group under control of a chief: it is found in many centralized states. But it is there under the control of the chief, who makes use of it as a means to enforce his judgments.[1]

The hostility that may be expressed in inter-group fighting is particularly that arising from conflict of interests between nuclear groups that are beyond the range of domestic kinship. This range is usually marked by the use of personal kinship terms between individuals; beyond it these give way to collective kinship categories only, under which individual ties are subsumed. Between these kin the killing of a fellow is fratricide, whereas that of a man less closely related is homicide. Fratricide is a sin, without humanly awarded punishment, although there may be rites of atonement and purification. There cannot be compensation, since property is usually held jointly to this range, and often the killer inherits the victim's widows and takes over much of his status in recognition of the tie of siblingship, as among the Lugbara. Between these kin marriage is forbidden and sexual relations are incest, a sin; whereas between kin beyond this range they are usually a form of remote clan incest punishable only if pregnancy results, and the offence

[1] An example is the Ankole (Oberg 1940).

is of a different order. Up to this range fighting is typically only duelling between individuals, and accusations of witchcraft may be made as an alternative to overt violence; beyond it fighting becomes feud or warfare, and the difference is often reflected in differences of weapons used. This range also generally marks the limit of hierarchically arranged internal administrative organization. Where the lineage is localized this range of kinship applies to large groups, even to the largest exogamous descent group. But where they are dispersed it tends to be smaller and to consist only of a small core lineage and close attached cognates. It seems generally that the greater the degree of lineage scatter the narrower is the recognized range of this kinship behaviour within the total system, consistent with the smaller range of accepted lineage values.[1]

Inter-group fighting in these societies is between units beyond this range of personal kinship which do not accept a common superordinate authority in political matters. We may distinguish two types of such fighting, feud and warfare. They shade into each other, but by the feud we refer to fighting between people as groups, usually undertaken as response to an offence, the groups being in such a relationship that although they fight they both accept the obligation to bring the fighting to a close by peaceful settlement, there being machinery to achieve this conclusion. The hostility between the groups is latent and becomes open fighting as a consequence of certain precipitating events. It is not the sporadic outbreak of fighting for a single offence that is soon settled and forgotten, as in Konkomba. If there is no such obligation or machinery to settle the fighting we refer to it as warfare. Feud is thus a condition that flourishes typically within the same jural community. All these societies practise warfare, but not all practise the feud. The outbreak of violence that we call the feud does not mean that there are no obligations to maintain law and order within the community. Indeed the feud may be the recognized means

[1] In Lugbara this range is generally coterminous with the major segment; in Konkomba with the clan; in Amba and Nuer with the village; in Dinka with the sub-tribe; in Tallensi with the inner segment. We have not given the relevant group a distinctive generic name, since it varies considerably in span even within the same society, and to do so reifies what is merely a cluster of individuals and nuclear groups acting together in certain situations in defence of their common interests, yet perhaps without any strong sense of unity or solidarity.

of maintaining law in default of a superior judical authority, and the only sanction for offences such as homicide.

One of the crucial features of the feud is that mentioned by Radcliffe-Brown (1940:xix). The relationships between the feuding parties is such that hostility between them, although permanent, must be inhibited in those situations in which they become allies in military, economic, ritual or other collaboration. If it were not at least temporarily inhibited mutual alliance would be an impossibility. It is thus typically found with a segmentary system, the feuding parties at one level being co-ordinate and politically equal segments that may unite at a higher level against more distant groups. The fact that a segment acts as a feud unit marks its separate identity as against other segments in one situation, and its joint unity with co-ordinate segments in others. As a permanent condition feud is one aspect of the continuity over time of a series of segmentary groups—it is, as it were, genealogical differentiation translated into action. Intergroup violence is resorted to in political situations within the jural community in societies of Groups I and III, in which the segmentary lineage system is of political significance.[1] In societies of Group II genealogical differentiation is not politically important and the overlapping fields of clanship composed of diverse maximal lineages are usually not arranged in a segmentary organization. Here the feud is not found, although warfare occurs.[2] In societies of this group there are often earth cults and similar institutions that inhibit the exercise of violence within a territorial unit. Earth cults reaffirm ties based upon territorial propinquity rather than upon descent and so are closely connected with the political importance of overlapping ties of clanship (as it is found in these particular societies) as against those based on lineage. The societies where clanship and other ties inhibit the feud have a

[1] We consider that the hostility between segments among the Tiv called warfare by Dr. Bohannan could rather be called feud.

The feud occurs typically in pastoral societies, all of which we know that lack centralized political authority being classed in Group I. Pastoral societies seem to have wide-scale segmentary lineage systems and a high degree of movement of lineages on the ground. The main exception known to us is that of the Fulani, who do not practise the feud; but then they do not form autonomous societies but are always part of a wider political system.

[2] Dr. Winter states that the Amba practise the feud. We suggest that the hostility to which he refers is better called warfare or blood-vengeance.

different kind of political structure, not being based upon a segmentary lineage system formed of political units, and without specialized political functionaries.

In societies of Group I self-help replaces superordinate authority at a very low level; in those of other groups it replaces it at a considerably higher level. In those societies with low cultural homogeneity the cleavages are such that exercise of self-help between segments would never be counterpoised by alliances of segments against others. We suggest that they therefore disintegrate unless, for some reason or other, chiefship is instituted and allegiance to a superordinate authority replaces self-help at the lower levels.

The feud is disruptive. Institutions that are often found with it, and which minimize its severity, are blood compensation, the institutionalized peacemaker and the right of sanctuary, which is a means of preventing an outbreak of violence until the occasion for it has been composed. Among the Tiv its place within closely related lineage segments is taken by disputes being expressed in terms of witchcraft: accusations are made and formal and institutionalized trials conducted between the segments concerned. The underlying hostility between segments is of the same order in both cases, but its expression in Tiv is covert rather than overt between units which recognize fairly close agnatic kinship. Settlement by ordeal replaces that by combat.

RELIGIOUS ORGANIZATION AND THE LINEAGE SYSTEM

Possession of political and other authority must be balanced by responsibility or accountability for its exercise. Formal responsibility of those who hold authority is rarely directed to those groups over which the authority is wielded. In uncentralized societies especially it is to the dead members of the group, the lineage ancestors, to God or to some vital principle from which this authority is thought to spring.

A cult has a congregation, whose members offer sacrifices together to the cult-object. The sacrifice generally has two parts—the offering to the cult-object and the sharing of food and drink among the congregation. The emphasis on each part may vary. Membership of a congregation enjoins that members must have peace in their hearts and have resolved enmity between them. To sacrifice together and yet to feel enmity is wrong and may be a sin, not merely a breach of everyday kinship behaviour. This seems to be true of any congregation, whether one gathered to sacrifice to an ancestor, to God or at an earth shrine.

The congregation is associated with a specific sacrifice and with a specific descent or local grouping. In most of these societies sacrifice may be of various types and to many cult-objects, and each may have a congregation of different span and composition. Certain rites may be recurrent, with the same congregation on all occasions, such as rites at harvest and other points in the farming cycle, at life crises, and so on. In other cases sacrifices are made to remove sickness or disaster brought upon an individual or group for an offence or in order to maintain the benevolence of a god or the fertility of the land. In the former instance, a rite is performed to restore a former structural alignment between statuses and groups which was disrupted by the original offence, or to validate a new one (as in the purification of incest that is followed by lineage segmentation). There is usually a direct connection between the social tie the breach of which has led to sacrifice and the composition of the congregation that attends it, as well as correlated differences in oblation and cult-object. Sacrifice serves to maintain a valued relationship.

The person ritually responsible for the offender may initiate this process by cursing or invoking, he may be responsible for making or supervising the sacrifice as the ritual head of the group, or both. His identity is significant in that from it we may see the group that is considered significant by the people in connection with particular offences. Usually the composition of the congregation is based on a descent group, including kin dispersed over several territorial sections. Congregations are overlapping and interlinked; by participation at sacrifices and other rites—a participation that is compulsory—the inter-group web of kinship ties is most significantly expressed and revalidated. The congregation may include close cognates living in the same residential group, which is hereby strengthened. The politically more important and more widely attended rites are often performed or led by holders of political office.[1]

It has often been pointed out that there is a close correspondence between the form of a religious organization and that of the social structure.[2] In systems where lineages are politically significant a segmentary cult closely associated with the lineage system is usually of greatest importance. The ancestral cult is usually connected with the main cult of the society, particularly in settled communities where there can be permanent association with grave sites. It is, however, only one type, although a common one, of segmentary cult associated with politically important and relatively self-sufficient descent groups of the type found in societies of Group I. The form of the cults is segmentary, but their contents vary widely. On the whole they reflect cultural and ecological conditions of the society, in particular the sense of dependence upon human and social forces or else upon non-human natural forces, and the control or lack of control of the environment which determines such features of the world-view. The Lugbara, for example, have an elaborate ancestral cult. But Nuer and Dinka have little regard for the ritual aspect of the ancestors and their main cult is that of God; sacrifices are made to refractions of God associated with the various segments of the society (Evans-Pritchard 1956). This may reflect their greater ecological insecurity, their sense of dependence upon extra-human forces and their realization of the weakness of human powers to influence nature in general; whereas the Lugbara are very conscious of the importance of human effort in their productive agricultural economy. The Tiv have no ancestral cult, but their beliefs about *tsav*, essentially a representation derived from human ability, again reflects the self-confidence which infects their view of the relations of man to nature in agriculture and other pursuits (Bohannan 1953). This does not imply, of course, that God cults are not found in agriculturally based societies—the Ganda and Kikuyu are well-known examples. Political and historical factors also play a part.

In societies of other types, and in particular of Group II, the land or earth cult may be important, and the strongest sanctions

[1] For example, see Fortes 1936.
[2] For example, Radcliffe-Brown 1945: 169.

on breaches of the peace by members of a congregation is that spilling of blood pollutes the land and threatens its fertility. Whereas the ancestral cult in particular is a ritualization of organization based on descent, the earth cult is a ritualization of organization based primarily on locality or community, with a high degree of political interdependence of descent groups. It is also, of course, one aspect of an agricultural society. In societies of Group III the main religious cults of political significance are those associated with the chief, who offers sacrifice on behalf of his subjects. In this way the bonds between chief and subject, which are not primarily those of kinship, are reaffirmed. As in societies of Group II, these cults are a ritualization of organization based upon a local community, and not upon a descent group.

INTEGRATION AND EQUILIBRIUM IN SEGMENTARY LINEAGE SOCIETIES

For a social structure to be stable the statuses and the groups the relations between which provide the political framework of the society must persist over time. Lineage systems, due mainly to lack of centralized and persistent political authority, tend to be in a condition of continual change and instability. There is no inherently stable system of this type: it would be a paradox. But these systems do acquire a degree of stability and of structural persistence, by definition: without them they would not be systems at all.

We have mentioned that in these small-scale African subsistence societies the basic residential and economic unit is usually based upon a three or four generation lineage, which may segment or fuse with others according to variation in size of its population and in ecological factors. The effect of this variation is tempered by factors such as the existence or non-existence of common lineage rights in land or other resources or in political, ritual or other statuses, of the institutions of clientship and tenantship, by differences in patterns of residence at marriage, and so on. Dispersal and segmentation occur but the structure persists: indeed, this persistence is a consequence of their occurrence. By segmentation divergence of interests within the small nuclear group is resolved. Change is then repetitive. When divergence of interests cannot be resolved by these means the composition and alignment of groups and statuses may change radically.

Rights in resources and the exercise of authority must be distributed within local and descent groups, which can persist in time only so long as this distribution is accepted by all members. Conflict of interests is countered by various institutions that provide for the affirmation of joint as against sectional interests. This seems largely to depend upon non-empirical factors, which include a common set of religious values, a common God or body of ancestors to whom constituent units and their representatives feel responsibility for their actions, and a common mythology. These affirm both common bonds and the values on which right mutual behaviour is based. Most potential conflicts of interests are limited by the common acceptance of social values of the members of the society, rather than by legal or other sanctions that come into operation only after conflict has been actualized. Religious values may, however, cease to have any great significance between distantly related or unrelated groups, although the overlapping of congregations, especially marked in units with interlinked fields of clanship, as in societies of Group II, lessens this tendency. Other common values may be weak or hardly held at all between culturally heterogeneous groupings, even though within the same total society.

Certain factors make for a degree of latent instability, which may be independent of and may exaggerate the divergence of interests we have mentioned. This instability in social structure is analogous to tension in kinship relations, which is often inferred by what seem to be the means for reducing it rather than by any indication of its actualization, which by definition does not occur under repetitive conditions.[1]

This latent instability may be the result of several factors, which may occur in isolation or jointly, depending on historical and ecological conditions of which we may have little knowledge. They include cultural heterogeneity; the scattering and interspersal of lineages among local groups; a considerable degree of attachment of clients or client groups to lineages; these

---

[1] The kinship tensions to which we refer are those assumed to be minimized by affinal avoidances, joking relationships, etc.

are all factors that minimize the effectiveness of common values as means to orderly coexistence of neighbouring groups. Those societies in which they are found may be assumed to disintegrate unless they are counterpoised by certain mechanisms, which may again be in isolation or in association. So many variables are concerned that it is misleading if not impossible to make simple connections between any one cause and any one effect. Such features are the recognition in behaviour of lineage and clan ties, chiefship, blood-compensation and non-empirical, religious sanctions. These have, in part, the effect of minimizing the resort to self-help between groups at lower levels of the structure. The splitting up of rights and duties among many levels of segment provides for a considerable degree of cohesion through the interlocking of lineage relationships. This seems significant especially in societies of Group I, which lack specialization of political authority. Also the bringing of the clan system into close association with the lineage system—often by the clan having some of the formal properties of the lineage— so as to provide stronger mythical validation for the genealogies and interrelationships of the latter, is relevant. The lineage structure is mainly a structural device, and lacks much of the ritual content of the clan system. It would seem that some systems of Group I especially gain strength from this factor.

In all these societies the range of the total society varies over time, just as does that of its constituent groups. The limits of the society are not known clearly to its members, unless defined by incidental environmental features. One important way by which a society is defined in space and in time for its members is by its clan system, the origins and relationships of clans being explained and validated by myths which are known and accepted throughout the society. Conceptualization of the society as a whole is of common interest to all its units, in the sense that sectional interests are not involved. Even though myth may validate the claim of one group or section to be regarded as superior to others, in a stable system all groups accept this validation and there is no conflict of interests with regard to it. The clan in varying forms and in varying ways generally remains the principal structural unit of the total social organization and it is about clans, as assumed permanent units, that mythological validation clusters. It is possible for a clan system

	Group I		Group II		Group III	
	Tiv	Lugbara	Amba	Konkomba	Dinka	Mandari
Total population (thousands)	800	240	30	45	900	15
Number of generations in genealogies (approx.)	12	10	6	6	12	10
Number of levels of lineage segmentation (approx.)	12	4	5	4	3	3
Type of chief	none	none	none	none	priest-chiefs	chiefs
Feud and warfare	both	both	war only	war only	both	both
Descent groups	compact	dispersed	compact	compact	dispersed	dispersed
Distinction into dominant and accessory descent groups	none	occurs	none	none	occurs	occurs
Inclusion of descent groups in jural community	single pyramidal system	single pyramidal system	multiple inclusion	multiple inclusion	multiple 'associated' inclusion	multiple 'associated' inclusion
Autonomy (A) or Interdependence (I) of main political groups	A	A	I	I	A	A
Political importance of clans	no clans	not polit. import.	polit. import.	polit. import.	not polit. import.	chiefly clan polit. import.
Religious cults. (A)—ancestral. (G)—God	'Fetishes'	A only	A and gods	A and G	G and totemic cults	A and rain cults

to be recognized over a field wider than any single society. Such a field is found where a society is only part of a wider cultural whole, the same clans being found across the whole. Consistent with this is the fact that genealogies are not necessarily traceable within the clan. It is not that clans need be so large that they are untraceable for that reason: they may be very small. But the tracing of genealogies is irrelevant.

The systems we have discussed have certain features in common. In all of them the segmentary principle is operative and relations between territorial groups are conceived in terms of descent, in terms of a lineage or clan system. The segmentary principle in its classical, pyramidal form, as in societies of Group I, is operative only when constituent groups can move freely on the ground and when there are no important rights over men or property inheritable only within wide-span descent groups, no clearly marked specialization of political authority, and no marked cultural heterogeneity of personnel. When these conditions do not occur we usually find the organizations of Groups II and III, with the recognition of multiple inclusion of constituent units within the jural community, with or without the institution of chiefship. In systems of Group I and to a less extent of Group III local and descent groups are more autonomous; political authority is distributed on the lines of territorial segmentation. In those of Group II local groups are more interdependent. The level at which acceptance of the decisions of a superordinate authority-holder gives place to self-help is connected with this distinction, as is the range of the society. The 'independent' organizations, those of the Tiv, Dinka, Nuer and Lugbara, seem able both to provide for generally larger jural communities, and also to extend loosely over a greater number and range of constituent groups; whereas the 'interdependent' organizations with their more complex way of linking groups into a system are less able to include a large number of units in a single political structure. Often these 'interdependent' organizations may form part of a wider system between whose units cultural boundaries are virtually indistinguishable: both Konkomba and Tallensi are examples, and Amba are one of several very similar small groups of the Ituri region. Societies of Group II, largely dependent for cohesion on the common recognition of the values of clanship, in general have smaller jural communities and are in totality smaller than those of Group I. The same is true of many of Group III, dependent upon the authority of many small chiefs, each with little physical force at his disposal and in permanent political competition or opposition to his fellow-chiefs.[1] The types of organizations of Groups II and III are more dependent on the observance of common ritual values and on attachment to symbolic office, factors that can link without conflict only a relatively small number of persons unless also backed by a stronger and more specialized political authority than is found in the uncentralized systems we have considered.

BIBLIOGRAPHY

BARNES, J. A.   1954.   *Politics in a Changing Society*, London.

BOHANNAN, L. and P.   1953.   *The Tiv of Central Nigeria*, London.

COLSON, E. and GLUCKMAN, M. (eds.).   1951.   *Seven Tribes of British Central Africa*.

DURKHEIM, E.   1893.   *De la Division du Travail Social*, translated as *The Division of Labour in Society*, 1947, Illinois.

EVANS-PRITCHARD, E. E.   1940.   *The Nuer*, Oxford.

——   1956.   *Nuer Religion*, Oxford.

FIELD, M. J.   1940.   *Social Organization of the Ga People*, London.

FORDE, C. D.   1939.   'Government in Umor', *Africa*, xii, 2, 129–162.

——   1947.   'The Anthropological Approach in Social Science', *Presidential Address to the British Association, Section H.*

FORDE, C. D. and JONES, G. I.   1950.   *The Ibo and Ibibio-speaking peoples of South-eastern Nigeria*, London.

FORTES, M.   1936.   'Ritual festivals and social cohesion in the hinterland of the Gold Coast', *American Anthropologist*, xxxviii, 4, 590–604.

——   1945.   *The Dynamics of Clanship among the Tallensi*, Oxford.

——   1949.   *The Web of Kinship among the Tallensi*, Oxford.

——   1953.   'The structure of unilineal descent groups', *American Anthropologist*, lv, 1, 17–41.

FORTES, M. and EVANS-PRITCHARD, E. E. (eds.).   1940.   *African Political Systems*, Oxford.

GLUCKMAN, M.   1950.   Preface to Mitchell, J. C. and Barnes, J. A., *The Lamba Village*, Communications from the School of African Studies, No. 24, Cape Town.

GULLIVER, P. and P. H.   1953.   *The Central Nilo-Hamites*, London.

HUNTINGFORD, G. W. B.   1953a.   *The Northern Nilo-Hamites*, London.

——   1953b.   *The Southern Nilo-Hamites*, London.

[1] The Dinka, numbering 900,000, are an exception, due perhaps to the high degree of mobility of territorial groups and lineages, consistent with their ecology.

LOWIE, R. H. 1950. *Social Organization*, London.

MIDDLETON, J. 1953. *The Kikuyu and Kamba of Kenya*, London.

—— 1955. 'Notes on the political organization of the Madi of Uganda'. *African Studies*, 14, 1, 29–36.

OBERG, K. 1940. 'The Kingdom of Ankole in Uganda', in Fortes and Evans-Pritchard 1940.

RADCLIFFE-BROWN, A. R. 1940. Preface to Fortes and Evans-Pritchard 1940.

—— 1941. 'The Study of Kinship Systems', *Journal of the Royal Anthropological Institute*, lxxi, 1–18.

—— 1945. 'Religion and Society', *Journal of the Royal Anthropological Institute*, lxxv, 33–43.

SOUTHALL, A. W. 1956. *Alur Society*, Cambridge.

WINTER, E. H. 1956. *Bwamba*, Cambridge.

31

POLITICAL ASPECTS OF
TIV SOCIAL ORGANIZATION

Laura Bohannan

INTRODUCTION

THE 800,000 Tiv who live on either side of the Benue River are the largest pagan tribe in Northern Nigeria. Of this number about 700,000 are concentrated in Tiv Division of Benue Province.[1]

The Tiv are bordered on the east by the Jukun and Chamba. To their west are the Idoma, and to the north the so-called 'broken tribes'—Angwe, Bassa, Koro—small, intermixed groups speaking mutually unintelligible languages. To the south, in Ogoja Province, are the people Tiv call Udam: a congeries of small, semi-Bantu speaking tribes—Bette, Otukwang, Egede, Bisseri, Bendi and Boki. Some of the Cameroons Bantu tribes— Mambila, Yukutare, Abo, Ndoro and Tigong—share certain linguistic and cultural traits with Tiv and Udam. Socially, there are a few striking similarities—exchange marriage, for example —and even more striking divergencies. Most of these societies seem to be made up of small descent groups—sometimes territorially distinct, sometimes dispersed—crossed and integrated by ties of reputed kinship, chiefship and religion. Segmentation in these societies could be compared with that of the Tiv only for content. In political organization the Tiv are in no way typical of the region in which they live.[2]

[1] In order to devote more space to the political, I am eliminating as much background information as possible. Further general data can be found in Bohannan 1953 and 1954.

[2] See Meek 1931a and 1931b; Abraham 1940: 45; Kingsley 1899; Migeod 1925.

Tivland is a rolling plain sloping from the foothills of the Cameroons and Sonkwala Hills in the south (about 1300 feet, with some hills of 4000 feet above sea level) to the banks of the Benue River (350 feet). Both are in the southern hills and along the Benue and Katsina Ala rivers the country is well-wooded grass land. In the central plains there is little wood and, at the end of a long dry season, water may become scarce. Along the Benue, the low-lying ground is a chain of swamps in the rains and a series of dust bowls during the harmattan.

There is tsetse. The few cattle kept are of the dwarf variety. Soil and climate, however, permit the Tiv to participate both in the grain cultivation of the north and in the yam farming of the south. Tiv are subsistence farmers.

A consistent and characteristic pattern of settlement makes Tivland readily recognizable from the air. Scattered about the countryside are the Tiv compounds, some of two or three huts, others of forty or more.[1] Each compound is composed of two rings of huts (sleeping huts and granaries outside, reception huts inside) concentric around an open yard and surrounded by fruit trees. Radiating from each compound, and connecting each with at least two others, are a number of paths. A few fade away in the dark rectangles of farms, which patch the intervening bush. Others—wide and well trodden—pass to the side of the compounds, can be followed for long distances and, in the south, lead into open areas with a few rectangular shelters: the market places.

Flying from north to south one notices the lessening proportion of bush, the smaller size of individual farms, and the drawing together of farm and compound that mark increased density of population.[2] But nowhere can one see any clustering of compounds, patterning of paths, or strips of no-man's land that might mark off territorial groups. Tiv boundaries are social facts.

There are a number of segmentary systems in Tiv social structure. The lineage system, though the most pervasive, is not

[1] 7–8 are average in the south, 8–9 in the north. Average population, 17–18 in the south, a few more in the north. Large but not maximum populations are 80 in the south, 140 in the north.

[2] The average for Tiv Division (64 per square mile) means little; there is a steady increase from the 25 or fewer per square mile north of the Benue to the 550 per square mile along part of the southern border.

34

in itself primarily political. But territorial and political organization of Tivland, the system of *utar* and *uipaven*, are expressed in its idiom, and the age-set system takes one of its dimensions from it. Markets are associated with political segments, and sometimes conflict with, sometimes support, the values attaching to them. Markets, in their non-segmentary nature and in their furthering of communications by ritual peace, form the conceptual bridge from the lineage system to the rather undeveloped and certainly unsystematic aggregation of peace treaties which cut across other political loyalties.

The order of presentation to be followed is in part a conceptual progression from interlocking segmentary systems to institutions not intrinsic to the political structure, though of great political importance. The territorial and political systems— *utar* and *uipaven*—characterize all Tivland. Age-sets, interlocking market cycles, and peace ties spread irregularly up from the south, and we believe their presence correlated with the higher degree of cohesion attained by relatively large populations in southern Tivland.

THE LINEAGE AND LINEAGE SEGMENTATION

The Tiv do not present that difficulty so common to Africa: identifying the tribe. A Tiv is a Tiv and can prove it. This proof consists in a genealogy through which every Tiv can trace his descent from Tiv himself. It is not in itself a record of ancestry—Tiv themselves consider it so only in connection with lineage—nor in itself a portrait of political structure, for its field of relevance is greater than that of the political while, on the other hand, not all political relationships are capable of expression in its idiom (Bohannan 1952).

Although they are stated in a common idiom, the referents of the named points of segmentation in this genealogy (Figure 1) are clearly not all of the same order. Chenge is a living man with sons and grandsons; Kunav, a territorial and political unit which formerly united in warfare; Ikor, the ancestor of Kparev and of two non-Tiv peoples, the Uge and the Utange; Tiv, the name of a linguistic and cultural entity which never (prior to British Administration) acted as a political unit; and Adam, the father of Batule, who begot all white peoples, and of Shôn, the

35

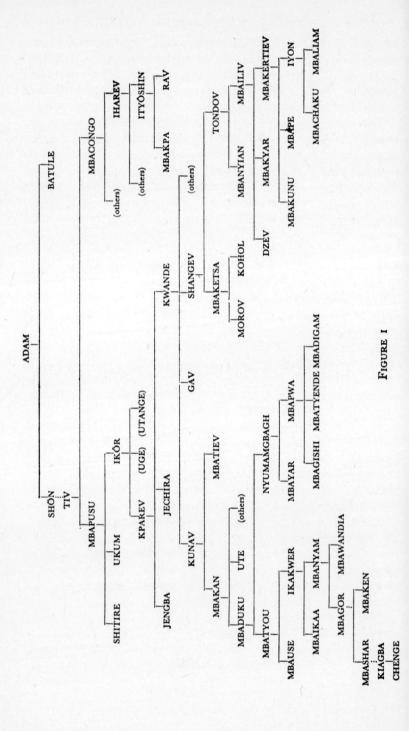

FIGURE I

ancestor of the black. The genealogy thus furnishes a common idiom for the statement of individual ties of kinship, political and territorial grouping, cultural unity, foreign alliances, and a general cosmological placement amongst the peoples of the world.

This genealogy, in so far as it serves to express relationships among the living by reference to the dead, represents a lineage system, each segment of which may be considered either in terms of span, i.e., as composed of living people (*nongo*), or in terms of depth, i.e., in its composition as a unilateral descent group (*ityô*). The segments form a system because the whole is comprehensible not as the sum but as the arrangement of the parts.

The Lineage Group, nongo

Nongo (literally 'line' or 'queue') may be used to enquire after or describe the component segments of any lineage. The *nongo* of MbaDuku (Figure 1) are MbaItyou and Nyumamgbagh; the *nongo* of MbaItyou, MbaUse and Ikakwer, and so forth. The referent of 'the same *nongo*' thus varies with the context of the statement: in terms of MbaDuku, or any lineage inclusive of it, a man of MbaItyou and another of Nyumamgbagh are of the same *nongo*; in terms of the component segments of MbaDuku, they are of different *nongo*.

Nongo refers primarily to the living representatives of a lineage. One's duties to one's *nongo* are one's obligations to living agnates. A man identifies his *nongo*, not by the name of the lineage segment, but by the name of some prominent man amongst its living representatives: a government chief, man of influence or prominent elder. Kiagba, a man known throughout Tivland, was frequently cited in the course of *nongo* identification, but the precise span of his *nongo* was given by social context: 'Kiagba's *nongo*' in Rav means Kparev, a lineage containing over half the Tiv; within Jechira, Kunav, MbaDuku, MbaGor or MbaShar, progressively smaller segments were identified by reference to his name.

The Lineage as Descent Group, ityô

That each man is automatically a member of all the segments inclusive of the smallest to which he belongs—that is, that

Kiagba is simultaneously MbaShar, MbaGor, MbaDuku, Kunav, Jechira and Kparev also means that he is descended from Shar, Gor, Aduku, Kuna, Jechira and Kpar and that, as his ancestors, they define his *ityô*.

Although the precise reference of *ityô* varies as does that of *nongo*, the two differ in that *ityô* cannot be used to describe the component segments of a lineage. It is a personal and particularistic (hence exclusive) term of identification, stating some individual's place among Tiv by identifying that lineage, filiation to which gives him his political citizenship, his rights to land and residence, delimits those persons who may bewitch him and whom he may not marry, and appoints the place of his memory after his death. Only his being sold into slavery can sever him from that place.

The *ityô* is a patrilineage. Tiv, attempting to define it, frequently explain that they 'do things on the father's path' (*er kwagh sa gbenda u ter*) and not, like some matrilineal Cameroons people known to them, 'on the mother's path'. In ideal, Tiv approach the patriarchal. In practice, they are overwhelmingly patrilineal.[1]

A man is connected with five patrilineages not his own (in order of decreasing importance): (1) his mother's *ityô*, whom he calls his *igba*, or rarely *igba ngô*; (2) his father's mother's *ityô*, his *igba ter*; (3) his father's father's mother's *ityô*, his *igba ter u tamen*; (4) his mother's mother's *ityô*, his *igba ngô u tamen*, and the *ityô* of his mother's secondary marriage guardian, his *igba tien*.

In any other context, a man speaking of his *ityô* may be speaking of any lineage included within the Tiv, but in context of comparison with his *igba*, his *ityô* is permanently fixed. A son of Kiagba whose mother was MbaIkaa, has MbaNyam as his *ityô*. Another son of Kiagba, whose mother was Nyumamgbagh, has MbaItyou as his *ityô*. The limits of *igba* and *ityô* are fixed by genealogical equivalence.

This feature is not without political significance. A man is safe amongst all and any of his *igba*, and it is the duty of his *igba* (especially his mother's *ityô*) to protect him from the injustice of his agnates. It is also a man's duty to his agnates to act

---

[1] A man's *ityô* are his agnates only if his father (*genitor* or *pater*) married his mother by exchange marriage or, since 1927, with bridewealth. Otherwise a man's *ityô* is that of his mother. Bohannan 1953: 23–5, 69–76.

38

as intermediary between them and his *igba*. The larger the lineages of a man's *igba* and *ityô*, the more important the affairs in which he is called upon to act as go-between, and the more likely he is to receive full protection against his agnates—for the genealogical distance between large lineages assures (or expresses) their enmity.

The man whose *igba* and *ityô* lineages are of small span, speaks of his '*igba* amongst his agnates' (*igba i ityô*) as a sign that his *igba* lineages are more often relevant to him as his *ityô* than as differentiated from it. That is, a man whose mother was MbaKunu and whose father was Iyon, has so many occasions to speak of MbaKertiev (a lineage including them both) as his *ityô* that the standing of one of its segments as his *igba* becomes almost irrelevant. Between two lineages so close, a mediator's office is seldom needed, nor do the elders of two such close lineages care to antagonize each other over individuals in any but the most clear cut cases of oppression.

It is these factors which explain Tiv preference for marriages between socially distant (but spatially adjacent) lineages, just as it is the obligations of kinship which turn a man's individual kinship ties into a relationship of occasional political importance to the community as a whole.

THE POLITICAL STRUCTURE

Among the Tiv the segmentary system of *utar* and *uipaven* respectively gives the spatial and social arrangement of political segments.

The Segment: ipaven

To determine the segmentation within a lineage, one can ask, indifferently, 'What are the *nongo/uipaven* of MbaKertiev?' One receives the same answer to both questions. But *nongo* is applicable at any genealogical level. *Ipaven* is not.

Iyon, MbaKunu and MbaPe are the *nongo* and *uipaven* of MbaKertiev (Figure 1). If one then asks for the *nongo* of Iyon, one is told 'MbaChaku and MbaLiam'. If one asks for the *uipaven* of Iyon, one is told flatly, 'Iyon has no *uipaven*; it is one and does not segment (*pav*).' If one then asks why, one is told, 'Iyon is one land (*tar*).' And, in demographic fact, the farms and

39

residences of Iyon (MbaChaku and MbaLiam alike) are inter-
mingled, whereas farms and residences of the peoples of Iyon,
MbaKunu and MbaPe each form a territorially discrete bloc—
a *tar*.

MbaChaku and MbaLiam are, however, lineages (*nongo*) and
may be called 'segments within the hut' (*uipaven ken iyou*), for
lineage segmentation is socially relevant even within the minimum territorial unit and indicates, amongst other things, the
possible lines of future fission into two *utar* or segments. These
'segments within the hut', just because they represent future
disunity, are hotly denied the political relevance which the term
'segment' (*ipaven*) would give them.

The reverse does not hold. Lineage transcends the political
system of *tar* and *ipaven*, and to apply lineage terms (*nongo*
and *ityô*) to political segments (*ipaven*) with a territorial
dimension (*tar*) is to apply lineage loyalties to political segments.
Furthermore, since lineage filiation determines political allegiance and since, in fact, 83% of the adult males resident in any
tar are of the *ityô* associated with it, Tiv readily say: 'MbaDuku
is my country (*tar*); it is my patrilineage (*ityô*).'

Land and Segment: Tar and Ipaven

Each segment, the members of which inhabit a continuous
bloc of land in terms of farm and residence, forms an *ipaven* and
a *tar*, and the social fission and fusion of segments is matched by
that of *utar*. MbaGor and MbaWandia are two segments and
two *utar*, which together compose the segment and *tar* of Mba-
Nyam (Figure 2). MbaNyam and MbaIkaa (similarly composed
of MbaKôv and MbaAji) combine to form the single *tar* and
segment of Ikakwer.

If this system is to work, companion *utar* must be adjacent and
in their fusion maintain the definition that the members of the
segment inhabiting it occupy contiguous land.

The system of *utar* is a system of juxtaposition defining the
relative spatial positions of segments. As long as this is maintained, they are, in Tiv expression, 'still in the same place'—
though they may all have moved several miles in terms of hills
and streams.

The *utar* are the spatial expression of the segments; these
segments in their turn express the social distance between *utar*

by the genealogically described order of segmentation. And it is this factor of social distance which makes an MbaKôv man (Figure 2) living on the very boundary of MbaWandia, say it is further to MbaNyam than it is to MbaAji.

The Political Meaning of Tar

Tar, like the English 'country', is a term of allegiance, of political as well as spatial relevance. A Tiv is born to his tar, for he has full citizenship there by virtue of its association with

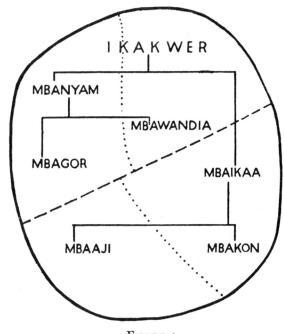

FIGURE 2

his *ityô* and his filiation with that *ityô*. The loyalties given to each overlap and support one another. In time of war, Tiv say, a man must return to his tar in order to assist his *ityô*.

The political connotations of tar can be further seen in such expressions as to 'repair the country' (*sôr tar*) and to 'spoil the country' (*vihi tar*). Any act which disturbs the smooth course of social life—war, theft, witchcraft, quarrels—'spoils the

country'; peace, restitution, successful arbitration 'repair' it.
'To repair the *tar*' is, thus, a phrase which refers to government
in its widest sense.

THE POLITICAL STRUCTURE AND LINEAGE SEGMENTATION

Important loyalties attach to lineage and country: 'He is of
my *nongo*; I help him farm', 'He is my *ityô*; we fight side by side',
'This is my *tar*; shall I allow the enemy to destroy it?' No such
loyalties attach to *ipaven*; the word is never used in political
rhetoric or emotional appeal; indeed, it smacks of a rather
lamentable disunity. Nevertheless, its alternate usage with *nongo*
in description of the genealogically phrased segmentary order of
utar is of considerable importance. It gives an idiomatic appearance of unity to the lineage and politico-territorial segments.
Nongo is a term of social ambiguity, a multireferent applicable
both to lineage and political segments. This ambiguity is essential to the strength of Tiv political loyalties. It is, however, an
ambiguity and not an identity. When it is necessary to distinguish between lineage and political segment, between the two
referents of *nongo*, Tiv enquire whether the genealogy cited is of
lineage—'father by father' (*ter a ter*)—or political—'segment by
segment' (*ipaven i ipaven*)—relevance and whether the *nongo* concerned have gone to 'eat together' or are truly 'one man'.

Tiv describe political segmentation in genealogical terms, but
the genealogy cited is often quite a different one from that given
in lineage contexts (Figure 3). Since the manner of this variation is diagnostic of the political workings of Tiv society—it
illustrates devices allowing for the political assimilation of
attached and stranger lineages and the mechanisms of change in
segmentary order to accord with real political relationships—I
shall cite four examples.

(1) *MbaKyar*. MbaKyar is a minimal territorial and political
segment (*tar* and *ipaven*). Its component *nongo* and 'segments
within the hut', the lineages along which future fission is believed likely, are MbaTsegher and MbaBar (Figure 3). However, one of the component lineages of MbaTsegher is Mba-
Chihin of Iyon (see below, (2)), and two of its sibling lineages
form part of MbaBar. MbaKyar explain that these two lineages,

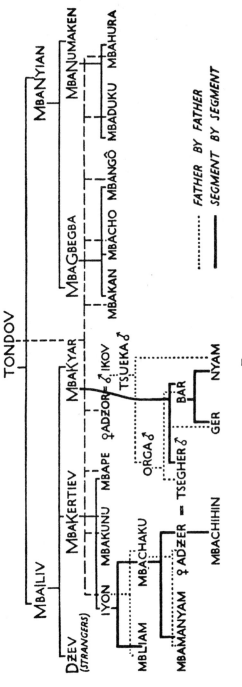

FIGURE 3

Gev and Bar, were small in number; so was Nyam. Gev, Bar and Nyam therefore joined together in certain spheres—they are an exogamic unit—in which they consider themselves the opposite and equivalent of MbaTsegher. And, indeed, in terms of number and strength, they are.

In Tiv words, 'Gev and Nyam went to eat with Bar'. They are not, however, 'one man', for they do not share an *all* inclusive ancestor. Their first common ancestor is Tsueka, but as a group they exclude the descendants of Tsueka's grandson, Tsegher. On the other hand, Tsegher and its sibling lineages Gev and Bar are not 'one man', because they do not 'eat together', that is, act as a unit. To be 'one man' the working unit and the unilineal descent group must be the same.

(2) *MbaChihin of Iyon.* MbaBar and MbaTsegher demonstrate the realignment of small lineages to match current strength in population and influence. MbaChihin demonstrates the position of a recently attached lineage.

Chihin is usually identified by Iyon as the child of Chaku and sibling of Manyam (Figure 3). As far as the standing of MbaChihin within Iyon is concerned, that is an accurate description. That Chihin is the son of a daughter of Chaku who was married to Tsegher of MbaKyar (Figure 3) affects only the relations between MbaChihin and MbaTsegher: in wars between Iyon and MbaKyar, MbaTsegher fought against Iyon, MbaChihin against MbaKyar, but in the battle MbaTsegher and MbaChihin avoided each other. They do not intermarry.

Both MbaKyar and Iyon describe the situation in the following words: 'Iyon is their *tar*, and MbaChihin *are becoming* Iyon. When a man settles down and all his children grow up around him, and he dies and they die, and their children's children live there until their children can say my father's father's father[1] lived in Iyon—then they have become Iyon; it is then their *ityô'. Ityô* and *tar* are ideally one. Tiv attempt to phrase the attachment to the one in terms of the other.

(3) *Tondov.* Those distinctions which Tiv maintain where the units concerned are of dual relevance become awkward and almost meaningless in connection with lineages of primarily political relevance. Between Tondov and its main political segments there are two levels of political segmentation (Dzev is an

[1] Cf. with the range of *igba* relevance, p. 38 above.

exception, Figure 3). In 'father by father' terms, Tondo herself was the mother of Iyon, Kunu, Pe, Adzor (MbaKyar), Kan, Cho, Ngô, Duku and Hura. But at this level there are very few occasions indeed at which ancestry rather than political alliance is of relevance. MbaKyar, Dzev and MbaKertiv, MbaIliv and MbaNyian as political units have a vivid and living reality influencing daily life, and in that reality MbaKyar's status as sibling lineage to MbaHura is of no moment.

Again, younger people name Dzev as one of the children of Tondo. Dzev's status as a stranger lineage is today largely irrelevant—thanks to general peace. As one elder remarked, 'Now that Dzev no longer ambush us MbaIliv on the path, sell us as slaves, or take our heads, they are no longer strangers.'

Alternate 'segment by segment' and 'father by father' genealogies explain anomalies of social status in different spheres of social life; when those anomalies no longer exist, the distinction is of no use and may even be an embarrassment.

(4) *Shangev*. Very large *utar* are seldom united except in warfare, and when they join to 'eat together' it is primarily because the disparity between span and depth, between manpower and political position, has grown too great.

In 'father by father' terms, Shangev is composed of three sibling segments: Morov, Kohol and Tondov (Figure 1). But, say Shangev Tiv, Tondo had so many children, and Kohol so few, that Kohol 'went to eat with Morov'. Together, Morov and Kohol matched the strength of Tondov.

The shift in segmentary order is easily expressed by stating a father–son relation as one of siblings, or vice versa; or, as here, by the insertion of another segment in a 'segment by segment' genealogy.[1] Where, however, political units are concerned fusion cannot occur by a simple merging of name, activity and population. There the spatial juxtaposition of the segments concerned must allow for their territorial fusion as a *tar*. Morov and Kohol, adjacent to each other and both to the north of Tondov, were thus ideally situated for this type of fusion: both in number and in situation they, as MbaKetsa, are equivalent and opposable to Tondov.

The principles governing the fission and fusion of segments in

[1] For other examples see Bohannan 1952.

45

the political system are influenced by factors non-operative in simple lineage fusion.

WARFARE

The operation of the political structure and its association with lineage segmentation are clearly manifest in Tiv warfare.

The Structural Limitation of Warfare

The spread of war is[1] determined by the segmentary order of the groups involved. The fighting spreads until equivalent segments are engaged and is limited to them.

In a remembered war between MbaNyam and MbaIkaa, the two component segments of Ikakwer (Figure 1), no other segment of MbaDuku concerned itself. Such intervention, say of a segment of MbaUse, would have transformed the battle into one between Ikakwer and MbaUse. When two of three equivalent segments fight, the third stands aside. MbaDigam (Figure 1), being equally related to the warring segments Mba-Gishi and MbaTyende, could come to the help of neither without repudiating its relationship with the other. MbaDigam took the only possible course—peacemaking.

The segments involved are those of the politico-territorial system and not lineages. When fighting broke out between Morov of MbaKetsa and MbaHura of Tondov (Figures 1 and 3), all MbaKetsa was engaged against all Tondov. The spread of the war thus followed the order of political segmentation. In lineage terms, Morov, Tondov and Kohol are sibling segments and by lineage values Kohol, like MbaDigam would have had to stand aside.

This segmentary limitation ceases to operate in wars between Tiv and non-Tiv, as by its very ideology it aligns all Tiv against the world. A system of traditional enmity based on territorial segmentation and traditional direction of migration somewhat mitigates the situation. Thus each segment of MbaDuku which borders the Udam has its traditional enemy in that segment of the Udam into whose territory it is moving. When one such

[1] War is, today, rare in Tivland. However, we observed warfare in 1950 and the principles here set forth were all evident at that time. Therefore the present tense is used.

pair of enemies is fighting, neighbouring pairs can in theory agree to keep the peace as between themselves. Such agreement is generally futile, if the fight lasts more than a day. Some Tiv segments have peace treaties with the foreign enemies of their adjacent *utar*. Again these treaties are tenuous against intra-Tiv solidarity and seldom limit the spread of war for very long. Occasionally, however, it does serve to delimit the battlefield.

The Focal Point of War

The personnel involved in Tiv warfare is dictated by the segmentary order of *uipaven*. The territorial position of the segments dictates the battlefield, and the combination of territorial juxtaposition with social distance determines the focal points of enduring hostility.

A given Tiv war may be described either in terms of the segments fighting or in terms of *utar* in which the fighting occurred. In 1934 a fight started on the Ute-Shangev border (Figure 1). All Kwande and all Kunav were soon involved, for the men of each flocked to the war. The scene of battle was, however, territorially limited and Tiv describe this war either as the Kunav-Kwande war or as the Ute-Shangev war.

This same distinction is also compatible with the formation of Tiv fighting clusters (the word 'unit' suggests an organization). The men of the *tar* first attacked flock to and stay within its borders. They move, however, in small groups of close agnates (five to fifteen men). The men coming to their assistance from allied segments travel in similar clusters. At the front, they attach themselves to any one of the local groups containing a close maternal or affinal relative. The fighting aggregation is thus composed of very small lineages, each hooking by a non-agnatic tie of kinship to a small lineage native to the *tar* on which they are fighting.

Tiv describe their wars as though they marched into battle segment upon serried segment. When asked to explain the blatant discrepancy between fact and description, they first comment that in the absence of any differentiation in language, dress or physical appearance personal acquaintance is the only means of telling friend from foe (they fight in precisely the same formation against non-Tiv), and then add that there is no real contradiction, for they are all 'one man'—or else they would be fighting each other and not side by side.

Causes of War

Many incidents form the ostensible causes of war, but Tiv themselves observe that any dispute can be settled unless the parties want to fight. Some elders, indeed, comment, 'After the first war, people are always ready to fight again.' From an analytical standpoint certainly, one can say that warfare is endemic between territorially adjacent segments which are

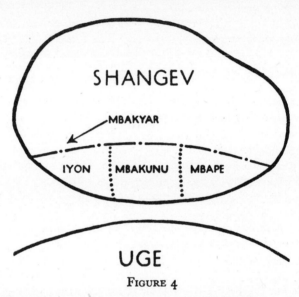

FIGURE 4

socially distant and is, in fact, a factor in the definition of that social distance. Nevertheless, certain incidents leading to war can be isolated and serve to illustrate important aspects of Tiv political relations. Since many of them are involved in the Mba-Kyar–MbaKertiev wars, I shall take them as my example.

In describing wars, Tiv always begin by drawing circles on the ground to illustrate the juxtaposition of the *utar* involved: scale is of no importance, and geographical features such as hills only of rare, tactical concern.

Fighting broke out when MbaKyar pushed against MbaKunu (Figure 4). Iyon and MbaPe at once came to the aid of their companion segment. One MbaKertiev man was killed, but MbaKyar was defeated; proof—MbaKyar ceased to push against MbaKunu. Instead, MbaKyar moved laterally into a position behind Iyon.[1]

In geographical terms, however, this move sufficed to bring MbaKyar's market into competition with Iyon market, held on the same day. Markets are political plums, and destroying a rival market by making it unsafe to attend, recognized tactics. There were some brawls. But when Iyon and the Uge began to fight, all Shangev came to Iyon's aid and all internal disputes were shelved. This war went on for some time, and Ityodu, the most influential man in all MbaKertiev, 'gave' Iyon market to Kwange of MbaKyar for the duration. That is, he ceased to hold his market and encouraged MbaKertiev people to trade in MbaKyar.

When the Uge war ended, Kwange refused to return the market to Ityodu: when Iyon reopened their market for trading, Kwange used all his force and influence to keep anyone from attending it. Furthermore, he claimed that the market magic—ensuring the peace of the market—had been given him by Ityodu, that consequently the peace of the market pact extended to the paths leading to MbaKyar market and that it was there that all diplomatic negotiations between members of the market pact should take place.

The stakes were high, and Ityodu led MbaKertiev to war against MbaKyar. He won. An MbaKyar man was killed in vengeance, and Kwange admitted that Iyon had the market magic and agreed to close his own market.

In these wars one can see that (1) war lies between equivalent segments, MbaKertiev against MbaKyar, (2) that this segmental opposition is an important factor in Tiv leadership (as against Kwange of MbaKyar, MbaKertiev automatically backed Ityodu); (3) that warring segments and political enemies nevertheless unite in the face of a common enemy, (4) that markets are a political factor, and (5) that vengeance lies between equivalent segments and may be taken only in time of war. An unavenged death increases the likelihood of further wars, but among the Tiv there is no institution of blood wealth and no blood feud.

[1] This move led to further difficulties. See Bohannan 1954: 45.

Some Factors of Social Distance

Tiv warfare expresses a political structure which classifies its constituent groups in terms of opposition and identification. Fighting spreads until equivalent segments are opposed to each other and ceases to spread when all the segments of the same order are involved: the principle of segmental limitation is the converse of the principle of segmental opposition.

The degree of hostility between segments is a function of the social distance between them, which determines (1) the manner of fighting—with clubs, arrows, poisoned arrows; (2) the bitterness of the fighting—'close' segments fight but do not attempt to kill in the fighting; (3) the frequency and seriousness of provocative actions, such as theft, abduction, etc.; (4) the degree of looting, burning and farm damage in time of war; (5) head taking and slaving in and out of wartime; and (6) the moral, social and religious consequences of homicide (Bohannan 1953: 25–30).

The social distance between segments (*uipaven*) is solely a function of their position. The social distance between lineage segments is also a function of their position within the system, but not solely. The qualitative differences between lineages, which allows some of them to be labelled as 'strangers', also influences the social distance between them. This differentiation may even perturb the general operation of reciprocal equivalence in values and behaviour among the component lineages of any lineage segment. Within the lineage system equivalence lies between *sibling* segments.

Dzev, MbaKyar and MbaKertiev are equivalent political segments, but Dzev is a stranger lineage. Dzev captured MbaKyar and MbaKertiev travellers as slaves or held them to ransom. Such acts did not occur between MbaKyar and MbaKertiev. No heads were taken in the MbaKyar–MbaKertiev wars; heads were taken in wars with Dzev. Finally, both MbaKyar and MbaKertiev would unite against Dzev in war.

There is then a qualitative difference in the moral values dictating behaviour by and to stranger (*mbavanya*) lineages. But it concerns only their behaviour *vis-à-vis* each other. Dzev is a stranger only within MbaIliv. Against its equivalent segment and against the world MbaIliv shows a united front.

Tiv lineage and political segments are then alike in that within each system the component segments are distinguished in the terms of the structural system of which they form a part. Within the politico-territorial system the juxtaposition of *utar* determines points of contact and focal points of hostility; the genealogically described system of segments (*uipaven*) determines the social distance between *utar*. Each *tar* is associated with a lineage segment which, by its own genealogical charter, validates the moral tone of inter-segmental relationships and gives the terms in which qualitative differences of behaviour between segments of equivalent position are described. In warfare we have seen the integration, in value and action, of these two systems.

THE AGE-SET SYSTEM

Tiv age-sets are a topic in themselves. Here only their political aspects can be described: the integration of age-set and territorial segmentation, and the role of the age-set in inquests.

Age-sets take as their members any man resident within the *tar*: slaves were formerly excluded, but no one else. They are formed approximately every three years, and within any given *tar* thus form a system of mutually exclusive segments which stratify the male population between twenty and seventy into eighteen or twenty groups. What we might call the vertical dimension of the age-set system is thus defined solely in terms of that system.

Horizontally, or in terms of span, Tiv age-sets segment in accordance with the system of *utar* and political segments (*uipaven*). Age-sets (*kwagh*) have their first formation within the minimal *tar*, and become identified throughout larger segments as the social horizon of their members increases with their age. Men of forty-five or so know their age-sets (and prominent men within them) through segments such as MbaDuku and Shangev. To know the age-set is to know its prominent members, for like *nongo*, age-sets are identified by the name of a man prominent within its number. Also as in the case of *nongo* identification, the span varies with the context and hence so does also the identifying individual. Uhô of MbaWandia and Kpeheka of MbaGor each gives his name to his age-set within his minimal tar, but when that age-set meets for MbaNyam, it is more often known as 'Those of Uhô', for he is, in terms of MbaNyam, the more prominent. However, the name of any member may be used to refer to an age-set; age-sets have no other names.

An age-set, then, is permanently limited in its vertical dimension,[1] but it is contextually variable in terms of span. And it follows the order of territorial segmentation and its rules: that is, Uhô's age-set may be MbaWandia or MbaNyam; it cannot be MbaGor, or MbaWandia and part of MbaGor.

The contexts determining the span of the age-set called out can roughly be divided into two: (1) when a man calls his age-set to defend him against witches or accusation of witchcraft, the inquest, then the span of the age-set is that of the lineage (*ityô*) concerned (see below, p. 56); (2) when a man calls out his age-set for a purpose (such as farm-clearing) in which it acts autonomously and not in opposition to any group, its span varies with the range of influence of the member who summons it; a prominent and generous man will command his age-set through a far wider range than a weak or mean man.

THE MAINTENANCE OF PEACE AND ORDER

The maintenance of peace and order within the minimal territorial and political unit is not simply described for it is not the function of a system or of a structural integration of systems, but the compound result of the rôles and values of various persons and institutions.

The compound, ya

The lineages composing that lineage connected with the minimal *tar* have no spatial expression. The members form, so to speak, a single village dispersed in compounds. These compounds are not correlated with genealogically defined *nongo* or lineage segments, nor is there any social structuring of inter-compound relationship: each is simply exclusive of the others.

Each compound is called after its head (*or u ya*, 'man of the compound') who, though almost always the most senior man within it, may be an agnate, non-agnatic kinsman, slave[2] or

[1] The age-sets of very old men merge together, but such old men seldom have reason to turn to the age-set.

[2] Though Tiv concur in the Nigerian law that no man today is a slave, slave genealogies—rarely mentioned—are remembered.

stranger in his relationship to the other members of the compound. The compound head is responsible for its members and their actions. Outsiders go to him with their complaints, to recover debt or stolen property, to receive compensation, for tax. Consequently, his permission is necessary for residence in the compound; he has definite authority over its members, and he can expel any of them for continuous trouble-making or insubordination.[1] For a stranger or non-agnatic kinsman, this means expulsion from the minimal *tar*—unless, and most unlikely, another host can be found. A member of the *ityô* associated with that *tar* can build for himself within it; his expulsion from the *tar* requires the consent of agnates and elders.

The compound is one of the strongest emotional centres of Tiv life. The solidarity of its members rests upon the thick clustering of the bonds uniting them: domestic ties of family and common residence; kinship; and the jural and economic loyalties and obligations of the compound itself. There are no ties between compounds as such, but the people living within them are united by (1) common residence in the minimal *tar*, throughout which their farms are scattered, and (2) membership in a single *ityô* or ties of kinship (cognatic and affinal), age-set membership, or hospitality with a member of that *ityô*.

The compound concerns us because the compound head is the only person in Tivland (outside the field of markets and the father-son, husband-wife relationships) with definite authority in specified fields over definite people.[2] The daily peace-keeping and settlement of troubles in matters of debt, theft, brawling, wife-beating, etc., is in his hands and it is in large part his firm authority and constant activity which allows the informal fluidity of other political leadership.

Elders and men of prestige

The processes by which and the qualifications through which a man becomes a person of prestige (*shagba or*) or an elder (*or vesen*) and by what stages such men in turn become men of

---

[1] For details on intra-compound social relationships, see Bohannan 1953: 15–19, and 1954.

[2] This statement holds in spite of the authoritarian roles established by the British Administration. Without administration such 'authority' would crumble, for it has little or no indigenous moral support.

wider influence or political leaders (*tyo-or*) are recorded else-where (Bohannan 1953: 32–37). Only a minimal sketch of their persons is necessary here, where we are primarily con-cerned with their activities.

An elder is an older man, generally the head of his compound, who has the qualifications necessary to maintenance of the Tiv peace: (1) knowledge of jural custom and of the genealogical and personal histories of his agnates; (2) the mastery of health and fertility granting magic (*akombo*), and (3) the personality and ability which in Tiv eyes mark the possession of witchcraft substance (*tsav*) (Bohannan 1953: 81–94).

A man of prestige, on the other hand, is a man whose wealth, generosity and astuteness give him a certain influence over people and formerly allowed the purchase of slaves and thus the formation of a 'gang' to furnish safe-conduct to those strangers who paid tribute and to rob those who did not. These men, then, had a certain measure of physical force (no longer avail-able to them) at their command. Unless they were also elders, however, they were ultimately controllable by the powers of witchcraft and magic lying within the hands of that geronto-cracy.

The Moot (*jir*)

It is in the power of the elders to deal with troubles arising from witchcraft, magic, curse and malice, troubles manifest in illness, omens and dreams, bad luck, barrenness and death. They may not, however, intervene wherever they see anything wrong; they wait until they are summoned to 'discuss matters' (*ôr kwagh*). And these meetings or moots form one of their constant activities.

Only agnatic members of the lineage may be among the elders of the moot (*mbaajiliv*). 'Women, slaves and the children of women cannot discuss matters.' They cannot do so because witchcraft lies among agnates and it is primarily in the idiom of witchcraft that the moot is conducted. An understanding of its political role therefore demands a knowledge of Tiv beliefs in witchcraft.

Illness, bad luck, poverty are the symptoms of being be-witched. Talent, power, luck, wealth, strong character—all these are manifestations of the possession of *tsav* (a witchcraft substance). Relative influence and relative wealth thus can be, and are, phrased as ranking in degree of *tsav*, and *tsav* is believed always to operate at the expense of others. A man is therefore thought to make his own way at the cost of those on whom his *tsav* can work, that is, on his close agnates who are also his neighbours. Consequently, no matter what benefit of prestige or material assistance a man of prominence gives his lineage, its other members fear him and try to whittle him down to their level. Tiv egalitarianism is manifest in the physical damage done to the possessions of an outstanding man. It is equally manifest if his crops are poor, his livestock die, and his luck turns bad: to Tiv it proves merely that his agnates have done the same work with *tsav* rather than with their hands.

A man bewitched looks for his enemy: someone known to possess *tsav*, hence someone influential, whom he has offended, wronged or given cause for envy. And he summons the elders to remedy the situation; this remedy consists in a wholly secular arbitration of the 'reasons' for his bewitchment, the ceremonial reparation of the damage it has already done to health or luck, and a ritual reconciliation between himself, the elders, and all possible witches. Any witch must then desist. The sanction upholding the decision of the elders in the moot is the statement 'We will let you be bewitched', and the expression in action of that statement is a refusal to come when summoned for arbitrations. The threat is so serious that it seldom need be uttered; when it is, Tiv crumble before it.

The purely secular aspect of the moot's arbitration is of course important to the smooth running of the land, but it is the fact that moots are concerned with witchcraft that makes them concerned with the distribution of prosperity and influence amongst agnates. Thanks to this aspect of their mediation, the elders exercise a restraining control not only on the trouble makers who disturb the community and its leaders, but on the wealthy and influential members of the community.

The association of witchcraft with all manifestations of good and evil, in man and in the world, expresses the ambivalence with which Tiv regard its exercise by any single man. The correlation of the power to bewitch with lineage membership corresponds to the mode in which the moot operates and to its restriction to the minimal *tar*, a unit divisible solely in lineage terms. The interrelation of lineage and political segment (the *ityô* giving citizenship in the *tar*) describes the manner in which this influence becomes political rather than purely domestic.

The Inquest (pinen kwagh)

Occasionally, especially when a man of very great influence is involved, the elders hesitate to act against him. Under such circumstances his victim turns first to his age-set and then to his *igba* to assist him by coming, as groups, 'to ask' (*pine*) the elders of his lineage why they are allowing him to be bewitched.[1]

The span of the age-set concerned is that of the lineage concerned. Most of a man's age-mates, therefore, are also his agnates. At the inquest, however, his age-set is opposed to the rest of his *ityô* and acts against it as a unit. Their sanction is the threat of physical force against witches (or suspected witches). Indeed, the age-set is the only group within the minimal *tar* which has this sanction of physical force within that unit. Collectively, Tiv youth is not defenceless, though as individuals they can oppose to the overwhelming moral force of older agnates only the threat of going elsewhere. It is not without significance that in the north of Tivland, where the age-set system does not exist, the manifestation of serious witchcraft within the lineage leads to panic—sometimes to the dissolution of the community. The protecting role of the age-set is an important factor in the continued existence of Tiv communities.

The span of the age-set is the span of the *ityô*, which, in its turn, is determined by that of a man's *igba*. An MbaKunu man, whose mother is Iyon, calls out his Iyon *igba* and his age-set throughout MbaKunu, and jointly they confront the *ityô*, which in this case includes all MbaKunu except the members of that age-set. The *igba* seat their daughter's son amongst themselves, and threaten to remove him to their own land unless his agnates do him justice; if it is just, they abandon him to the severity of his lineage. The readiness with which they allow themselves to be convinced is closely correlated with the span of the two lineages. The elders of Iyon and MbaKunu have been known to sacrifice the interests of the individual concerned,

---

[1] A man's age-set usually turns out for a moot in which he is concerned, but do not 'ask' unless the elders seem partial.

for their solidarity as MbaKertiev is considerable. Conversely, when the younger brother and approved heir of a government chief found himself helpless against his *ityô*'s malice and witch-craft—for no one within that *tar* (of some 8500 people) would defend him—his *igba*, an equivalent segment, marched over, some 300 elders strong, to take up his defence. They did so successfully, and his continued existence on the political scene was largely due to their intervention.

Initiative and Intervention

Both moot and inquest are concerned with the protection of an individual against persons of influence, and both take their idiom from Tiv notions of witchcraft. Neither is capable of dealing with affairs between political units as such, nor, indeed, with all individual disputes.

When witchcraft is not involved, people seek less cumbersome and more direct remedies. Two men of equal standing, unable to agree, seek out some elder and ask him to arbitrate; they often go to several in succession until they have heard a solution pleasing to them both. If something has been stolen, Tiv, having found the thief, go to demand compensation from the latter's compound head. In cases of negligence, such as farm damage done by livestock, a Tiv generally confronts the culprit himself. The sanctions against most anti-social acts of this nature lie in the many links of mutual dependence between the co-residents of a minimal *tar* and in the moral obligations of lineage.

A compound head can intervene in the affairs of his people of his own initiative. A market master, the market police, have and exercise the right of intervening in market affairs. Tiv morals dictate that any elder step in to make peace if he sees men fighting. But in all other cases, unrequested intervention is meddling and resented as such; Tiv elders and leaders alike must be asked to intervene before they do so. The significant difference lies in the fields of such requested intervention: the elders are called *en masse* to mediate between suspected witch and be-witched, between the average man and those with influence and power over him. Tiv leaders and men of prestige are asked to intervene in disputes between equals and to enforce the claims of their 'own' against 'others'—at any level of segmentation.

57

POLITICAL LEADERSHIP

Among Tiv there is no indigenous fixed association of political leadership with given lineage segment; indeed, there is no office[1] of leadership. If and when a man attains influence within his minimal *tar*, or any part of it, people outside that *tar* make use of his good offices in their dealings with other members of that political unit. Sometimes no man of influence exists within a given minimal *tar*. Even less commonly there have been men who, like Kiagba, can make their influence felt throughout a segment of considerable span. Normally, a man's influence amounts to leadership only if he acts *for* a segment *against* its equivalent (in war, inquest, etc.) Such a man was sometimes called a *tyo-or*.

In the present system of Native Administration there are, however, offices associated with fixed lineages (Bohannan 1953: 30–42). The most important of these is also called *tyo-or*. The origin of this word is obscure—Tiv do not agree on its meaning. It is certain that it was a descriptive term, not a title. It seems to have meant something like 'leader' in the past; today it is used by the administration to translate their notion of chiefship, completely lacking among Tiv, and has been made a title.

A Tiv leader (whether in the old or new sense of *tyo-or*) is considered within his legitimate role when he furnishes safe conduct to travellers, leads his *tar* to war or represents it in peace negotiations, arbitrates between his people and 'others'. He steps out of his role if he concerns himself with the internal affairs of any segment to which he is not filiated or as soon as he favours the cause of 'others' at the expense of 'his own'. And these are the reasons one must talk of such political figures in terms of 'influence' and 'leadership', rather than in terms of chiefs.

Who 'the others' are varies with the situation. If segment B (Figure 5) is at war with A, then X is the *tyo-or* of B. If anything has been stolen by a man of B, from any member of A, then the victim comes to X for restitution, for to A, X represents B. But within B, X represents 4; within 4, h. All too often if he attempts to recover stolen property from e, he will be accused of meddling in e's affairs.

[1] I follow Weber's definition (Weber 1947: 302).

X can extend his influence through I only by sometimes favouring A at the expense of B, yet every time he does so he risks his popularity and influence within B. As long as he is representative of his segment (of any order) against its equivalent, he is approved by it. If he fails to be so, he is suspected of evil practices—bribery or witchcraft. His intervention in the affairs of segments not his own are equally suspect. Men of influence try to limit this suspicion by making use of every cross-segmental tie available: age-sets; kinship ties with *igba* and affines; 'best friend' (*hur-or*) ties; connection with a market. And wherever such a tie exists, he phrases his intervention in its terms rather than in those of political leadership.

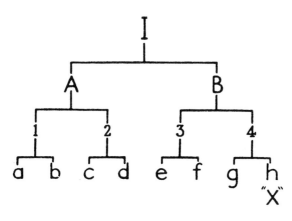

FIGURE 5

The Mystical Idiom of Tiv Leadership

Valid leadership is in idiom correlated with the legitimate possession of *swem*, the emblem of truth and mystical protection against the evil of man and hence of witches. *Swem* prospers the land (*tar*) in all its meanings of farms, people and government: crops grow well and abundantly; rain falls and sun shines at the proper season; man and beast are fruitful and multiply; kinsmen live at peace and in amity with one another; no blood is shed; none die but the one child every woman owes the land that its (mystical) sacrifice may renew the forces (*akombo*) which promote health and fertility.

But the nature of *swem* interacts with the character of its holder. *Swem* diminishes in the hands of a weak man until a perjurer may swear on it with impunity. A true *swem*, in the hands of an evil man, will turn upon him and kill him. When one sees evil men in control of a *swem*, one then knows that *swem* has been 'faked' or 'stolen'. Such accusations are also made when there has been a transfer of influence from a weak man with an inherited *swem* to a newcomer of strong personality. It is said that Morov seized MbaHura's *swem* in the course of the Tondov-MbaKetsa war which transferred the balance of power to Mba-Ketsa. Since then, Tondov say, the crops in all Shangev have been poor, the women have borne few children, and thieves have multiplied. Indeed, many elders say that all Tivland is now spoiled because all the *swem* are in the hands of witches.

This contention is more than a reference to a golden past. Under British Administration, the chiefs (*tyo-or*) of the Native Authority have authority (rather than influence), and have it through all the segments of the political unit to which they are appointed, even in the internal affairs of segments not their own. Inevitably such men are considered witches.

All prominence is an indication of *tsav*. That, to Tiv, is in the nature of things, just as it is in the nature of things that close agnates have the power to bewitch each other—and sometimes do so unwittingly. It is also believed that a man can increase his *tsav* to enormous proportions by eating the flesh of those killed by witchcraft. Witches are believed to share these feasts, and a man who has once participated in such a feast must in his turn provide one. X (Figure 5) may, Tiv reason, have been invited to such a feast in lineage A; he owes his host a similar feast but he himself can kill by witchcraft only within his close agnatic lineage h. If a man, well-liked and respected, without known enemies, dies in h, X will probably be accused of having caused his death for that purpose. If all a man's close agnates die, one after the other, it is known that he is involved in a series of such flesh debts. If he is a man of influence, the motive ascribed to him is that of seeking to place the witches of other lineages under his obligation. If he is a man of no influence, it is believed that he lies under such an obligation and that, lest eventually he have to provide himself as victim, he becomes the willing tool of the 'foreign' witch to whom he is indebted.

A man who sacrifices the interests of his own to gain influence with others is probably engaged in a series of flesh debts and is a witch leader. Since a man sacrifices the interests of his own in some narrower span or segment whenever he is approached for restitution and often in the course of arbitration, he is often called a witch leader. When Upev of Morov tries to concern himself with the affairs of Tondov, he may be called a witch; but even Tondov speak kindly of him when he successfully furthers the affairs of Shangev against others.

Tiv leadership is thus an expression both of the segmentary political structure and of Tiv cosmological views. Just as any segment is one and indivisible when opposed to its equivalent, so any man of influence in his dealings with that opposed segment appears as the representative of its equivalent and, so long as he furthers its interests, its legitimate representative. Only when he contradicts or attempts to surmount segmentary cleavages in his political role (he is allowed influence as kinsman, friend, etc.), does he appear as a witch leader, anti-social because no matter how politically expedient his action may be, it goes against the grain of the society that he should perform it.

TREATIES AND PACTS

There are two ways in which segments of political relevance can be united outside the terms of their own system: peace treaties (*ikul*) and market pacts. Both are limited in number and distribution.

Ikul Treaties

Ethnographically speaking, *ikul* treaties are strongest among the tribelets to the southeast of the Tiv, and the strongest of those in which Tiv are concerned lie between Tiv and these peoples. Indeed, the model, to Tiv, of them all is that between Kunav and the Utange.

These treaties are not only variable in strength, but in content. Some, for example, forbid intermarriage; others do not. Two features are common to them all: (1) they forbid the shedding of blood of the contracting parties and any act which might lead to it (such as shaving); (2) they are made between segments which would otherwise be free to capture and kill travellers from one another. The Tiv statement, 'We make *ikul* treaties with those who might kill us but amongst whom we often travel', adequately describes their function. Like so many Tiv institutions, these pacts are concerned with trade communications and safe conduct.

Such treaties mitigate the hostility resultant from the social distance between political segments, but they do not surmount segmentary loyalties. There is no known instance of two parties to an *ikul* treaty joining in war against a segment more closely related to either. That distinction is reserved to the contributing parties of a market pact.

Market Pacts

A market, both as a channel of wealth and as a centre of social communication, offers obvious advantages to anyone interested in the acquisition of influence. Indeed, the history of many markets is a tale of transferred ownership from one man of influence to another: sometimes his successor, sometimes his rival within his minimal *tar* or from another segment. Kwange's attempt to steal Iyon market for himself and MbaKyar is an incident paralleled in the history of most Tiv markets.

Each market is associated (1) with that *tar* on whose land it is held, (2) with that lineage (*nongo*) a member of which owns it (through inheritance or some other means), some of whom act as market police and others as market judges; (3) and with that segment which initiated the market magic (which maintains peace in the market place) and the market pact (which unites several segments in upholding the market peace both in the market and on the paths leading to it).

Tiv do not consider maintenance of peace in the market an easy task. Even today men go armed to market, though there is an injunction against it and some market authorities demand that weapons be 'checked' with them. Women sit in markets with their backs to the direct path home to allow unimpeded flight. Men from many different and distant segments attend; most of them are young men, and much beer is drunk. No one is surprised if a disagreement over price or the amount of change turns into a brawl. Market police are there to keep words from turning into blows; market judges settle disputes on the spot and while they still concern individuals only. At a well-run market, this organization works smoothly, but it works with constant appeal to the values of the market peace.

Men of influence and prestige make a point of attending such markets. In part they go to hear the news. They also go because at market one can find one's affines, one's debtors (or their close agnates), those responsible for the actions of thief, or runaway lovers. And the successful outcome of such meetings depends in large part on the association of the market with a man of character and influence as market master or owners.

Such a man in control of an important market is in a very strong position: men used to pay him tribute for safe conduct; as market owner he is approached on disputes occurring in the market and if his opinion is thought generally valuable has legitimate standing as an arbitrator in troubles between people of segments where his influence would otherwise not extend; the market tribute is a source of wealth; a consecrated market is a channel of diplomatic negotiations between contributing segments at all times and between others at war on their own grounds.

Tiv of Shangev and MbaDuku and the Uge are associated in Iyon's market pact. Uge and Tiv conduct 'international' negotiations at that market: individual Tiv-Uge disputes; general agreements, such as permission for Shangev Tiv to cut firewood in Uge territory. They act as channels of communication between groups not in direct contact, and assure the safety of discussions between emissaries of warring segments.

The supreme importance of these pacts is shown by the fact that on occasion they supersede the segmentary political structure. Among others, Shangev, MbaYongo and Otukwang had contributed to the pact of Atsar market (in MbaDuku). The only occasion on which MbaDuku ever went to war against Tiv on behalf of foreigners was an occasion many years ago when MbaYongo violated the market pact by killing some Otukwang on their way to Atsar market. MbaDuku Tiv joined Otukwang in a war against MbaYongo, for the latter had broken the peace of the market pact.

The importance, in political terms, of Tiv markets is thus dual. Their organization furnishes a means of increasing the range of legitimate influence of individual political figures.

Through the medium of market pacts political groups are united across the lines of the segmentary system, and united as groups.

CONCLUSION

The political structure of the Tiv takes its individual tone from the interrelation of the two segmentary systems of lineage and politico-territorial segments.

Within the segmentary system of *utar* and *uipaven*, one segment can be distinguished from another only by its place within the system as a whole; such segments vary in order, but not in kind. They cannot be defined in terms of a division or specialization of social tasks, nor as individuated by cultural symbols of taboo or totem. They exist only in terms of the total system, and the system is in turn capable of description only in terms of the functioning of its parts in such spheres as warfare or in terms of the arrangement of its parts, among Tiv, genealogically expressed.

Within the lineage system too each segment forms an externally undifferentiated whole, but the component lineages of such a segment are *vis-à-vis* each other differentiated as to their status as siblings or strangers.

In genealogical idiom the two systems are united, though where they differ appreciably enough in structure and moral values, each follows its own charter. They are also united by the use of *nongo* as a multi-referent, by the association of lineage and political values consequent to the correlation of political citizenship with lineage membership. But there are two systems. The lineage system is of far wider relevance in a far greater area of Tiv life. A man can leave his *tar*; he can emigrate and transfer his political allegiance, and Tiv see stranger and attached lineages as the outgrowth of just such individual emigration. But even when the elders met and formally severed a man from his *ityô* and sold him into slavery, he could never wholly rid himself of it. (He was, for example, no longer able to marry a free woman, but his exogamic restrictions were unchanged.)

Territorial organization is an important element of any political structure, and it is generally accepted that the expression of the political and territorial structure is to be found in the fields of law and warfare.[1] Certainly and obviously this general definition has determined the topics discussed in this article. Yet it is also obvious that those institutions which emerge in the light of activities relevant to this definition are by no means limited to or even predictable from a discussion of political structure (taken from the same definition).

I believe this consequent to the far less general (it does not even approach the abstract) notion we hold of political activity in law and warfare. We have used, in this definition, the sphere of relevance of that aspect of social organization which also determines territorial loyalties. But a simple reversal of definition, using the activities so defined to find the organization in another society, is not necessarily a happy analytical procedure.

Where, as among the Tiv, there is no purely political and governmental organization—I refer to a patterning of statuses and institutions and their correlation with arrangement of groups we refer to as structures—there is no clearly delimited sphere of political affairs. The Tiv language contains no word which might be translated 'political'. There is no culturally organized sphere of activities which might enable us to say that so-and-so has taken up politics. If, on the other hand, we abide by the relevance of anything concerned with the maintenance of peace and the waging of war, then we must also say that there is no single inter-group or inter-personal relationship in Tiv society which does not some time serve political purposes nor any aspect of Tiv affairs not at some time of political concern.

If we try to isolate certain attributes of the roles of elders or men of influence as political, we falsify their true social and cultural position, for we give not a précis but a digest of their roles. The same statement holds of the roles of such institutions as markets, marriage and moots in Tiv society.

Finally, I mean this in a positive and not a negative way: a segmentary system of this sort functions not despite but through the absence of an indigenous concept of 'the political'. Only the intricate interrelations of interests and loyalties through the interconnection of cultural ideology, systems of social grouping, and organization of institutions and the consequent moral enforcement of each by the other, enables the society to work. To

[1] See Radcliffe Brown 1940: xiv.

LAURA BOHANNAN

isolate part of it as 'political' may be correct, insofar as our definition of the political is concerned, but to do so robs the society of those very factors which endow it with vitality.

ACKNOWLEDGMENT

Field work among the Tiv totalling 26 months between July 1949 and January 1953 was carried out under the auspices of the Social Science Research Council and the Wenner-Gren Foundation for Anthropological Research, for whose assistance grateful acknowledgment is made.

BIBLIOGRAPHY

ABRAHAM, R. C.   1940.   *A Dictionary of the Tiv Language*, London.

BOHANNAN, L.   1952.   'A genealogical charter', *Africa*, xxii, 4, 301–315.

BOHANNAN, L. and P.   1953.   *The Tiv of Central Nigeria*, London.

BOHANNAN, P.   1954.   *Tiv Farm and Settlement*, London.

KINGSLEY, M.   1899.   *West African Studies*, London.

MEEK, C. K.   1931a.   *A Sudanese Kingdom*, London. ,

—— 1931b.   *Tribal Studies in Northern Nigeria*, London.

MIGEOD, F. W. H.   1925.   *Through British Cameroons*, London.

RADCLIFFE-BROWN, A. R.   1940.   Preface to Fortes, M. and Evans-Pritchard, E. E., *African Political Systems*, Oxford, 1940.

WEBER, M.   1947.   *The Theory of Social and Economic Organization*, London.

66

THE MANDARI OF THE
SOUTHERN SUDAN

Jean Buxton

INTRODUCTION

THE Mandari live in the broad-leaved woodland and savannah forests of the Equatorial Sudan. They are predominantly pastoralists, but also practise horticulture. Their Nilo-Hamitic language, although differing in many respects, resembles dialects spoken by the Bari and related tribes, with whom they are considered to form one stock.[1] Many features of Mandari culture and social organization, however, suggest Nilotic influence or even direct Nilotic origin. Since the establishment of peaceful conditions under the Sudan Administration, a close economic interdependence in pastoral activities has grown up between Mandari and their neighbours, the Aliab Dinka and Atuot, which has furthered their contact with Nilotes as opposed to other Bari speakers, who have largely given up a pastoral mode of life.[2]

The Mandari comprise two groups occupying separate countries and claiming to be of different stock. Those to whom the name 'Mandari' appears undisputedly to belong live in an inland territory about ninety miles west of the Nile, bordered by the Atuot in the north and the Moru and Nyangwara in the west and south. On the east they are separated by a broad stretch of uninhabited thorny savannah from the riverain peoples who, although generally referred to as Mandari, call

[1] The peoples of the Bari group are the Bari, Nyangwara, Fajelu, Kuku, Kakwa, Nyefu and the riverain Sera and Köbora.

[2] With the exception of Sera and Köbora, and to a lesser extent the Nyangwara.

themselves Sera[1] and Köbora.[2] The grouping together of the latter peoples with Mandari would appear to be relatively recent. It has resulted in the river-dwellers and Mandari coming to have a vague sense of being one people, although there is little social intercourse between them. They cannot easily reach each other, owing to the difficulty of the territory by which they are separated. In this short account I consider only the inland group who themselves claim to be Mandari.

Mandari country is flat woodland and grass savannah. In the dry season good supplies of surface and river water are found in a few areas only, and this strict localization may compel whole villages to move to temporary encampments near pools during the last two months before the rains. When these begin in early April, the country is rapidly covered with pools and streams, deeper channels becoming swift-flowing rivers. The soil in most parts of the country is light and sandy, and Mandari do not have to face extensive flooding, since surface water dries up rapidly, except in low-lying areas.

In the west the iron-stone plateau provides a rich red loam, and larger woodland trees including shea-butter, ebony, mahogany and tamarind grow among low bush and creeper. The iron-stone belt culminates in the south-east in Mount Tindalu, a rocky ridge, which is very important in the mythology of the Mandari. Eastwards beyond this point is waterless scrub with some grassland, parts of which are grazed by herds during certain months, but which is not suitable for habitation because of lack of permanent water.

Mandariland is small and has a low population, probably not exceeding 15,000 souls.[3] Its people are scattered over the homeland in isolated groups in order that inhabited areas may be near streams and rivers which provide relatively permanent water, and to facilitate shifting horticulture. The isolation of

---

[1] The Sera (Shyr or Shiara as they have been called by early travellers to the area) claim to be indigenous to the Nile Valley. Later other immigrants, including certain Mandari groups from the inland territories, came and settled with them on the Nile.

[2] Köbora (Böri or Liene on the east bank) came to the Nile in a series of migrations from the east beyond Lafon Hill. They may have been of Luo or Anuak origin. Köbora, who fought with many of the earlier river-dwellers, formerly spoke their own language, and the Sera people claim to have had theirs. Both now speak a dialect containing a very high preponderance of Bari words.

[3] With the riverain groups, Mandari may number 33,000.

groups of villages is also related to the division of the country into small independent chiefships. Millets, groundnuts and pulses are the chief crops, with some maize, cassava and tobacco. Fields, and finally village communities, are moved to uncleared woodland, or back to land which has been lying fallow for several generations as plots become exhausted and unproductive. This movement is possible because each chiefdom has its own areas of unexploited territory over which its people have rights of horticulture. There is also as yet no overall land shortage in Mandari. Products of the forest, particularly the oil-bearing fruit of the shea-butter tree, are gathered seasonally, and hunting and fishing are minor activities which supplement diet during the hungry months of the late rains before harvest.

The care of their herds, however, is the chief occupation of Mandari. They are pastoralists by tradition and inclination. The necessity for part of the population of each chiefship to be almost continually on the move over country which is uncompromising for herder and beast is an important factor for breaking down the isolation of political groups. The exclusiveness of small territorial units under rival chiefs, based on the village and horticulture, is counteracted by the wider scale co-operation necessary for protecting and pasturing the herds. Co-operation between these isolated chiefdoms is made necessary by limited sources of water and scarcity of sedge swamp which forms the basis of dry season grazing at a time when forest land is devoid of water and grasses. Widescale sharing of resources is exemplified in the grazing of Aliab Nile grasslands by Mandari in the dry season, and the sharing of Mandari woodland grazing by Aliab Dinka and Atuot herds during the rains.

Historically, the Mandari regard themselves as being composed of different levels of incomers superimposed on earlier populations. This building up has been the result of immigration and absorption, which is clearly shown in the histories Mandari relate about the origins of their present-day clans and lineages. The Mandari are not a tribe, but a people—a cultural and not a political group. There is no single Mandari founding ancestor, but certain groups consider they have a more rightful claim to Mandari country because they occupied their land prior to people of later advent. The most important people of early Mandari stock say that they are descendants of a sky being, and that their ancestors separated out of a single homeland close to Mount Tindalu named Mandari Bora. The people of Bora extraction represent the largest group who claim a single ancestor, and clans of this stock are found throughout the country. They base their right to land and their religious superiority on an important myth known in some form to all their descent groups.

The essence to the myth is that in the early world the earth was joined to the sky by a rope, and God, together with the people of the sky and those of the earth, went up and down the rope, the two societies of earth and sky being complementary and united. At about this time, two sky beings arrived on earth, in some versions, down the rope, in others, by direct fall. Of these two, who were brothers, the one named Rueli went back to heaven and left the other, Mar Nykwac Jakda, on earth, where he eventually begat a number of sons who are said to be the founders of present-day Bora clans. In the myth we are told that Mar Desa, the ancestor of the clan which still bears the name Mandari Bora, killed his younger brother Jangdor because he was jealous of his miraculous powers. This act brought about the separation of earth and sky and introduced suffering and death into the world. At the separation of the cosmos, the senior Bora ancestor divided his sons, 'because', Mandari say, 'they became many and were always quarrelling'. Each son with his people was allocated a different territory over which he was placed as religious and temporal head, *Mar*, he also being given power to intercede for rain and perform rites for the land and forests.

On one level this myth is a justification of political and territorial divisions which exist at the present time; on another it vouches for the religious powers which are hereditary in chiefs of land-owning lines. Bora descent groups hold chiefdoms in all parts of Mandari, and their heads perform rites for the land as well as holding it by political ascendancy.

Mandari also say that there were people in the country prior to the arrival of the Bora. Small lineages which have since been absorbed by Bora or other incomers say they originally lived by hunting and cultivating and had no chiefs; others who are still powerful and land-owning say they kept cattle. Both Bora and pre-Bora populations consider themselves to be true owners of land. Their holding of it is vouched for mythologically, and also by right of primary occupation, their ancestors having been the first people to exploit it.

Groups considered by these landowners to be of more recent advent, or who admit this fact, may try to usurp land-owning status when they have political and numerical supremacy in a chiefdom, but they lack religious association with the soil and cannot perform valid forest and rain rites. These 'pseudo' land-owners are often descendants of migration leaders who came in from outside Mandari and settled on unoccupied land, establishing chiefships on the Bora pattern. Others were formerly 'clients' with people of Mandari stock who, superseding their hosts in numbers, gradually assumed political dominance. The lines of their patrons became weak, retaining only the privilege of performing land rites which could not be taken over by outsiders. Immigrants from Moru, Nyangwara, Lugbara, Dinka and Fajelu now hold powerful chiefships of this kind in Mandari.

POLITICAL UNITS

(i) *Territorial organization*

Mandari never had any form of centralized political organization. Before the recent formation of six administrative chiefships, Mandari country was composed of a very large number of small chiefdoms between whom relations were friendly, competitive, or openly hostile. These little territories varied a good deal in size; some were hardly more than a few miles across and comprised a few hundred souls, others, from what can be seen of remaining boundaries, stretched for ten to fifteen miles and their populations numbered several thousands. Although these indigenous divisions have now been merged politically into larger units, each land-owning group and its people is acutely conscious of its separateness from those with whom it has been linked administratively, and these known historic divisions still form the basis for social interrelations and religious activities which are not related directly to government. They are the only divisions that have importance for Mandari and it is the organization of these former chiefdoms which I describe here and not that which has recently been imposed from without.

Each chiefdom typically comprises the straggling villages and hamlets of the land-owning core and its satellites with cultivations, forest land and wet season grazing; it is ideally separated from neighbouring groups by areas of unoccupied bush. Dry season grass-lands, although found on the territories of specific groups, are utilized by a number of chiefdoms on a co-operative basis. Land boundaries are jealously guarded, and this is primarily related to the economic value of natural phenomena, the most important of which are rivers, pools and natural plantations of shea-butter trees. These have hereditary owners who may perform rites for their productivity and for the safety of those using them. Added to this, land which has once been occupied is always incorporated for all time in the chiefdom, even if it is not used again for several generations. Homeland and landowners are bound together by ties of a religious kind, regardless of how the land itself may be divided up within and between owners, clients and settlers. Thus while Mandari know that movement has taken place, and later groups have filled in the unoccupied stretches between chiefdoms, they consider that the boundaries of the main land-owning groups have remained unchanged since the creation of the country. This way of looking at land sections as permanent and fixed by religious charter is very important. Mandari groups *in situ* never fought for the possession of land, but only for cattle and retainers. This follows from the belief that undifferentiated land is of no value. Only the specific owners of a country can exploit its resources effectively because they have hereditary power to do so; that is why where land has been taken over by immigrants from outside the new owners either leave the former inhabitants to perform land rites, or they try to validate their own performance of them by reference to another supporting myth. In some cases ill feeling between the two sets of occupants has resulted in the rites no longer being performed.

(ii) *Descent groups*

Each Mandari chiefdom has been built up round a nuclear land-owing descent line of Bora, pre-Bora or immigrant land-owning stock. These dominant lines which founded or took over territories attracted and absorbed a non-related population of clients and settlers, as well as maternal and affinal kin. Each chiefdom is therefore a heterogeneous collection of small lineages and extended families linked by ties of mutual inter-dependence to a dominant core of landowners who hold together the total population in a single polity. In every chiefdom the group of related landowners are said to own the land. They are known as *komonyekak*, *komonye* meaning 'owners' or 'fathers', *kak* 'country' or 'earth'. I have called these descent groups of land-owning agnates 'land-owning clans'.[1] Their chief characteristics are that they are always territorially defined groups between whose members intermarriage is forbidden. Residence through attachement to land being strongly patrilocal, herds and other property are identified with the agnatic descent line. These factors help to perpetuate the territorial stability of land-owning groups. In cases where small extended families of agnates have moved from their land to another chiefdom, land-owning status is lost, the group becoming related settlers or clients. A man can only be a landowner in the country where his clan have this status; for this reason, permanent settlement outside one's own territory is rare, except for fugitives and wrong-doers. Temporary residence with the mother's brother or affines for a few generations is quite common, however, and is related to the economic interdependence which exists between many types of kin.

Land-owning clans always segment into named lineages, each of which occupies its own land within the chiefdom. Groups of hamlets, accommodating members of one such lineage and its satellite lineages of clients and settlers, form a straggling village which may be separated in a large chiefdom from the villages of collateral lines by several miles of bush. The hamlet is the day to day economic unit and its labour is based on mutual assistance between close kin. The village is also an economic unit, but as many of its members have no real blood ties, the labour of a village is rewarded with beer or tobacco.

Members of the owning clan have a common name which is also the name of the total territory. Lineages of the clan are also named and the land on which they build in like manner bears this name. Land and its owners are linguistically identified at all levels of segmentation, but lineages of clients and settlers who

---

[1] I use the word clan to define a segmented group of agnates who trace descent from a common ancestor. Small unsegmented groups living with landowners I call lineages.

73

have the perpetual usufruct, but never the ownership, of land, do not name country in this way.

It is possible to speak of a genealogical principle in Mandari, because each member of a territorially based clan can, if necessary, show his exact relationship to every other member by reference down the lines from the clan founder. I should stress, however, that genealogy tends to be bounded by country–kinship ties which are land based taking precedence over kinship ties outside the territory which are widely separated in time. In any chiefdom, each lineage of the land-owing clan has equal political representation, although some are known to be senior to others, having segmented from a common ancestor farther back in the line. Thus named lineages which represent groups of living people see themselves as sharing equally in power and representation. Because lineages see themselves in this way, they do not combine to form politically important larger groups within the chiefdom, or divide into factions under political pressures. There is no hierarchical lineage system because all lineages always come to the centre—to the *Mar*—in a political situation. A clan is continually segmenting and Mandari see this quite clearly: they say that division into what become further-named groups is related to the number of surviving sons born to an ancestor at a certain point on the line. If the groups stemming from these sons become large, each will be separated off after four or more generations, and named after the natal lineage of the woman who bore the individual founder. Although people know that some lines segmented farther back or more often than others, the different generation levels of lineages are irrelevant in a political situation, as also is closeness or distance in lineage time, which in Mandari does not necessarily imply closer or more remote distance territorially. Principles of internal unity are co-ordination round the central figure of the hereditary chief, whose lineage is either that descended from the first son of an important clan ancestor, or the line which has emerged historically as the strongest and most suitable to chiefship. This line is always the point of cohesion for its collateral lineages and for non-related clients and small lineages sharing the territory.

In external relations between chiefdoms it was the balance of power—co-operative or hostile—between individual *Mar*, backed by their land-owning lines, which was the basis of the political system.

Each Mandari chiefdom has an internal structure based on a segmented land-owning clan as described. A proportion of these chiefdoms consider themselves completely separate from their neighbours, while others feel themselves to have links of kinship through their land-owning lines to descent groups which are ruling nuclei in other parts of Mandari. Chiefdoms linked in this way are those occupied by lines of Bora stock who claim one sky founder, and say they separated from the Mandari Bora homeland. Non-linked chiefdoms belong to lines of pre-Bora or immigrant stock. Linking is, therefore, based entirely on common ancestry.

In assessing the importance of descent ties between Bora chiefdoms, it must be remembered that, because of the territorial basis of all land-owning clans, agnation in Mandari tends to be largely reckoned in terms of sharing a common territory. The limit of the individual chiefdom occupied by a Bora group is narrower than the widely stretching ancestral line which provides the nuclei in many different chiefdoms. There is, therefore, a pull between actual allegiance to land segments as represented by the individual chiefdoms, and feelings of 'ideal' kinship based on a historical linking through descent. The historical Bora line is truncated at many points by the territorial pattern, Bora people having not only divided into different chiefdoms in Mandari, but penetrated as far as the Nile valley where they have settled with Sera and Köbora. For this reason, the Bora line as a factor for active political and kinship cohesion is weak. In one chiefdom, segmentation within the owning clan leads to new lineages being formed whose members always know and give social recognition to their blood ties, but lineages which fragment *away* from a chiefdom to new homelands, as in the dividing up of the Bora people, give rise to new political units, and also form what eventually become independent kinship groups. Exact ties of agnation between these split off clans and the original parent stem are in most cases forgotten. Some Bora segments occupying chiefdoms widely separated by peoples of other stock have ceased to give direct recognition to their common origin, although this knowledge is kept alive by reference to versions of the Bora myth. Those segments, on the other hand,

75

which occupy territories directly adjacent continue to act in their relationships with each other as if they were still lineages of one clan. From the political point of view each has its own *Mar* and separate country, but unlike more widely separated Bora clans, these segments consider they remember their exact relationship to each other, and do not intermarry. A block of Bora clans who act in this way dominates the country round Mount Tindalu, where outsider chiefdoms have not been established.[1]

In Figure 1 I give a chart of the Mandari Bora clans.

It is, therefore, apparent that Mandari distinguish between two types of agnatic descent. That which exists between people of the lineage of one land-owning clan within a single territory always receives social and religious recognition. It prohibits marriage and sex relations, and people linked in this way are one *kakat*, the descendants of one 'door'. The other type of descent links Bora clans. This is primarily ideological; putative agnation put forward for a special reason. Links between Bora clans do not make their people one *kakat*; they may not prohibit marriage; they are no basis for political and territorial solidarity. Knowledge of them is important because it validates rights to parts of Mandari country, and supports the hereditary religious powers of Bora chiefs. Bora chiefdoms have a historical association which is explained in a kinship idiom; they are also tied sentimentally to the original Bora country and Mount Tindalu, a factor which is important to the overall unity of Mandari country.

In every chiefdom, whether occupied by Bora, pre-Bora, or other landowners, there is the land-owning nucleus and the non-land-owning population of settlers and clients. Only one lineage of owners provide the chiefship, but all collateral lineages consider themselves of chiefly descent in relation to the outsiders who can never be either landowners or chiefs. This does not necessarily impose disabilities on settlers, although with regard to one type of non-landowner, the client, disabilities exist; but land-owning status is a factor for prestige in a particular territory, and lack of it a lessening of prestige depending on the role the settler plays.

[1] The clans are Boreng, Rume, Mandari Bora, Sömmöring and Migigi. All of these occupy territories bearing the clan name.

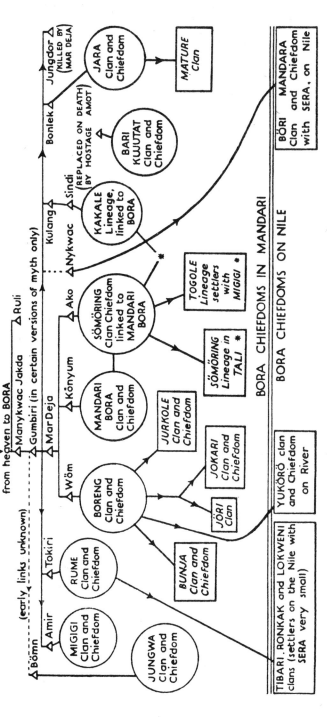

Names in Circles: Clans formed by first separation of Bora.
Names in Squares: Clans or lineages formed by further splits in Bora line. Some of these groups do not marry with parent groups.

* = Clans or lineages which do not have chiefdoms. ⟶ Indicates movement away (fragmentation).

FIGURE I—Diagram of the Bora Clan Group and Bora Chiefdoms in Mandari

Lineages which in time grow out of client or other affiliations are grafted onto the main line and give the appearance in everyday life of being related segments. It is known, however, within the chiefdom that the people have no blood tie, and this fact is also known to some extent outside the territory, because their marriage prohibitions are different from those of the land-owners. Attached lines also perform separate rituals to their own family ghosts. Marriage can take place between non-related outsider lines, and between these lines and lineages of landowners, although a landowner will not marry his own clients. This provides brides near home and within a unit which can exercise political and jural sanctions. In spite of this, the greater number of marriages are outside the chiefdom, and external ties based on affinity are important in regulating political relations between chiefdoms.

An attached lineage is always spoken of as stemming from the main line through the original host to whom the client or other settler attached himself. Attachment is always to specific individuals, and thus every person in the chiefdom has a kinship link of a sort to some other persons. These lineages are often given a 'brother' or 'sister's son' status. A land-owning line with attached lineages of clients may be represented as in Figure 2.

In any chiefship, the land-owning line should present the largest block of agnates.

A line strong numerically can hold the political balance between its attached lineages, which are usually small unsegmented groups who have no corporate unity, their point of common interest being the *Mar* or other elder to which all are attached. Members of client lines automatically support their land-owning nucleus because they depend upon it for their rights as citizens. They also unite with it against rival factions which may form within the chiefdom and threaten to usurp power; for instance, a faction led by a powerful brother of a weak chief. Only where a land-owning line for some reason has lost its numerical strength can a client or outsider line gain political superiority.[1]

[1] This has happened in what is now Mokido chiefdom. The land-owning Lorogak were superseded by a group of settlers whom they took in after a famine in Moru. In Jabour, descendants of clients from Dinka were supported as government chiefs by the Administration in preference to the land-owning Wejur, a small line of pre-Bora stock.

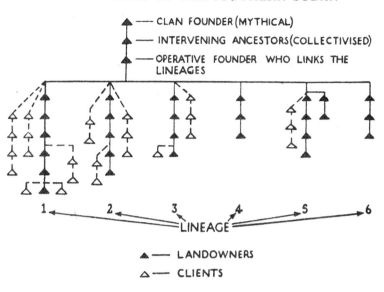

FIGURE 2—Land-owning Clan and Satellites

Note: Line 1 is the line of the Chief and has the greatest number of client lines. Line 4 has died out, and Line 6, being the junior line, has as yet no clients. It will be noticed that client lines are always at least one generation shorter than their host's line. This relates to the late marriage of the client, who may not acquire a wife until middle or later years. Client lines over a depth of 3 or 4 generations are named.

LEADERSHIP AND POLITICAL CONTROL

(i) *The Mar*

I have explained how ideally a *Mar* should be a member of a land-owning line which can exercise full religious powers, and in most chiefdom lines of this kind are the dominant nuclei.

The *Mar* is spoken of as *Mar Lo Bay*, 'chief of the country', or *Mar Lo Toket* of 'the meeting tree'. The office is hereditary, passing either from father to son, or along a line of siblings to the son of the eldest. While primogeniture is considered a factor for eligibility, suitability of character is also relevant as is whether the accession of a particular son is supported by the old *Mar* and the elders. If a line cannot provide a suitable male heir, a member of a collateral lineage may take over, because these people are also landowners and of chiefly status. Mandari consider that the succession of the true *monyekak* lines is ultimately vouched for on a religious level, and can never die out 'because God would arrange it'.

While a *Mar* assumes office by hereditary right, the successful fulfilment of his role is largely dependent on whether he can please his people and build up a strong group of retainers. Although, once installed, Mandari say a *Mar* can never be deposed or killed by his own people, his position can, however, be weakened by the non-co-operation of the elders of the council, or the withdrawal of support of powerful collateral lineages, who in the past sometimes fragmented away to found new chiefships, particularly as a result of quarrels between powerful siblings. From a study of the genealogies of the main landowning lines, however, most of them appear to have been relatively stable for the last eight to ten generations. Mandari say that in fact the *Mar* were 'good', indicating by this they mean strong, rather than of good moral attributes. A 'bad' *Mar* was one who was weak, who could not feed his people, and was defeated in war. Apart from the interest of all lines in the chiefship, the *Mar* himself is chosen because he conforms to a preferred social type. The degree to which Mandari think of the *Mar* as belonging to the people, as well as acting as their ruler, is shown in the saying 'he is our *Mar*, we put him there so that he can talk and we can eat (off) him.'

A *Mar* always had a large number of people round him in the territorial sense as well as linked to him by ties of descent and clientship. His homesteads and the meeting tree of the country were surrounded by the homesteads of close agnates and trusted clients and the goat kraals where the young men slept. This settlement pattern is still marked at the present time. The *Mar* is always physically in the centre of the group because there was formerly no greater disaster than for a rival chiefdom to succeed in killing him. Although this was so, chiefs and their sons were war leaders who led their people against other chiefdoms for raiding cattle and settling homicides. According to Mandari folklore many were killed in this way, and up till recent times, violent deaths of *Mar* are recounted.

The *Mar* gives judgments within the chiefdom. *Kutuk na mar*, the 'mouth' of the *Mar*, meaning his utterances, is said to be given by God, and for this reason people hear him. The *Mar*

crystallizes and expresses the views of the elders after general discussion when people came for help over settling their cases. The
Mar and the group of elders, many of whom are closely related
to him, have a close bond, and while each supports the authority
of the other, each is likewise a check on the power of the other.
The council of elders under the *Mar* is known as *toket*, a name
derived from the word for the shade which is thrown by a meeting tree belonging to a chief or important personage; this is referred to as *toket* as opposed to the shade of an undifferentiated
forest tree, which is *tilimet*. The *toket* of the *Mar* has always been
the appropriate place for male activities not specifically associated with horticulture and herding. Youths and adults whose
homes are within reach of the meeting tree come to spend the
day there, repairing and fashioning weapons and artifacts and
hearing the discussion of cases and the affairs of the chiefdom.
In the past, senior men attending the *toket* ate with the *Mar* and
drank beer there. They came to gain protection and be enter-
tained and also to ensure that the *Mar* was protected.

The *toket* in the context of a group of elders does not constitute a council in the sense of a specially selected or regularly
meeting body. The people who compose it are spending the day
at the tree with the *Mar* and at such times complainants come
and put their cases. Those who take the most active part in
assisting others to solve their conflicts and award compensation
are important heads of land-owning lineages, heads of client
and outsider lines of long standing, paternal uncles, brothers
and adult sons of the *Mar*, and personal clients who are respected for their age and because they have the ear of the *Mar*.

When the people of a chiefdom are widely scattered, heads of
land-owning lineages preside over their own village meeting
trees, but come to the central tree over serious matters, such as
homicide, cases affecting members of more than one lineage, or
the land as a whole. Offensive warfare and raiding were thus in
the past carried out on the level of the chiefdom under the *Mar*
and central *toket*, whereas defensive fighting by nature of its
unexpectedness was on a local lineage basis, collateral segments
in a chiefship rallying if necessary when news of an attack
reached them.

Of equal importance with the power of giving judgments is
the obligation of the *Mar* to feed his people. 'The hand of the

Mar', *Köyn na mar*, is a phrase still heard in spite of the dimin-
ished wealth and prestige of chiefs. The *Mar* is expected to give
assistance to those in need as well as providing food and entertainment for the elders of the *toket* and visitors. In theory, a *Mar*
should never refuse a request for shelter, food, implements or
weapons for hunting, and because chiefs are anxious to keep
their dependants, and in the past, to attract new clients, they
give economic assistance where they are able.

Various sources of wealth and labour are available to help the
Mar to meet his obligations. He is able to draw on a working
force of clients and wives from his many homesteads, and this
work-group is supplemented at certain seasons by men and
women from different parts of the chiefdom, who come to prepare his fields for sowing and to cut the harvest. This latter help
is traditional and is rewarded with beer and meat. The lineage
of the *Mar* also holds the majority of the cattle in the chiefdom
and these are augmented by the marriage of daughters and
female relatives to rival chiefs and by the claim of the landowner to a portion of the bridewealth of the daughters of
clients who have themselves married wives with cattle from the
herd of their protector.

Part of the shea-butter harvest is brought to the *Mar* at an
annual ceremony in acknowledgment of the sacrifice he performs for the forest. A portion of the kill at every hunt is also his
due, and gifts of fish, honey or grain may be made by persons in
order to become 'known to the *Mar*' as a surety against future
want. These offerings are not obligatory, but they are customary
and show good manners. They confirm that the right to accept
gifts is appropriate to the office. In recent times economic demands made on *Mar* have become increasingly difficult for
chiefs to meet. The loss of retainers has coincided with a level-
ling out of status and wealth which Mandari recognize when
they say 'in the past big men were from God, now everyone
thinks he is *Mar*'.[1]

Apart from acting as the pivot of economic, jural and political
relations within the chiefdom, the *Mar*, in degree to which he is
the rightful descendant of the original landowners, has duties in

---

[1] Clientship has been discouraged by the Administration. The cessation of warfare and raiding has reduced destitution, and when famine conditions threaten
government assistance in grain is forthcoming. There are, therefore, few persons
seeking protection from a chief.

relation to the land. There are two important religious personalities in Mandari—the doctor, *bunit*, who assists the individual in his sickness and misfortune, and the *Mar* who is the
guardian of the rain, the land and natural phenomena. *Mar* and
bunit act as intermediaries between man and different manifestations of Spirit *Nun*, and both are considered in different degrees to derive their power from this source. The sacrifices made
by *Mar* are offered to Spirit as universal creator, whereas offerings made as a result of divination by a doctor are made to
spirit as minor phenomena or Ancestor Ghost. The religious
personality of the *Mar* is superior to that of the doctor, and his
duties are automatically performed at regular intervals and are
unrewarded. He is effective because of his intrinsic spiritual
qualities. The services of the doctor are solicited and paid, and
his prestige depends largely on his own efforts.

The *Mar* performs the annual rain sacrifices which include
those for the forest, rivers and shea-butter trees.

In some chiefdoms additional rites are also made for the latter,
and delegation of specific religious duties may occur where rites
for different natural phenomena are performed by a collateral
line of the *Mar* or by a group of client origin. Delegation may be
justified by a story of the handing over which was sometimes a
reward to a favoured client, or a recognition of particular
aptitude for office. It differs from usurpation by an outsider line,
which is never valid, because in the former case the *Mar* and his
line remain ultimately responsible, the new operator and owner
acting for them. A spreading of religious power through delegation is sometimes found in a large chiefdom where different
people may be *Mar lo kudu*, 'chief of rain', *Mar lo kumuri*, 'chief of
shea-butter trees', or *Mar lo tör*, 'chief of the rivers'. In Bora chiefdoms it is usual for the *Mar* to fulfil all these roles. Bora *Mar* are
thought to have the hereditary power of *Ki*, which is spiritual
power associated with The Above. This power was thought to
have been brought into Mandari through the early ancestors
who were religious founders. Territories whose chiefs do not
have *Ki* or other religious powers, often employ rain experts
who are practitioners of the same order as the doctor.

The fact that the office of *Mar* is a sacerdotal one is emphasized in the installation ceremonies through which the *Mar*
passes. Mandari say that if he were not installed, he would be no

different from any powerful elder who has retainers and influence.[1]

(ii) Installation of a Chief—Guida na Mar

On the death of a *Mar*, the country was without a head for a year to eighteen months, until the completion of the mortuary ceremonies for the dead chief. During this time, leadership of the chiefdom was in the hands of elders of the land-owning lineages, close agnates of the dead *Mar* and the *Mar*-elect. These people 'hold the land', '*mogga kak*', and guide the affairs of the chiefdom till the *Mar* is installed. The ceremonies at which he took office were held immediately following the mortuary ceremonies and were a time of feasting for the people of the chiefdom and for visitors and relatives who attended. Persons of other chiefdoms took an important part in the procedure, and this is shown by the fact that certain acts during the ceremony were performed by members of a rival chiefdom; sometimes by a group said to be traditional enemies, although never one whose people were actively in the process of exacting vengeance for a homicide. The *Mar* of a chiefdom which wished to show friendly respect to the new ruler, or had received hospitality from the deceased chief, sent his elders to annoint his successor.

In the central part of the ceremony of installation, the new *Mar* and the client who had been chosen by the elders to become his close assistant and mouthpiece were placed on a mat and bathed in water and milk by old women of the visiting chiefdom. The visiting elders then anointed them with simsim oil, at the same time calling for spiritual protection and assistance for the new *Mar* and exhorting him to rule well and look after his people. The hands of the *Mar* and the client were joined together by the elders, who emphasized the new bond between them, by saying such words as 'you are brothers, you must stay together'; then they instructed the client 'you are *Mar* also, if the *Mar* is absent you look after the people'. After the washing and anointing, *Mar* and client passed a five-day seclusion in a hut during which time close relatives of the *Mar* killed oxen for the visitors and ceremonial dancing took place. While he was in

[1] At present, chiefs no longer pass through these ceremonies, automatically taking office if put forward by their people and supported by the Administration. Information about past procedures was obtained from elders of various chiefdoms.

the hut, the *Mar* was given a new name selected from the names of ancestor *Mar* by the elders of his lineage by which he would thenceforth be known. When the *Mar* re-entered the community, a sheep was sacrificed and prayers were offered for his safety and the support of his office.

At installation the *Mar* acquired a new personality and the seclusion which followed was a period of rehabilitation before he took up his new duties. The change in his personality was reflected in the way he must speak and act as the *Mar*, and the sensitivity of his person to hostile actions and to malignant ritual forces, and in his receiving a new name. Moreover, a very intense relationship was established between *Mar* and client because of their sharing of the rites of installation. 'The client', Mandari say, 'is the *Mar*. He speaks for his master when the *Mar* is not present; he is treated with respect and addressed as *Mar* by people of the chiefdom and visitors.' The client, in fact, became the operative aspect of '*mar*ship' in connection with any unpleasant duties in place of the *Mar* himself. From the time the latter was installed, he had to stand aside from argument and never use harsh words, but only speak, as Mandari put it, 'good and agreeable talk'. The client, as his spokesman, was responsible for giving the commands of the *Mar*, for keeping order in the *toket*, and for summing up cases and speaking for him in his absence; 'he knew what the *Mar* would say and said it for him'. This conjunction of two personalities led to the establishment of a special type of intimacy between *Mar* and client which allowed the client to joke with the *Mar* and take liberties with his possessions.

(iii) *The client—Timit*

Clientship was formerly an important adjunct to chiefship and land-owning status. At the present time there are few individual Mandari clients, and most dependants of this kind are Aliab or Atuot Dinka who come to Mandari seeking for rich patrons. Each land-owning line, however, has its attached lineages of client origin, whose people remain with their original hosts.

In the past, the typical client was a man who through misfortune or misdeed had lost or been expelled from his kin group and sought to attach himself to a chief or notable from another political unit who would act as his protector. Clientship involved the performance of duties in exchange for protection which amounted to mergence in the kin group of the host. Being *timit* was not only a condition of poverty, it was also a status which an individual acquired when he exchanged his personal liberty for the protection of a powerful land-owning line which gave political, legal and economic rights where these had been relinquished elsewhere. This change of status thus implied change of country, because within a chiefdom poor persons could claim assistance from the *Mar* or from more prosperous relatives. When a man left his country, however, the only way in which he could be absorbed was by making himself acceptable as a client.

Clients in Mandari appear to have been of mixed origin. Some semi-client groups were the remnants of a previous people who attached themselves to more powerful incomers; such persons, because of their numbers, were an asset to the new landowners and were never in the dependent position of the individual client, nor were they called upon to perform the same kind of menial duties. Other clients were fugitives from neighbouring tribes. Apart from war and famine, bloodshed between kin, persistent theft and accusations of witchcraft led people to become clients when their lives were no longer safe in their own group.

Clients are a well known institution, and stories relating to their finding are always variations of a theme; they tell how the host finds the client wandering in the bush or grassland, sometimes with a cow, at other times with a wife or dependant. The saying that clients 'come from the bush' is a conventional way of stating that their origins and antecedents are unknown.

The position of the client is full of ambiguity and the type of behaviour considered suitable towards him as a kinsman of a type, but not of one blood, has been considered elsewhere. It should be remembered, however, that after a period of service, the client was assisted in finding a wife, built his own homestead and cultivated fields alongside those of his host. In time he founded his own line, which was distinguished by name but remained grafted onto the land-owning lineages through his original association. The position of people of client lineages of land standing is similar in most respects to that of land-owners,

86

except that the individuals tend to be poorer and the groups smaller. They no longer perform specific duties for the landowners, these being undertaken by newly incoming clients. They are, however, under a moral obligation to remain with their hosts, who still give political and jural protection, and sometimes assistance with bridewealth.

While individual clients assisted their hosts in cultivation, building and herding, it was in the attachment of the client to the person of his host that his duties distinguished him from other dependants or poor relations. Because of this constant attachment, the client was not free to move or utilize his time in the same way as a non-client.

It was usual for clients to marry women of client lines, because of their inferior economic position. But women of client lines also married landowners, and these marriages and the mutual exchange of brides between lines of clients helped to unite different groups in the chiefdom, non-related persons becoming linked by affinal ties, and people of client status becoming in-law relatives of landowners.

Landowners never married into their own clients but married those attached to their collaterals. Marriage with one's own clients would have merged lines which essentially had to be kept apart, as well as violating the conception of kinship embodied in the relationship.

The client always enjoyed the protection of his host against persons of other chiefdoms, and it is said that 'the *Mar* will go to war over his client'. On the other hand, when involved in conflicts with the group of his host, the legal disabilities of the client were pronounced. Clients in serious conflict with their masters had no other course than to escape and try to pledge allegiance elsewhere. Apart from having jural disabilities in relation to landowners, clients and outsiders tended to suffer under the suspicion of having bad ritual traits. Because clients 'come from the bush' and their background is never satisfactorily known, it is in accordance with logical thinking that when illness and other misfortunes occur, which Mandari believe may be caused by malignant individuals, the client with his unsatisfactory history should be suspected. The way in which Mandari believe the evil-eye and witchcraft to be inherited keeps the agnatic line of landowners generally free from suspicion, while at the same time conserving this stigma in outsider and client lines. While every client line is not thought to be ritually dangerous, people expect witchcraft to run in subordinate lines, and know that beneficial powers for the earth run in lines of landowners.

(iv) *Judicial institutions*

The *Mar*, with the backing of his land-owning line and the important religious powers vested in his person, was a mechanism for maintaining peaceful relations within the chiefship. It must be remembered that the *Mar* never initiated litigation, but waited for persons to put their petitions to him for consideration and judgment. The carrying out of pronouncements made by the *toket* were in most cases left to the individuals concerned, although where cattle were handed over following a case, this was done in the presence of the *toket*. Settlement was often, however, dependent on the ability of the injured party to exercise self-help in getting his dues. If a complainant was persistent in his demand for help in this respect to the *toket*, the Mandari say the *Mar* might instruct his young men, accompanied by the elders, to seize and hand over the property awarded in compensation.

Mandari also say that many cases were never satisfactorily settled and people would wait until the *Mar* was absent to take their own revenge on their enemies. Bloodshed, though strongly condemned within one chiefship, sometimes occurred, even within the land-owning line itself. It was, however, impossible for fighting to persist within one chiefdom without it leading to the complete disintegration of the group; for this reason the *Mar* and other land-owning lineages always combined together to intervene between warring segments.

The people of one chiefdom paid recognized scales of compensation for injury to person and property. Whether in fact compensation could be paid depended on the kind of kinship relation which linked the two parties. Wrongs within the landowning line could in theory never be compensated because the people concerned were agnates. Killing or sexual offences within the clan which shared a common territory also constituted serious sins demanding purificatory sacrifice, and almost always led to the complete separation of the people concerned; the guilty party or the one which was weakest fragmenting away from the chiefdom and settling with relatives elsewhere or attaching themselves as clients to another land-owning line. People who were not agnatically linked paid compensation between them which varied according to their status as clients or landowners and the pressure the injured group were able generally to bring, and the necessity for preserving peaceful relations within the chiefdom. Killings between unrelated persons were formerly compensated by the handing over of a female child and are now effected in cattle.

The chiefdom was the largest unit which had permanent machinery for maintaining law and order. Between two separate chiefdoms minor wrongs remained unsettled, and serious wrongs led to fighting. Hostilities ranged from war to regulated revenge killings. The latter might be initiated by a number of people under the *Mar* and his land-owning line, or by a kinsman of the dead man, depending on the latter's position in the chiefdom. The type of action taken in revenge killings and the number of persons affected on both sides always depended on the position and status of the dead, and whether a friendly or hostile relationship already existed between the two chiefdoms concerned. The heads of two friendly polities would sometimes share a common *toket*, forming a combined council to try and settle major wrongs in order to prevent the breaking up of important economic interdependence which was vital to both. Sharing of a common *toket* also took place between adjacent Bora chiefdoms, or between non-linked chiefdoms whose land-owning lines had intermarried. These chiefdoms tended to be those which were also closest territorially. Chiefdoms which were far apart and which, therefore, had few economic ties in common, and between whom intermarriage was less frequent because of distance, never came together for peaceful settlement of disputes.

(v) *Political configuration of cattle camps*

The degree to which people of separate chiefdoms come into contact with each other has always varied according to the time of year and the economic activities which are associated with particular seasons. Pasturing the cattle in the dry season enforces movement outside the homeland, or imposes co-operation with the people of incoming chiefdoms in the case of certain groups having dry season grazing in or near their territories. For this reason, no chiefdom is able to remain entirely unaffected by the movements of its neighbours. As the dry season advances, villages are left empty except for old people and young mothers, the unmarried girls and children following the cattle, provided the grasslands are within reach of the homeland. They do not go to camps in the Aliab. In areas where water does not last out the dry season, total villages move to temporary encampments near watering places.

A dry season camp is always based on the cattle of a chiefdom under the charge of a proportion of the young men. The nuclear group, and the one which gives the camp its name and corporate unity, is composed of the cattle fires round which are pegged the cattle of the *Mar* and his close agnates. These fires are placed in the centre of the camp and round them are the fires of other land-owning lineages with their satellites and clients. On the outside are sited fires of settler and client lines of long standing who have their own cattle as opposed to individual beasts tied with the cattle of their hosts. People on the outside are less protected in every way and are those who are less closely related and less significant politically. A number of cattle at any fire belong to maternal or affinal kin. People like to separate out their herds as a safeguard against disease and raiding, and also so that potential in-law relatives cannot easily assess the numbers and attributes of their cattle.

The constituent elements of fires, like the agnatic lines (*kakat*) on which they are based, are dynamic, continually segmenting and forming new fire groups. When a lineage of about four generations has accumulated a number of cattle, heads of extended families break away and form their own fires, then other people come and peg down with them. Lineages which are wealthy may have a number of separate fires.

Elders only visit camps for short periods and the care of the herd is in the hands of the young men under the *Mar lo lisuk*, 'head of the camp', who is usually a son or younger brother of the *Mar* of the chiefdom or his close agnate. The *Mar* of a camp is not an office; the youth in this position is merely a relative whom the *Mar* has put in charge of his own cattle. Because he had under him a greater number of fires than other groups in the camp he is automatically the leader, and other people are there with their cattle because they have come round him and under his protection in the same way that the lineages of which they are members accrete round his land-owning line in the chiefdom. Because he is a relative of the *Mar*, is experienced in the care of cattle and has a strong personality, he can command respect and represent the interests of all other segments in the camp. He is responsible for keeping order, talking over disputes, and for the defence of the cattle.

Even when camps are far away on the grassland, contact with the chiefdom is never completely severed; people are continually going backwards and forwards. The *Mar* and elders are informed of conditions in the camp and it is they who decide when the cattle should be brought back to the villages; they can evaluate the needs of the herds and those of the people who remain behind. Because of the necessity for sharing summer grazing, people in the camps come into much closer contact with those of other countries than they do during the time spent in villages. Herdsmen from different political units attend dances together and co-operate under their camp leaders in the sharing of grazing and water. The camps of hostile chiefdoms are sited apart with the camps of friendly ones in between them.

In pre-Administration days, movements were different from those made at present, because Mandari did not use Aliab grazing. Herds were smaller, according to Mandari, and the bulk of cattle belonged to the *Mar* and land-owning lines. Movements to Mandari summer grazing were regulated by friendly relations between *Mar*, and by the outbreak of hostilities or cattle epidemics. These factors are still relevant today. Friendly groups in the past formed semi-permanent pacts for the movement of cattle and travelled in large concentrations accompanied by armed men. At present, movement to the Aliab involves a long trek made in slow stages. The cattle move at the same time, those of one chiefdom following a few miles behind those of the one in front. Moves are made in this way for protection, because the journey is through uninhabited country and ends in the territory of an aggressive and warlike people. The resources of the Aliab belt is almost limitless and herds usually remain on it until the first rains at the beginning of April, when they are withdrawn to Mandari forest camps near villages, so that the work of cultivation can begin. During the rains, movement continues but is more individual, the cattle of each chiefdom moving separately as convenient, taking into consideration the layout of villages, the needs of garden work and the distribution of water and grazing. A camp may break down into smaller units composed of the cattle of each land-owning lineage so that the herders can be closer to their hamlets. Youths walk down every day, or spend short periods in the villages till the gardens are completed, then the cattle are taken off again in one camp to areas of salt grazing, returning at harvest to forest camps in their independent chiefdoms.

CONCLUSION

In relation to neighbouring peoples, Mandari do not see themselves in terms of a political whole. The contrast themselves on the basis of language, and of beliefs and practices common to all Mandari. They also have a strong feeling for their land, comparing what they consider its perfection with the poorness of their neighbours' countries. When travelling in any one direction, Mandari can say where their country ends and that of the next people begins, and because Mandari is a small country, the majority of male adults know in general the configuration of its boundaries and can name natural features or villages which mark the ends of these. They will also, if questioned, suggest that they and the Bari-speaking tribes may at some time have been closely connected or even of common stock, and will speak of '*baŋ geleŋ*', 'one homeland', right through to the most distant Bari speakers. This linking up is introduced when they want to show the difference they believe to exist between themselves and other Bari speakers, and the Nilotic group of Atuot, Aliab and Bor Dinka. In a context directly referring to Bari, on the other hand, they stress differences in language and custom.

This way of placing themselves in a larger Bari-speaking world has no practical application. While there is some intermarriage on the east with Nyangwara and Sera, these people cannot easily come into contact with Mandari. Ecological factors enforce separation and make sharing of grasslands in most cases inconvenient.[1] In outlook, most Bari speakers are

[1] Mandari Bora clans and Rume sometimes share camps on the edge of the Aliab with Sera and Köbora.

orientated away from what Mandari consider to be the ideal life; the western and southern Kakwa and Fajelu are also far from Mandari and largely christianized, the majority being employed as wage earners.

When comparing Mandari political organization with that of other segmentary societies in the Southern Sudan, typified by Nuer and Dinka, it is apparent that we have a very different form of segment and of inter-segmental relationship. The structure of Mandari political units in many ways is closer to the small segmentation of Anuak and Shilluk, than the widely spread pattern of the former.

Mandari political relations were not based on political relativity, arising from the existence of powerful agnatic lineages which were also political segments, the constituent parts of which constantly changed in relation to varying political pressures. Lineage segments in Mandari did not form a wide network stretching beyond the territorial boundary; on the contrary, they were defined by territorial limits. They were always of the same order, that is, each individual segment, a lineage, was a unit with an unchanging value, and never part of a number of lineages built up in a hierarchy. Each segment was a permanent part of a well-established territorial pattern under a head, and relations between defined groups of segments which composed a clan and its subsidiary groups were dependent on the friendly or hostile relations between their heads.

The autonomous chiefdom of which these segments were the basis had a genealogical structure in that a land-owning clan was dominant in each, to which small lines of non-related persons were affiliated as clients and settlers. Unlike Nilotic societies where widely separated hierarchical lineages of dominant clans had a political value, in Mandari agnatic links beyond the chiefdom, such as those of Bora, had no immediate political significance. Because of *Mar*ship, differences of status were more pronounced in Mandari than among Nuer or Dinka, where nothing resembling the division into landowner and client was found.

The relations between Mandari states ranged from co-operation to hostility. Semi-permanent pacts of friendship were formed between adjacent chiefdoms which had strong affinal ties, or whose lands bordered summer grazing. Hostility was also inherent because of the equivalent structure of the village states and the desire to raid cattle and attract retainers, the only two commodities which gave prestige. Rivalry, apart from being openly expressed in fighting, was formalized in social usages, the most important of which was the performance of installation ceremonies by people of a different chiefdom. This theoretical dependence, whereby a new chief could not take office without the assistance of people from outside, shows how the independent heads of political units were linked by a common interest in preserving chiefship in general. Chiefship retained its desirability, because each chief was surrounded by rivals weaker or more powerful than himself.

Competition is still exemplified in the taking of dances by one group to a notable of a neighbouring one, to receive food and gifts in exchange for giving entertainment; and in the custom whereby valuables pass between *Mar* when one chief makes a visit to acquire an object he has seen in possession of another, the latter making a return visit to claim some other object after a suitable period. These exchanges are governed by strict etiquette. Intergroup rivalries are also expressed at the mortuary ceremonies of chiefs and notables, when visiting parties from neighbouring chiefships present material tokens of their grief to the bereaved family, at the same time singing war songs and making mock attacks on the grave.

In the past, Mandari fought the Aliab and, to a lesser degree, the Moru. In these fights occasional alliances were formed between neighbouring Mandari polities. These alliances were haphazard, the small independent chiefdoms having no definite pattern of combination. For this reason they tended to fare badly in their encounters with Aliab, who, with their age-set system and wider scale political units, had a strong basis for making war. In Mandari both offensive and defensive actions were based on territorial and kinship divisions within one chiefdom, adult men dividing up into fighting groups based on land-owning lineages and their satellites. There was no way in which the organization of a single chiefdom could be extended to cover a larger unit, and when alliances were formed between chiefdoms, each fought as a separate entity under its own leaders.[1]

[1] While lacking in the past an age-set organization, present-day youth has adopted

94

The largest segment with jural and political effectiveness was very small. To balance this, social bonds of a different kind were a force for overall cohesion. Their nature was economic, ceremonial and religious, and in the case of Bora, the awareness of common ancestry. Common ancestry evoked feelings of sentiment rather than furthering direct political solidarity. There was no common territory occupied by Bora clans apart from Mandari country as a whole, and no means of combination between the majority of Bora segments. While it is said that friendly relations existed between them, fighting is also known to have occurred. The presence of these dispersed groups of a common stock helped to map the country and to give Mandari a consciousness of being one people, and to weld together the many alien groups which settled round Bora segments.

The importance of Bora must be assessed on a historical level rather than in the relationship between political segments as a functioning whole at any one point in time. All political units, whether of Bora or non-Bora origin, are potentially equivalent in power and composition. The fact that some chiefdoms are 'religious' with true land-owning *Mar*, while others are secular, is only relevant in relation to certain beliefs about how nature and society should interrelate in the performance of land rites, and in the division between landowner and client. Ultimately we may, I think, speak of all indigenous land-owning groups as being opposed ideologically to all dominant outsider ones, and this opposition is apparent in conversation and expressed in opinion, particularly in the way landowners speak about themselves in relation to established groups from outside. People who came into Mandari formed states with no ties between them. Their roots were not in a common territory rich in historical associations, but in individual homelands in other tribes. It is significant that it is these alien states who intermarry with and co-operate most closely in economic activities with Aliab and Atuot. Bora stands for the overall nexus of traditional values, which compensates for the pulling apart of the individual political units because of different origins and mutual rivalry.

and adapted a form of initiation known as Pyita from the Atuot. Initiation is followed by entry into 'bead-sets'—*rem*—whereby groups of boys who were initiates together wear waist-bands of coloured beads whose colours are changed progressively. Bead-sets are related to courtship and have no political significance; none of the senior groups alive at the present time has been initiated or divided into sets.

95

ACKNOWLEDGMENT

I should like to acknowledge the valuable assistance and co-operation given me by the Government of the Anglo-Egyptian Sudan during my stay in Mandari.

THE WESTERN DINKA

Godfrey Lienhardt

INTRODUCTION

THE Dinka are a Nilotic people, numbering some 900,000, whose country fringes the great region of swamp and open savannah of the central Nile basin in the Southern Sudan. In any typology of African political systems, that of the Dinka must be considered at the side of that of the Nuer, which is already familiar to anthropologists through the work of Professor Evans-Pritchard. His analysis of the segmentary lineage structure of the Nuer forms a point of departure for all subsequent studies of political systems based upon the principle of lineage segmentation; but it does so more particularly for a study of the Dinka.[1]

Variations in detail between conditions in different parts of Dinkaland cannot be described without confusing this summary account, and I therefore refer in the main to some tribes of the Rek and Abiem tribal groups of the Bahr-el-Ghazal Province of the Sudan.[2]

ECOLOGY

Western Dinkaland is bounded to the south and west by the ironstone rim of the Nile basin in the Sudan. The Dinka live in

[1] Partly because it is produced under his teaching, and with the benefit of his advice, and partly because his account of the Nuer (1940) is the first full description of the class of political system to which the Dinka also belong. Some specific characteristics of the political system of the Dinka can therefore now be established only as they differ from the characteristics by which, through accounts of the Nuer, the class is already recognized.

[2] For a general description of the Dinka and their country see Seligman 1932, Titherington 1937, and Stubbs and Morrison 1938.

a broad band of open savannah (*toc*) and savannah forest (*gok*), which forms an intermediate zone between the southern iron-stone and forest, generally unsuitable for their cattle-herding, and the rich pastures of the Nuer to the north-east, and of the cattle-Arabs to the north across the Bahr-el-Arab. These two warlike peoples have prevented the expansion of the Dinka in their directions.

The year in those parts is divided into clearly marked wet and dry seasons. The rainy season starts in March or April and lasts until the end of October, after which there are but a few light showers until the following year. By July, the many rivers and streams which cross the country, from the south and west to the north and east, begin to flood the open grasslands found inter-mittently along their banks and at their confluences. Tracts of savannah forest which lie between these flood-plains of the rivers are then water-logged in many places where drainage is bad and rainwater stands on the surface of the land. At the end of the rainy season, the floods subside. The main rivers dwindle eventually to strings of lagoons and mere pools, and the savan-nah forest between them becomes scorched and arid.

The Dinka are mixed farmers, who supplement their diet by fishing at the beginning and after the end of the rains, when the fish are moving with the rising or falling rivers. Cattle-herding, however, is their main interest; and to combine herding with cultivation they have to be transhuman, moving each year between higher and better-drained land, where they build per-manent settlements and cultivate millet in the rainy season, to riverain pastures where alone the cattle can live in the dry season.

Permanent settlements may consist of up to a hundred or more homesteads, each homestead comprising one or more sleeping huts and perhaps a cattle-byre, all built around an un-fenced courtyard.[1] Every homestead is situated in its own two or three acres of millet gardens. Dinka settlement-patterns differ from each other somewhat according to the two broadly different kinds of country in which the homesteads can be built —the savannah forest country, which probably carries most of the population of Western Dinkaland, and the open savannah. Savannah-forest settlements may straggle for many miles at a

[1] Stockaded homesteads are sometimes found in lion-infested country.

stretch, skirting depressions in which rainwater collects in the wet season, preventing quite continuous settlement. Boundaries between different political communities are often not apparent to the eye in such savannah-forest areas. Permanent homesteads can also be built on mounds and ridges in open savannah country; settlements built in such places are clearly isolated from each other, since the lower ground between them is extensively flooded in the rainy season.

Most Western Dinka tribes have settlements in both kinds of country, but the Dinka characterize themselves as a people of savannah-forest settlement, from which some have established colonies in open savannah. In comparing themselves with the Nuer, they draw attention to the fact that Nuerland is, from their point of view, all open savannah.

The density of population of some of the more thickly populated areas of settlement has been estimated in the past as reaching 60 people to the square mile. The figure should be treated with reserve as it is almost impossible without elaborate survey to make any calculation of the area settled, and a figure arrived at by considering the total area would be of doubtful significance. It was calculated, for example, that about two-thirds of Aweil District is unsettled.[1]

After the rains, in December or January and sometimes earlier according to local conditions, all but the very old people begin to move with the herds to pastures near the rivers, and camp out there in temporary shelters until April or May. The Dinka say that in the past each tribe claimed and would hold by force its own dry-season pastures, admitting to them members of other tribes only on grounds of kinship or friendship, and on sufferance; but efforts on the part of the Administration to share out the best pastures equitably have now resulted in a concentration of Dinka of different tribes there. Those tribes which traditionally claim these pastures as exclusively their own, say that many of those whom the Administration now admits into them would have had to content themselves, in the past, with their own inferior pastures on the banks of rivers nearer to their permanent settlements.

[1] These calculations were made several years ago by Capt. J. M. Stubbs, who was then District Commissioner of Aweil District and left notes of great anthropological value.

99

In April or May, most people return with their cattle, to hoe and plant in the settlements.[1] It is a difficult time, for the early rain which has made the ground soft for cultivation may not have been enough to provide enough grass for the herds around the settlements. By July, when the crops are established and the river-flooding is beginning, the older men remain with the women in the homesteads to tend the gardens, while many of the young and middle-aged men form themselves once more into cattle-camping groups.

These Dinka cattle-camps of the wet season spend the rest of the rains moving between a few traditional camping sites, where the herds are tethered and the herdsmen sleep at night, in the savannah-forest country of each tribe. At first the camping groups may consist only of members of two or three related extended families; but as flooding reduces the area available for grazing, such small groups are drawn together and converge on the few best sites in their neighbourhood. Towards the end of the rainy season, the herdsmen of each tribe are concentrated in several subtribal camps.

This second phase of transhumance in the wet season is characteristically Dinka. It is not found among the Nuer, living in open savannah, who at this period are forced back by the wider flooding of their country into the isolation of their separate villages, the sites of which alone provide dry standings for the herds.

In many parts of Western Dinkaland, the savannah-forest pastures on which the herds graze in the wet season lie between and around permanent settlements. The herdsmen are then never very far away from their own homesteads, and visit them frequently. Where, as for most of the Rek Dinka, camping areas are thus situated near areas of permanent settlement, the sites at which the herdsmen spend the nights are often on the outskirts of villages. Among the Malwal and Abiem tribal groups, on the other hand, the savannah forest pastures of the rainy season lie at two or three days' journey away from the permanent settlements, in uninhabited forest between the

---

[1] The Dinka prefer to leave most of their cattle with some of the young men in the riverain pastures until flooding drives them back. Some young men, despite official attempts to promote cultivation, still have the custom of remaining in the open savannah during the early cultivating season to become enormously fat on the plentiful milk and fish of the season.

settlements just north of the river Lol, and the Bahr-el-Arab. The herdsmen are thus separated from their homes for most of the rains, and their wet-season camping-groups are less identified with particular areas of permanent settlement than among the Rek. Wet season camps break up after the harvest. The cattle of each homestead are taken back to graze on the millet stalks left in the cultivations where they are tethered at night. For a month or more, the whole population is together in the permanent settlements.

Whether the wet season camps of a tribe be in and near its areas of permanent settlement, or situated at some distance from them, the Dinka always distinguish between the cattle-camp (*wut*, pl. *wot*), and the homestead and settlement (*bai*).[1] In speaking of their political communities they use the idiom of the cattle-camp, and cattle-camps are more fluid in composition, and less fixed in their spacial relations to each other, than are permanent settlements.

In general, Western Dinkaland in the dry season does not impose upon its people the range of movement and degree of concentration described for the Nuer, whose sources of water and pasture at that season are less widely distributed over the whole country. In the wet season, on the other hand, the whole Dinka population, unlike the Nuer, is not dispersed in separate and isolated village communities, since pastures are available for the Dinka in unsettled savannah-forest, and mosquitoes are not so troublesome as to drive men and beasts into smoke-filled byres at night, as in Nuerland. Many Western Dinka cattle are never taken into byres unless they are sick or in calf, and some of the Dinka do not construct cattle-byres at all.[2] Dinka country sets less rigid limits to movement in the wet season, and to the expansion of settlements, than are set by much of Nuerland for its people. These different ecological conditions are consistent with some differences between Nuer and Dinka political segmentation.

---

[1] For the Nuer, the 'camp', *wec*, and the 'home' or 'village', *cieng*, are the same in the rainy season.

[2] The cattle of many Agar Dinka are never brought into the settlements at all; but the Agar fall outside the scope of this essay.

CONSPECTUS OF SOME OF THE SEGMENTS OF DINKA SOCIETY

(i) The Dinka People and Tribal Groups

The Dinka form an ethnic and linguistic group among the Nilotic peoples. Their closest affinities are with the Nuer, but they are related also to the Lwoo-speaking Nilotes of the Sudan —the Luo (Jur) of the Bahr-el-Ghazal Province, the Shilluk, and the Anuak, to mention only the most important. With the Luo and the Shilluk those Dinka who are their neighbours have considerable social contact and there is some intermarriage between them.

The largest divisions of the Dinka people are some 25 named tribal groups,[1] each with its own well-defined territory. These are the divisions of the Dinka usually marked on tribal maps of the Southern Sudan, and have sometimes been regarded as the 'tribes' of the Dinka. They are not so regarded in this essay, for each is, as C. G. and B. Z. Seligman correctly wrote, a 'congerie' of independent and autonomous tribes (1932: 135). Tribal groups occupy continuous stretches of Dinkaland which tend to be distinctly separated from each other by natural boundaries—by rivers, swamps or waterless forest. Their total populations of the tribal groups vary from under 3000 people in the smallest to well over 150,000 in the Rek group, which is much the largest. The tribal groups I have here called the 'Western' Dinka are the western Luac, estimated at some 14,000 people, the Rek (156,000), Abiem (13,800), Paliet (4370), Malwal (37,640) and the Palioupiny (8530).

(ii) Tribes, Subtribes and Sections

A tribal group is an aggregate of tribes, each with its own areas of permanent settlement and wet and dry season pastures within the land of the tribal group. The Rek group, for example, has 27 tribes, the Abiem group has 10 and the Malwal 6. The territories of tribes, unlike those of tribal groups, are not invariably continuous. Different settlements of the same tribe, or the wet and dry season pastures of a tribe, may be partially

---

[1] I do not know whether some of the small central groups—the Thoi, Rut and central Luac—are more appropriately regarded as 'tribes' or as tribal groups.

separated from each other by intrusive settlements of other tribes. Natural boundaries are generally less well-marked between tribes than between territories of tribal groups. Tribes vary much in size, from less than 1000 to up to 25,000 members.

A tribe is divided into subtribes, its largest political segments. One of the largest of the Rek Dinka tribes, Apuk Patuan, has nine subtribes; smaller tribes have three or four. I use the term 'subtribe' rather than the more usual 'primary tribal section' for these largest sections of a tribe because, in many tribes, they are the only political segments.[1] In any tribe, segments of the order which I call 'subtribes' stand out clearly in function both from smaller political segments which may be comprised in them, and from the tribe in which they are comprised. The subtribes have now been used for administrative purposes and have official subchiefs. This arrangement may have increased, but it is not the cause of, the emphasis which the Dinka themselves place upon subtribes, an emphasis which undoubtedly led the Government to select them as manageable units of their own system of rule.

The subtribes are the largest fully corporate communities. Young men of each subtribe gather in the wet season in a single subtribal camping area, after ending the rainy season together at one or two large subtribal camping sites, from which they fan out in the daytime, or for a few days at a time, in smaller groups, to find grass for the herds. It is within the subtribe, and not within the tribe, that age-sets are opened and named.[2] These age-sets are opened and closed by a religious chief (*beny bith*— master of the fishing spear), generally acknowledged to be the most influential of several such priests living in the subtribe.

In small tribes, the subtribes may not be further segmented into units which, without causing confusion, one could call 'political'. A subtribe in this case is composed merely of groups of members of several related extended families. In larger subtribes, however, between this domestic level and the subtribe there is a further political division which I here call simply the 'section', a permanent and formal segment of the subtribe. It is sufficient for a description of the political segmentation of the

---

[1] The use of the word 'primary' suggests that, as with the Nuer, they necessarily include others of a lower order.

[2] Dinka age-sets, unlike those of the Nuer, are organized only at a subtribal level.

Dinka to refer, within any tribe, to segments of either one or two orders—the subtribe, or in larger tribes, the subtribe and the section.[1]

The degree of political segmentation of any group of Dinka is undoubtedly related to the number of its members, though ecological factors may also enter into the reckoning. The larger the tribal group, the more tribes it comprises; the larger the tribe, the more numerous its subtribes; and the larger the subtribe, the more likely it is to contain political segments of a lower order, the sections. An examination of the population figures in relation to the degree of segmentation of Dinka political groups suggests this; also, as will later appear, it is part of Dinka political theory that the increase in size and expansion of their political groups, and increase in their segmentation, go together.

(iii) *Descent groups*

Among the Western Dinka alone, there are well over a hundred different clans, patrilineal and totemic, which for the most part are unrelated by any original tie of agnation or cognation, and which are, with few exceptions, theoretically exogamous. Among the Dinka people as a whole, the number of unrelated clans is very much greater.[2]

Some clans are known all over Dinkaland; others are smaller, with a more restricted distribution, and their members may not be found far outside a particular tribal group, or even outside a single tribe. Clans are of two categories. Members of the first, called collectively *bany* (sing. *beny*), have special religious functions, and from them come the priests of the Dinka. The symbol of religious office of these priests is the sacred fishing spear (*bith*), and the members of priestly clans, mostly older men, who actually function as priests may be addressed as *beny*, chiefs (or

[1] It will be remembered that for the Nuer Professor Evans-Pritchard had to allow for three orders of segmentation within a tribe, primary sections (my 'subtribes'), and secondary and tertiary sections.

[2] Some clans, particularly one group of clans of priests sometimes called collectively *menh dyor*, regard themselves as ultimately linked to a common ancestor, but their ways of tracing the link are various and uncertain.

It is to be noted that, in relation to the total population, both the 'clans' and the 'tribes' of the Dinka are more numerous than are those of the Nuer, where there are only relatively few tribally important clans and many small lineages of Dinka descent.

as I prefer to call it, 'master') of the fishing spear. I refer to priestly clans as clans of spearmasters. The second category of clans, the members of which have no special hereditary religious functions, are called collectively *kic*. The word might be translated as 'commoners'; but since these clans are also described as 'people of the war spear', *koc tong*, in relation to the spearmasters who are 'people of the fishing spear', *koc bith*, and are distinguished from the latter by political function rather than by rank, I call them 'warrior clans'. The warrior clans among the Dinka as a whole are more numerous than the clans of spearmasters, but the latter form a large minority.

Every tribe contains descent groups from many clans of both categories. I find it convenient to use the term 'subclan' for the largest lineage of his clan which a Dinka recognizes. A subclan consists of those members of a single clan who can trace their relationship genealogically. The larger and politically more significant subclans are segmented into further named agnatic descent groups, the largest of which I call 'main lineages'. Smaller formal segments of main lineages I call 'sublineages'. These three orders of clan segmentation, into subclans, main lineages and sublineages, are found to be enough to describe the formal structure of Dinka descent groups.[1]

It should be made clear that subclans, main lineages and sublineages are agnatic descent groups of varied, but in any case determinate, depth, which Dinka themselves abstract from their total genealogies. Looked at from the logical point of view only, all the agnatic descendants of any one man form a lineage, so that if he can trace his ancestry back for ten generations, he can logically refer to ten orders of lineage segmentation. It is not this, which one might call logical or theoretical segmentation, which concerns us here. Subclans, main lineages and sublineages are functionally defined in ways I later mention, and are named segments of the clan, standing in fixed genealogical relations to each other. The agnatic genealogical structure of his whole clan, however, is not known to a Dinka; he knows that there are likely to be many subclans of his clan, all descended from wives or sons of the clan-founder whose names and existence have been forgotten long ago by members of his own

---

[1] Whereas for the Nuer it was found necessary to find terms for four orders of segmentation within the clan, into maximal, major, minor and minimal lineages.

subclan. A Dinka is as little surprised to find a previously unknown subclan of his clan in some more distant part of Dinkaland as we are to find families with the same surname in England and Wales. Hence, subclans in different territories are usually known there by the name of the whole clan to which they belong, for they do not, for the most part, need to be distinguished in relation to each other. The case with main lineages and sublineages is different. They have to be distinguished by name within the subclan to which they belong, for they are seen as complementary parts of a known genealogical structure.

The more important subclans may have a depth of from seven to eleven generations; the main lineages of such subclans will spring from ancestors of from five to seven generations back; and the sublineages may be only some three generations in depth. I should mention that Dinka genealogies are often very confused, and that while a man may be prepared to name some twelve or more generations of ancestors, there will then usually be several ancestors at the top of his genealogical tree who form merely a single line of descent, the branching occurring first at a point several generations nearer to the present. As will later appear, Dinka clans do not perform the same political function as do Nuer clans, and this fact is consistent both with the more muddled genealogies of most of the Dinka, and with the fewer orders of formal segmentation into lineages, though the total generation depth of many Dinka clans is as great as that of the politically significant Nuer clans. Many Dinka take pride in the number of agnatic ancestors they can remember, but their memory, or fictions, in this respect are independent of the number of formal orders of lineage segmentation which appear in their clans.

DINKA POLITICAL THEORIES AND PRACTICE

The Dinka are able to give some account of how their communities developed, and of how they are characteristically composed and regulated both internally and in their relation to others. They have notions also of what their society ought, ideally, to be like. They have a word, *cieng* or *cieng baai*, which used as a verb has the sense of 'to look after' or 'to order', and in its noun form means 'the custom' or 'the rule', and they well know that this rule and custom differ from one place to another, even in Dinkaland. I have heard it said of a renowned master of the fishing spear of the past that he led (*kwath*, the word for driving cattle) his people, and ordered (*cieng*)—'ruled' would be too strong a word to use of anyone among the Dinka—the whole country. Dinka who are favourably inclined towards the Administration use the same expression for its rule. In this section, I describe how the Dinka represent to themselves the regulation of their political life, trying to describe and distinguish between what they recognize as the usual or common situation, and what they regard as desirable. In a final section, it will be possible to review what the Dinka say in the light of what can be known of them by the systematic investigation and comparison which we ourselves undertake.

When we speak of 'the Dinka', we represent the people as a totality, known from the outside, so to speak, and, to the extent that they are all Dinka, all equally differentiated from those who are not Dinka. No Dinka knows his whole people in this way, unless he has received education and been given opportunity to travel. A Dinka knows, not *the* Dinka, but 'Dinka'— 'some' Dinka; not *the* Nuer, but 'Nuer', and so on.[1] So, when the Dinka speak of 'Dinka', *jieng*, they cannot have in mind *all* Dinka, as we know them to be. Though the names of some tribal groups, particularly in my experience the Malwal, the Agar and the Bor, are widely known throughout Dinka country, no Dinka knows the names of them all, or their number, or, with any certainty, the outline of their distribution. They know only that their land is vast, and their people innumerable.

It is only when Dinka from different parts of the country meet together among foreigners that their common culture and language may draw them together, simply as Dinka, in opposition to foreigners whom they understand less well than each other. In their homes, they have no consciousness of themselves as a nation, and a Bor Dinka travelling in Rek country may well find himself insulted as a foreigner rather than accepted as a fellow-Dinka. On the other hand, foreigners who settle with the Dinka—for the most part small families and lineages of Luo—

---

[1] The absence of the definite article in the Dinka language in this context in a sense makes this inevitable, though I do not base my statement on this grammatical point.

are accepted as fellow-tribesmen. 'They were once foreigners, but now they are Dinka', I have heard people say of them. The fellow-feeling which develops among individuals from widely separated homes when they meet among strangers is thus not based upon any well-marked sentiment of the unity of all Dinka against the world. In the 19th century, when much of Western Dinkaland was pillaged by slavers and adventurers, there was little wide-scale co-operation against the common enemies. It is known that neighbouring tribes of Dinka harried each other in temporary alliances with the invaders until they began to understand the scale of the subjection which they were all inviting. Even now, however, many Dinka recognize that Nuer are able to unite on a larger scale than are Dinka.

The Dinka word for the large regional groupings of their people, the tribal groups, is *thai*.[1] The meaning of the word is simply 'kinds of people', or 'folks', in the social sense. The Nuer, Europeans and other peoples the Dinka know, are similarly *thai*, though the Nuer, unlike the others, are not also 'foreigners', *jur*, and are sometimes spoken of almost as though they were one of the Dinka 'peoples'. Real foreigners are distinguished by the colour of their skins as *jur col*, black foreigners or the Luo, brown foreigners (the Arabs) and red foreigners (Europeans). There are also opprobrious terms for the Azande and other Sudanic-speaking peoples, whom the Dinka seem scarcely to regard as 'people'.

A tribal group, like the Dinka people as a whole, is not in any certain way unified. It is true that Rek, for example, are theoretically opposed to Agar; but neither tribal group is organized in such a way that the sentiment of opposition could be expressed in action by the whole of each tribal group. In such a large tribal group as that of the Rek particularly, the definition of what is and what is not Rek depends upon the situation of the speaker. Though on one plane of thought all the Rek know which tribes are in the Rek tribal group, on another, members of one tribe of the Rek will approximate distant tribes of the Rek to the other tribal groups in whose direction these distant

---

[1] Fr. A. Nebel, 1936, translates the word as 'people—popolo, gente'. R. Trudinger, 1944, gives some translations of the word 'people' which are found among the Northern and Eastern Dinka. He there translates *thai* as 'section of a tribe'. This is not a normal Western Dinka usage, but it may be that Dr. Trudinger's definition of 'tribe' and 'section' is not that given in this paper.

tribes lie, and by whose influence they have been culturally affected. Thus, the eastern tribes of the Rek often say that the north-western tribes of the Rek are 'Malwal' and indeed their relations with the Malwal are closer than their relations with the eastern tribes of their own Rek group. The north-western tribes of Rek describe the eastern tribes as 'Agar', for the Agar Dinka are known to lie beyond them. Old men who take an interest in tradition may say that the Paliet, and even the Malwal, tribal groups were originally Rek. It is supposed that they split off from the Rek at some distant time to find their own land and pastures. There is a general tendency for those tribal groups further west to be derived from the eastern neighbours, for the Dinka have the impression that they have spread across the Bahr-el-Ghazal Province from the east to the west. It may be suggested by some that all the tribes of a tribal group were children of a single mother long ago; but the Dinka know that this is a manner of speaking, and cannot indicate any genealogical basis for the suggestion. In other situations, they are equally inclined to stress what they see as the historical basis of their tribal groups, which is that different tribes, and at different times and by different routes, settled in common areas in the course of westerly migration, and there proliferated and spread out over the present territory of the tribal groups. The Rek tribal group is held to have been composed of two quite different stocks of Dinka, the Apuk stock and the Kwei stock, who were hostile to each other. Sometimes it is thought that these were two original cattle-camps. Dinka are not consistent, however, in stating which tribes of today came of which stocks, and one might spend long in their country without hearing of this division.

The Dinka themselves do not regard the tribal group as being of the same kind as a tribe. It is an unorganized aggregate of tribes which have settled in a defined territory; and a man will more usually say that he is a Dinka of Rek country than that he is a Rek. The tribe is logically prior to the tribal group, in that there are thought to have been tribes before their present aggregation in tribal groups.

The largest organized political groupings of the Dinka, the tribes, are the largest groups which the Dinka call *wut* (pl. *wot*), which in its simplest physical sense means a cattle-camp. An understanding of the ranges of meaning of this word is the key to the understanding of the Dinkas' view of their political organization. A *wut* is any cattle-camp, any site upon which cattle are usually tethered or which is associated with camping in the past, any group of cattle with or without their herdsmen, or any group of herdsmen even without their cattle if it is understood that the purpose of their association is the tending and protection of a herd. By extension from this, *wut* denotes the section (the smallest formal political unit of a tribe), the sub-tribe, and the tribe. Larger groupings, the tribal groups, are not *wot*, and they are not based upon the notion of all herding cattle together.

If a stranger should ask a Dinka to describe a *wut*, he would almost certainly give an account of the physical lay-out of a cattle-camp, probably of a wet-season camp. The arrangement, organization and segmentation of any such camp is the paradigm, for the Dinka, of some features of the segmentation of members of a tribe into different descent groups and of the tribe into its subtribes and sections, and we therefore describe it here.

The site of a large subtribal camp in the rains is an area some two or three hundred yards square, where it has been found by experience that drainage is good. The site will usually consist of a number of slight mounds, built up higher by the accumulation of the ashes of dung smudges and the debris left by generations of herdsmen. On these mounds are low shelters built on stout piles and thickly roofed with branches covered by sods and earth. Each shelter is surrounded by cattle-pegs, and while the herdsmen sleep and sit in the protection of the shelters, their cattle are tethered around them. A large subtribal camp may have ten or twelve such shelters.

Each shelter with its surrounding pegs belongs to members of a subclan represented in the camp, and their kinsmen who have joined them for the camp. Sometimes two groups of members of different subclans share a single shelter. On the best-drained mound or mounds in the camp, and usually in a fairly central position, are the shelters of members of those subclans (sometimes one, sometimes two or even more) whose ancestors are thought first to have established the camp on that site. These form a nucleus for the whole camp, and it is to be noted that this nucleus may be composed of two, and sometimes even

three, different descent groups. In Dinka, these central groups
are 'the people of the middle of the camp' (*koc wut cielic*) ; or the
'originals' (*koc*) who first staked their claim to the best position
in the camp by driving in slightly decorated and notched
(*nguek*) cattle-pegs. Further, most usually, in my experience, in
the case of nuclear descent groups of spearmasters, the people
of the middle of the camp may be called 'the maternal uncles
of the camp', *naar wut*.

The descent groups present in such a subtribal camp are
called *gol* in Dinka, so that the social segments of a camp, *wut*,
are distinct descent groups of cattle-herders, *gol*. The word
again has a range of different, but related, meanings.

In the simplest sense, a *gol* is a cattle-hearth—the place
where herdsmen make their smudge of dung to smoke away
insects, either in the centre of a cattle-byre in the homestead, or
among their cattle outside. It is the fire of the men of the homestead, while the cooking fires and their hearths (*mac thook*) are
the fires of the women and their young children and daughters.
So, in a polygynous household, there will be several cooking
hearths, one for each wife, and one cattle-hearth for the husband, his adult sons and his male visitors and kinsmen. Such an
arrangement, in Dinka eyes, persists down the generations, so
that a *gol* means also a group of agnatic kin, the children of one
father, caring for the common herd, and joined in this task by
other kinsmen who are members of the *gol* socially but not by
descent.[1]

As in a polygynous household the men who share the cattle-
hearth are united as sons of the father, but divided into different
groups as the sons of different mothers, so a *gol* in the sense of an
agnatic descent group is divided by reference to different wives,
or sons, of the founder, from whom members trace their descent.
It consists then of different *mac thook*, 'cooking hearths', or
different *ghot thook*, literally 'mouths of the hut', 'doorways'. In
general, where the internal divisions of an agnatic descent
group are explained in terms of descent from different wives of
an ancestor, the divisions are referred to as 'cooking hearths';
where the division is explained by reference to different sons

[1] Where it is necessary (for example, in religious ceremonies) to make a clear
distinction between membership of a *gol*, socially, and by descent, the word *dhieth,
dhien*, 'born of', may be used.

of the founder, the genealogical segments are spoken of as 'doorways of the hut'.

These terms for the genealogical segments of a clan are obviously relative to each other. In relation to other segments of his clan which a Dinka supposes to exist, but does not know, his subclan, the largest descent group to which he effectively belongs and of which he knows the genealogical structure, is a 'cooking hearth', or 'doorway of the hut', the whole clan being the 'cattle-hearth'; but in relation to its main lineages the subclan is the 'cattle-hearth' of which they are the constituent 'cooking hearths'. Similarly, a main lineage is a 'cattle-hearth' in relation to its sublineages, its 'cooking hearths'.

The nuclear agnatic descent group of a subtribal camp or, where two or more different agnatic descent groups form the nucleus, each of these nuclear groups, may be composed either of members of a main lineage of a subclan, or of members of different sublineages of a subclan. This comes about because not all subclans in a tribe have the segments which I here have called main lineages, and between which there is greater genealogical difference and distance, within the subclan, than between sublineages. In the view of the Dinka, only the largest subclans have main lineages; some subclans remain formally unsegmented down to the level of sublineages. The Dinka see the formal segmentation of their descent groups as a matter of size and function. What I have here called 'sublineages' are those formal genealogical segments, each only two or three generations in depth, which have theoretical claims on each other in the collection and division of marriage cattle for a member of any one of them. What I have here called 'main lineages' are larger genealogical segments, found in some subclans and not in others, which have ceased, even in theory, to have such claims on each other in the sharing of marriage cattle. Such claims are made only within the main lineage. The tests of genealogical distance and proximity of the formal segments of Dinka descent groups are two. Genealogical segments which consider themselves near enough to each other to take a common interest in the marriage cattle of the members of any one of them are what are here called sublineages. Genealogical segments which have formally divided for purposes of sharing marriage cattle, but which remain near enough to each other to prosecute the feud together, and to have, in theory, claims on each other for help in the payment of compensation for homicide are main lineages. Subclans are more distant from each other than are main lineages, in that members of different subclans may not know their genealogical relationship to each other, nor even of each others' existence. Main lineages of larger subclans may sometimes become 'far apart', as the Dinka say, to such an extent that intermarriage is permitted between their members.

Using these functional criteria of the Dinka, then, we may say that the nuclear group (or each of the nuclear groups, if there are several) of a subtribal cattle-camp of the rains, may be a main lineage of a subclan, the subclan being represented elsewhere in the tribe, and perhaps in neighbouring tribes, by other main lineages; or it may consist of members of several sublineages of a subclan which is not formally segmented into main lineages, and of which merely other subclans may be found in other tribes.

Each section, subtribe and tribe has its central agnatic descent group, or descent groups, by reference to which its members explain their coming together to form a single community. One, or two sublineages, of different clans, may form the nucleus of a section; one or more main lineages, or a main lineage of one subclan and sublineages of another, may form the nucleus of a subtribe; while at tribal level, the nuclear agnatic group is usually (though not invariably) a single subclan. That is, most tribes are said clearly to 'belong', as whole tribes, to a single subclan, and the subclans thus central to whole tribes are in almost all cases subclans of spearmaster clans.

Among the Dinka, a sublineage which forms the agnatic nucleus of a section is not necessarily a sublineage of one of the subclans, of which the members form the nucleus of the subtribe to which that section belongs. Again, the descent group or groups, whether main lineages or subclans, which form the nucleus of a subtribe do not necessarily come from the subclan which forms the nucleus of the tribe as a whole. That is, the agnatic descent groups with which the segments of a tribe are severally associated are not inevitably related to each other, in a single agnatic genealogy. Further, as I have suggested, segments of lower order than the tribe, and sometimes the tribe itself, may be politically identified with two and sometimes more descent groups, forming in association, with each other, a dual or multiple agnatic nucleus for the political group.

Tribal structure is a relationship between opposed segments, particularly between the subtribes, which are in opposition to each other but combine, to form the tribe, in relation to other tribes. But among the Dinka, this fusion and fission is not usually expressed simply in terms of the unity and segmentation of any single agnatic descent group, a 'dominant clan'. Consequently, the basis of the opposition of subtribes (not to refer to political segments of lower order), and the basis of their fusion, are not to be sought throughout in the same agnatic genealogical system, and fusion and fission are not simply of equal and complementary force. The subtribes, with their separate age-sets, their own nuclear agnatic groups which may not be represented in every subtribe of a tribe, their close co-operation in their several wet-season camps, and their own distinct masters of the fishing spear, are more united internally than they are united with each other in the tribe as a whole in opposition to other tribes.

It is part of Dinka political theory that when a subtribe for some reason prospers and grows large, it tends to draw apart politically from the tribe of which it was a part and behave like a distinct tribe. The sections of a large subtribe similarly are thought to grow politically more distant from each other as they grow larger, so that a large and prosperous section of a subtribe may break away from the other sections, with its own master of the fishing spear, its own separate wet-season camp, and eventually its own age-sets. In the Dinka view, the tendency is always for their political segments, as for their agnatic genealogical segments, to grow apart from each other in the course of time and through the increase in population which they suppose time to bring.

It is clear that such a theory—I do not yet discuss how far it may be considered as founded in fact—could only develop among a people who know themselves free to move away from each other; to occupy further tracts of empty or weakly occupied country, and to find new pastures. The Western Dinka as a whole do indeed think of themselves as people who have in the past, in the course of migrations, first segmented and eventually fragmented. It is by such a notion that they explain why there are now tribes which bear the same name, but which are separated from each other by intervening unrelated tribes, and why even whole tribal groups which, it is thought, were once together, are now widely separated, like the Twij Dinka of the Bahr-el-Ghazal Province and those of Bor District, several hundreds of miles away. This notion of segmentation and ultimate break-away also explains to them why subclans of the same clans are found scattered far and wide over Dinkaland. The Western Dinka in fact have a firm impression that their dispositions in the past were very different from what they are now, and in talking to them one is encouraged to suppose that their past has been one of many migrations and upheavals, that they have increased vastly in numbers of people and of cattle, and that the invaders of the later part of the 19th century, 'when the earth broke up', were only the last and most bitter of their vicissitudes.

It is characteristic of the way that the Dinka introduce the cattle-camp as a model of the explanations of their political communities, that the segmentation, and finally fragmentation, mentioned above should be referred back to what happens when a cattle-camp increases in size. I have said that the nuclear agnatic group or groups of the camp, and others who have been early associated with it, are in possession of the best-drained sites. Later-comers will be less advantageously placed, since in a wet-season camp the land up to the very edges of the camping-site may be frequently water-logged. The Dinka point out that when a group of later-comers to such a camp becomes rich and large, its members no longer have enough space to tether their cattle on dry-standings, and resent the superior position of the first-comers. It then happens that, among such later-comers, an ambitious man, perhaps a master of the fishing spear, gathers to himself a group of his own kin and perhaps others whose places in the camp do not satisfy them, and sets off to form his own camp. In time, the Dinka say, his new camp grows into a subtribe, and he is prepared to create his own age-sets.[1] It may happen that the leader of such a splinter-group is a member of a sublineage of one of the nuclear descent groups of the camp, and also of one of the subclans which are thought of as first

[1] This separation at the present day is often expressed by a demand for the recognition of a new official sub-chief.

settlers in the tribe as a whole. In such a case, the new segment will have as its agnatic nucleus a genealogical segment of one of the central descent groups of the original subtribe and the tribe. It may also happen, however, that such a leader is a member of a subclan with no such subtribal or tribal importance, and in this case, the new subtribe which he has formed will be weakly linked genealogically, if at all, to these other nuclear groups, only by such members of those groups as have been prepared to follow him, or by his relationship through women.

So far, I have emphasized the cleavages between the political segments of a Dinka tribe, particularly between different sub-tribes, because the Dinka themselves stress this aspect of their behaviour. 'It became too big, so it separated' or 'they were to-gether long ago but now they have separated' are common Dinka accounts of present divisions between descent groups and political groups. As I have said, in fact the largest tribes, and the largest descent groups, are those which are most segmented.

It is time now to explain how, despite these cleavages, the Dinka conceive of the unity of a tribe and the principle of fusion of its segments. In the rainy season, as I have explained, each subtribe exploits its own tract of pasture, and the units which are closest to each other and have most contact are the subtribes of one tribe. It is between them that fighting can most easily break out, and in general it is the convention that fighting between subtribes should be with the club only, though sub-tribes of a large tribe may be so distant from each other politic-ally that the spear is used. Fighting with the club reduces the danger of homicide, and is a sign of the recognition of the de-sirability of peace between subtribes of a single tribe. Fighting between tribes is not governed by any such conventions, nor do the Dinka think that peace between them should be the rule. In the dry season, the reasons for such a convention of peace between subtribes is clear, for then the Dinka are not only re-quired, by the reduced areas which provide water and pasture, to concentrate more closely, but also in the open savannah are more vulnerable to large-scale attack. It is then that they defend themselves as whole tribes, and each tribe, as the largest unit called *wut*, cattle-camp, claims like any other cattle-camp its own pastures. The dry-season pastures are spoken of as the pas-tures of whole tribes—*toc Apuk*, the dry-season pasture of the

Apuk tribe, *toc Awan*, the dry-season pasture of the Awan tribe, and so on—though within these tribal pastures the subtribes have their own customary areas.

The tribe is thus the political unit for defence in the dry-season pastures, and is so regarded by the Dinka. It is also, in their theory, the largest group of people among whom it would be possible and desirable to settle cases of homicide by the payment of compensation in cattle, rather than by the self-help and feud which were not only inevitable, but principles of honour, where members of another tribe had killed one's kinsman.[1] The tribe, then, marks the limits of the possible recognition of any convention that disputes should be settled peacefully. I have frequently been assured that in the past people would not have dared to travel in the territories of neighbouring tribes of their tribal group, perhaps only a couple of days' journey or less away from home, unless they were given safe-conduct by kinsmen or friends there.

The Dinka positively value the unity of their tribes, and of their descent groups, while also valuing that autonomy of their component segments which can lead to fragmentation. The basis of this occasional contradiction of values lies in each Dinka's ambitions, and in the necessities of their cattle-herding. A man wishes to belong to a large and united tribe and subtribe, because they have the strength which enables them to claim and hold the best pastures either in the dry season or the wet. A large and prosperous tribe or subtribe, however, may come to require more pasture than is available, and therefore, the Dinka think, tribes and subtribes divided and sometimes scattered in the past. A man similarly wishes to belong to a large descent group, because the greater the numbers of his agnatic kin who have still not formally segmented into separate agnatic groups, the wider the range of people from whom he can hope for help in collecting marriage-cattle, and the wider the range of kin upon whom he can for certainty rely for help in quarrels either within the tribe or outside it. On the other hand, each man wants to found his own descent group, a formal segment of the subclan which will for long be remembered by his name,

---

[1] Blood vengeance is still taken by the Dinka on occasions, but the effectiveness of the Administration is such that feud can no longer develop, and for knowledge of it one depends upon hearsay.

and wants to withdraw from his more distant agnatic kin in order not to be required to help them in their marriages. These values of personal autonomy and of co-operation, of the inclusiveness and unity of any wider political or genealogical segment and the exclusiveness and autonomy of its several subsegments, are from time to time in conflict. Then, as the Dinka see it, a lineage formally severs itself from its collateral lineage,[1] a subtribe from its tribe, or a section from its subtribe, each to form a new unit equivalent to the whole of which it was previously a part. A tribe, or a clan, is thus a system of equivalent segments formed, as the Dinka see it, by such a process of proliferation and division in time. They see their history as a spreading-out and separation of peoples on the ground, and hence in terms of cattle-camps, and hence, often, of age-sets, for since the age-set is a feature of the subtribe, the division of a subtribe may be seen in terms of the creation of a new age-set.

For the Dinka, this model of proliferation of equivalent political segments includes the notion of a measure of personal leadership. Fission is not thought of as simply occurring mechanically or haphazardly, but as the result of the action of ambitious and dissatisfied individuals who gather around them followers. Based upon this notion of personal leadership, there is another Dinka model for the relationship between political segments which supplements that already given. A common account of an ideal polity for a tribe is as follows. Each subtribe should have its own master of the fishing spear, whom all its members acknowledge as the first among several masters of the fishing spear who may live in its territory. One of these subtribal masters of the fishing-spear should be acknowledged as pre-eminent throughout the whole tribe, and in times of tribal difficulty all the others, led by him, should provide spiritual guidance for the warriors of the tribe as a whole.[2] Further, each subtribe should have an outstanding warrior, the *keic*, to lead its warriors, and in times of crisis for the whole tribe, one of these subtribal war-leaders should emerge as the war-leader of the whole tribe. The task of masters of the fishing spear is to ensure

[1] To permit intermarriage between members of the same clan whose lineages have 'grown far apart', a bull is divided into two equal parts longitudinally.

[2] This model is that which C. G. and B. Z. Seligman emphasized in writing that there was in all tribes a master of the fishing spear, 'consulted and deferred to on every occasion and his word is law' (1932 : 142).

victory in war and prosperity in cattle by their prayers and invocations, directed against human and animal foes; in the Dinka view, this prayer is supplemented by the physical combat of the warriors under their war leaders, for while prayer and invocation may succeed by themselves, the warriors will not succeed unless they are supported by them.

According to this model, then, each subtribe should have as its nucleus a descent group—it might be a subclan or a main lineage—of spearmasters, and also a descent group of warriors. The tribe as a whole should have a central, pre-eminent subclan of spearmasters, and a pre-eminent subclan of warriors, just as each subtribe should have its own master of the fishing spear and its own war-leader, though it is not expected that all subtribal leaders will come from the central spearmaster and warrior subclans of the tribe.

In Dinka thought, if such dual leadership, either of the tribe or the subtribe, is to be harmoniously maintained, the master of the fishing spear and the war-leader should be maternal kin, and in any subtribe or tribe, those descent groups which traditionally have provided the master of the fishing spear and the war-leader should have a classificatory kin-relationship through a woman. The pattern of such relationships is that of an agnatic descent group and the descendants of one of its women, that is, of a maternal uncle and his nephews or of a maternal grandfather and his grandchildren. Among the Dinka, all relationships through women have the quality of that of the descendants of a man and his sisters, or of a man and his daughter. Such kinship through a woman is thought to be in some respects closer than agnatic relationship, and kin of these categories are ideally supposed to live together in amity, showing each other a courtesy and even affection more markedly that agnatic kin. The maternal uncle—who often brings up his sister's eldest child in his own home—is the peacemaker between his own children and those of his sisters, and is the pivot of relationships between members of his own and other exclusive agnatic groups living in community. The sister's son is similarly the peacemaker between the children of the different wives of his maternal uncle, since he stands in the same relationship to all of them. So, in this Dinka model of the dual leadership of their tribes and subtribes, it is implied that in each case one of the descent groups is peacemaker in relation to the other, and it will be remembered that a nuclear group of a tribe or subtribe may be referred to as *naar wut*, maternal uncles of the camp. In most cases, those spoken of as 'maternal uncles of the camp' are members of a descent group of spearmasters, and the connection between their peacemaking functions within the group as priests and as 'maternal uncles' is explicit. I have been told on many occasions that where such a classificatory relationship is recognized between a nuclear warrior descent group and a nuclear spearmaster descent group of a subtribe or tribe, they will be united, strong and prosperous for 'they will all listen to one word'. This model of the Dinka political system with its emphasis upon the relationship between warriors and masters of the fishing spear, both individually and as descent groups, is thus somewhat similar to what has been called in other parts of the world 'dual chieftainship', and the Dinka represent their leadership in such a way, though the real picture, as will be seen, is much more complex than this particular Dinka theory of it.

A final way in which the Dinka conceive of the relationship between certain tribes, and between subtribes of a tribe, is based upon their conception of the relations between the eldest, middle and youngest sons of a family. There are, for example, three different Rek tribes all called Apuk—Apuk Patuan, Apuk Padoc, and Apuk Jurwir. One of these is spoken of as the eldest, one as the middle, and one as the youngest son. As may happen in a family, the eldest and middle 'sons' left their original home, and settled in distant places. The youngest son, as in a family, stayed behind in his mother's home. This account has an aetiological and historical rather than a practical relevance, for these tribes have now no opportunity of effective combination, and it is only the older men who remember the tradition.

The model of the three 'sons' is somewhat more important when it is used to explain relationships between subtribes of the same tribe. The Dinka may explain that certain subtribes of a tribe, considered together, are the eldest 'son', others together the middle 'son' and others the youngest 'son', so that the relationships of the subtribes are conceived on the model of the three brothers. Among the Dinka, the eldest son of a family usually takes over the management of his family when his

father dies, and, representing his father and his agnatic ancestors, he is thought to have the greatest share of the totemic
spirit of his descent group, the *yath*. When a tribe is conceived
on this pattern, one subtribe is spoken of as the 'subtribe of the
totem' (*wun yath*) and its function, ideally, is to look after the
tribe as an eldest son looks after his deceased father's family,
making peace between the other 'sons' when they quarrel.

In a final section of this account, I try to suggest what common structural principles we ourselves may see to underlie these
different Dinka models of their political system. First, however,
I give a purely descriptive account of some specific examples of
variations in detail between the composition of one tribe and
another. In generalizing, I have so far had to allow for such
variations, possibly at the expense of some appearance of
confusion.

The first example, which may be seen in text Figure 1, is the
Apuk Patuan tribe of the Rek Dinka. It is one of the largest of
the Rek tribes, and according to the figures I have available
may have some 22,000–25,000 members. The tribe as a whole
is clearly recognized by everyone to be the tribe of a single subclan, a subclan of the spearmaster clan Paghol. Paghol means
the House (*pa*) of the Thighbone (*ghol*), and is so called because
the first master of the fishing spear gave the thighbone as a totem
to the ancestor of this clan. The whole tribe is known as *pan
Paghol*, the home or country of Paghol, as well as by its proper
name Apuk, which, like other proper names of Dinka tribes and
subtribes, is thought to have been originally the name of a cattle-
camp.

The Apuk tribe consists of nine subtribes, one of which is now
so small that for all practical purposes it is merged in one of
the others, its neighbour. One consequently hears in recent songs
of 'our eight-segmented tribe' (*apung dan bet*). According to
tradition Apuk Patuan is the 'eldest son' of the three Apuk
tribes, all of which were at one time living together. The eldest
and middle 'sons' left home to search for better pasture and
settled in their present lands, where they have on the whole lost
touch with each other. This theory of relationship is tenuously
supported by known genealogical links between the central or
nuclear groups recognized in these tribes at the present day.

In the past, it is said, Apuk Patuan consisted of only three subtribes of which one, Abaga, was the 'eldest son', and also the 'maternal uncle' of the tribe, and kept peace between the other sons, Amakir and Aluala. Again, this is a manner of speaking, for these names are the names of original cattle-camps, not of persons. Amakir and Aluala then each comprised four sections

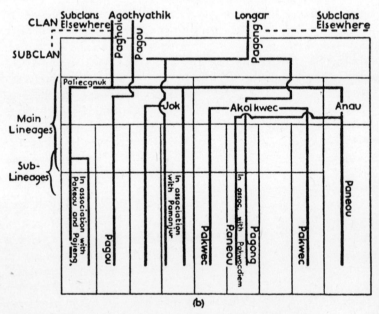

TRIBE	APUK PATUAN								
Original SUBTRIBES	AMAKIR				ALUALA				ABAGA
SUBTRIBES	Abior	Apol	Abwok	Ador	Amuk	Boyar	Biong	Nyarr-emung	Abaga
SECTIONS shown for 2 Subtribes only	Abior Dit / Abior Ryau			Tayou / Kwoc / Amermith					

(a)

DIAGRAM SHOWING (a) Tribal Segments, Apuk Patuan

(b) A few of the associations of descent groups found in the tribe, especially of the subclans of Paghol and Pagong.

FIGURE I

(to use the terms introduced into this account—in Dinka they are simply 'cattle-camps'), and each of these two groups of four sections is similarly seen as grouped, in the forms of three 'sons'. Aluala consisted of Amuk, the youngest 'son', Biong and Boyar together as the middle 'son', and Nyarremung, the eldest 'son'. Amakir consisted of Apol and Abior together as the youngest 'son', Abwok as the middle, and Ador as the eldest 'sons'. Again, these names are not names of men of descent groups, but of mixed cattle-camping communities, and only in some cases can older Dinka suggest uncertainly any distinct genealogical basis for these relationships in the genealogy of particular descent groups.

It is thought, then, that the present nine subtribes of Apuk Patuan developed from the three original subtribes, Abaga, Amakir and Aluala. Abaga, the 'eldest', is still spoken of as though it were a subtribe equivalent to the other eight, though it has now so dwindled in numbers that for age-sets and wet-season camping it has joined its neighbouring subtribe, Apol. The others—Apol, Abior, Abwok and Ador, who know themselves to have been originally Amakir, and Amuk, Boyar, Biong and Nyarremung, who know themselves to have originally been Aluala—are the present subtribes, in the sense in which the word has been used in this essay. Each of them is further subdivided into a number of sections, in some cases two, in some, three.

The tribally central subclan Paghol, called simply Paghol like the whole dispersed clan of which it is a part, consists of four large main lineages called Panoeu, Pakwec, Pajok and Paliecnguk. The first three of these are descended from and named after three sons of the clan founder. The fourth, Paliecnguk, is said to be descended from the wife of the maternal uncle of the others, from a son who was begotten by the father of the other three. According to older men of this Paghol subclan, Paneou, the lineage of Anau, the eldest son, was originally the lineage of spearmasters in the Abaga subtribe, the subtribe of the totem, the peacemaker, and also the *ner wut*, the 'maternal uncle' of the whole tribe. The present subtribe Abaga is still identified with Panoeu. The original subtribe Aluala was the subtribe of the Pakwec main lineage, and the original subtribe Amakir was the subtribe of the Pajok main lineage. From these main lineages of the tribally central subclan came the masters of the fishing spear of its three original subtribes.

The Dinka recognize that this simple correspondence between political and lineage segmentation, in a single subclan, no longer fits the facts. The fourth main lineage of the Paghol subclan, Paliecnguk, born of the wife of the maternal uncle of the others, now provides the masters of the fishing spear of the subtribe Abior, where its leadership is acknowledged in conjunction with two warrior subclans, Pakeou and Pajieng, the first of which is regarded as the warrior descent group with which Abior is identified. It has so happened, however, that the Paliecnguk spearmasters have lost influence, partly because they have not produced a master of the fishing spear of great spiritual reputation, and partly because they have for some time been on bad terms with the warrior subclan Pakeou, with which they have no clear classificatory relationship. Their classificatory relationship through a woman is with the second warrior subclan, Pajieng. Consequently, one section of the Abior subtribe which neighbours the powerful Agwok tribe has tended to call in for religious occasions a master of the fishing spear from the subclan Pabuol, important in Agwok, and who is a son of a woman of Abior. An influential faction of this section has now even started to go to the dry and wet season pastures of kinsmen in Agwok. The other section of Abior is also drawn towards a renowned master of the fishing spear of the neighbouring Ador subtribe of its tribe, and it is doubtful if in fact, in political relations either with the Agwok tribe or the Ador subtribe, the Abior subtribe could be effectively rallied round the Paliecnguk main lineage, which, in any attempt to relate the genealogy of the Paghol subclan to the whole tribal segmentation of Apuk Patuan, should form its nucleus. Again, the division of Abior into two distinct sections, separated for wet season grazing, is said to have occurred in the last few years, and represents within the subtribe a cleavage between the two main warrior subclans, Pajieng and Pakeou, whose rivalry is thus pulling the subtribe apart more successfully than the comparatively weak Paliecnguk spearmaster lineage can hold it together.

The largest and most prosperous subtribe of Apuk Patuan at the present day is the Ador subtribe; and though there is present in it a sublineage of the main lineage of the tribally central

Paghol subclan, the Pajok main lineage, it is not with this lineage that Ador is politically identified today. Ador is said by all to be the country of a master of the fishing spear of a subclan of the clan Pagong, and his sister's sons, a subclan of the warrior clan Pamanjur. The spiritual reputation of this Pagong clan is very high over all Western Dinka country, and, in the Apuk tribe, I have heard it said that Pagong was the descent group with which the whole of the original Amakir subtribe was identified, Aluala and Abaga only being the subtribes of Paghol.[1] On this view, the tribe was always divided between two different subclans of spearmasters, just as today a group of spearmasters different from that which is identified with the tribe as a whole is identified with its largest subtribe. Abaga, the subtribe which is 'eldest son' and 'maternal uncle' of the whole tribe by being identified with the senior main lineage of Paghol, now consists of perhaps some 400 people, while Ador, the subtribe now identified with a subclan of Pagong, has some 3000. Yet, in Dinka theory, Abaga is still formally equivalent to Ador, and was at one time equivalent to the whole of Amakir, which now consists of four much larger subtribes. The Ador subtribe is now far more tenuously connected, genealogically, with the tribally central subclan Paghol through Paghol's weak main lineage present in Ador than are other subtribes of Apuk. When I was there it was hinted that Ador would grow increasingly distant from the others, behaving more and more like a separate and quite independent tribe. From this example it will be seen that what emerge as the most important descent groups of a particular subtribe do not necessarily, as with the Nuer, give one a clue as to the genealogical structure of the 'dominant clan' (for the Dinka, 'subclan') of the whole tribe. Still less would the nuclear sublineages of particular sections of subtribes suggest to anyone that the whole tribe was drawn together in this agnatic genealogical pattern of a single subclan.

Examples showing such associations, among the Dinka, of subtribes with descent groups of different origin from the tribally

[1] Pagong is one of a group of related clans thought to be descended from the first master of the fishing spear, the Dinka culture hero Aiwel Longar, and its religious prestige is greater than that of other clans of spearmasters. I have heard it said that Pagong is 'the maternal uncle of all Dinka' (*Pagong aa naar jieng eben*), and there is a suggestion that this and its related clans might better be expected to compose differences between different tribes than any other clans of spearmasters.

central descent groups, are very numerous, and in many it is
difficult even to decide which of two fairly evenly balanced subclans can be said to represent the whole in relation to other
tribes. Nor is it always a senior lineage of the tribally central
subclan which is identified with the senior subtribe, the 'subtribe of the totem'. The Awan (Pajok or Rup) tribe of the Rek,
for example, consists of three subtribes, the senior of which is
identified with a subclan of the well-known spearmaster clan
Patek, while the other two are identified with two main lineages
of the spearmaster clan Payi. In this case, other complications
are present, for the senior subtribe, and one of the others, are
related by the presence in them of lineages of a single important
warrior subclan, Pajieng, while the third, related to the second
by its main lineage of Payi, is divided from both the others by
its identification also with a totally different warrior subclan.
Again, the tribally central subclan Payi in this tribe is clearly
segmented into three main lineages, just as the tribe as a whole
is segmented into three main subtribes. Only two of these main
lineages, however, are identified with subtribes; the third main
lineage is sparsely represented in the tribe and its real home is
in the country of the neighbouring tribal group of the Western
Twij Dinka. To take another example, the subtribes of the
Abiem tribe Akainyjok are severally identified with the main
lineages of a single subclan, in this case a warrior subclan
Paliec, said to be of Nuer origin. But though they are thus united
by identification with the segments of one single subclan, they
are divided into two groups by reference to two different subclans of spearmasters, one of which is identified with some of the
subtribes, one with the others.

It is clear that a Dinka tribe has a kind of lineage structure,
since any of its segments is politically identified with one or
more agnatic descent groups. It is equally clear that the relationships between all its segments—even between the largest,
the subtribes—cannot invariably, or even usually, be explained
by reference to the agnatic genealogy of a single descent group.
That is, all the subtribes do not stand at fixed and known distances from each other corresponding to the fixed and known
distances between descent groups in a single agnatic genealogy.
It is interesting to note how the Dinka themselves represent,
when illustrating their tribal structure by lines of the ground, a

difference between their lineage system and that which we are familiar with among the Nuer. It will be remembered that the Nuer indicate, by lines converging on a point and standing at various distances from each other, the fixed relations of distance

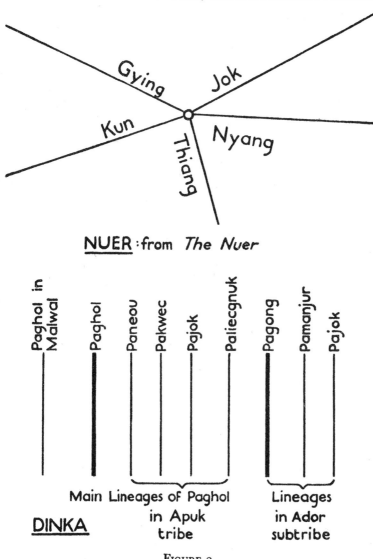

NUER : from *The Nuer*

Main Lineages of Paghol in Apuk tribe

Lineages in Ador subtribe

DINKA

FIGURE 2

and proximity between different lineages. If their representation, reproduced in Figure 2, be compared to that of the Dinka also reproduced there, it will be seen how the Dinka think in terms of the association of lineages, linked to each other in various ways, while for the Nuer a single agnatic principle is enough to explain all significant political identification of lineage with territorial segmentation. If the structure of a Nuer tribe be considered as a single, or simple, agnatic lineage structure, that of a Dinka tribe must be considered as a compound structure of associated lineages, since the relationship between its segments can only be represented genealogically by the associations with each other, in varying classificatory relationships and at different levels of tribal segmentation, of lineages from different clans. This Dinka structure of associated lineages seems to me to be consistent with other features of the political system of the Dinka which have been referred to in this account, particularly to the generally aggregational, rather than congregational, nature of the various political segments which have been described. This is particularly marked at the level of the whole people and of the tribal groups. It is found also in the tribes, particularly in the largest, where the political distance between subtribes makes them in some ways act as separate tribes. It is found, moreover, in the way the Dinka see the historical formation of their political groups, not as the grafting of strangers on to a single original descent group, but as the division of their land between a number of equivalent original groups which have spread out and displaced each other on the ground.

THE DINKA POLITICAL SYSTEM

Though the Dinka political system, like that of the Nuer, may be characterized in general terms, as 'an expanding series of opposed segments', from the smallest cattle-camps to the whole Dinka people, the principles upon which segmentation at different levels is based and the functions of segments of different orders are not the same. All segments, from the smallest to the largest, have a territorial basis, it is true, in that the permanent settlements and cattle-herding circuits of the members can be plotted in relation to each other on the ground. As I have said, however, segments smaller than the tribal group are not necessarily isolated from each other territorially in the permanent settlements, nor are their settlements necessarily in a single continuous area. The basis of their unity is less the occupation of particular settled territories than the exploitation and defence of particular pastures, by their members, in the wet and dry seasons. I have never heard in Dinkaland of an attack by one 'village' (*bai*) on another. Organized fighting is always said to take place in the pastures, between 'cattle-camps'.

It is therefore only those segments of Dinka society which, as whole segments, claim particular areas of pastureland, which are organized political units. As a whole people, the Dinka have no such defined pastures known to all of them; and where, as on the borders of the Western Twij Dinka with the Bul Nuer, there may be conflict between the Dinka and another people over pastures, it seems that it is by no means expected that all Dinka within call will rush to the assistance of their fellows against members of a different people. Tribal groups similarly (except, perhaps, the smallest and in special circumstances) do not collectively as undifferentiated groups claim specific areas of pasture. The largest segment which is identified as a whole with particular pastures is what we have here called the tribe, and this is the largest politically organized segment of Dinka society. It is the largest segment also within which there is any systematic relationship between descent groups, and the defined territories they, and those who have joined them, exploit. There is thus no answer, at the level of the whole people, or of the tribal group, to the question 'which are your pastures?'. That association begins at the level of the tribe, and distinguishes that segment from the larger ones.

Among the Dinka, the known and effective lineage relationships of members of any agnatic descent group tend to stretch across tribal boundaries. We have seen that in fact the Dinka clans are more widely dispersed than the Dinka know, so that subclans of the same clan may be found in different parts of Dinkaland. Also, however, main lineages of the same subclan, whose exact genealogical relationship to each other is known to their members, and who may feel bound to assist each other in the feud and in the payment of compensation for homicide, are found in different, neighbouring, tribes. This is particularly the case among the Malwal and Abiem tribal groups, where, on account of the situation of their pastures,[1] there is less identification between herding groups and the populations of particular areas of settlement than among the tribes of the Rek. Since the genealogical structure of any agnatic descent group, and especially of those larger ones which are politically more significant, is thus likely to cut across tribal boundaries, tribal exclusiveness like subtribal exclusiveness, cannot be entirely conceived in terms of the exclusiveness of any single descent group. This extension of agnatic lineage ties outside the political group is associated, in part at least, with the smallness of many tribes, and the realignments of many of their descent groupings made possible by their detachment from the fixed areas of permanent settlement in their long periods of mobility in the pastures.

It is for this reason that the exclusiveness of Dinka tribes, and still more of subtribes and sections, is represented in terms of different associations and combinations of agnatically unrelated lineages, and their inter-relationship is consequently less systematic and stable than if they were identified simply with the single system of agnatic lineages of one dominant descent group. Two subtribes united in relation to the main lineages of one nuclear subclan are divided by the presence in them of associated nuclear groups from different clans. One of these other nuclear groups, however, may relate one of these subtribes to a third subtribe, in which there is no important lineage of the subclan which relates the first two.

This is why it seems appropriate to describe Dinka political structure as an 'associated' lineage structure; and such a structural principle is clearly consistent with the fact that leadership, in any Dinka political segment, necessarily involves the presence of members of two different classes or categories of clan, the warriors and the spearmasters, which are of equal and complementary status. There are, strictly speaking, no 'tribal aristocrats' among the Dinka, and one may note that there is not among them, as there is among the Nuer, a higher rate of compensation required for the killing of one of the tribally or

[1] See above, page 100. It may be mentioned in connection with this that, at meetings of District Commissioners from different Dinka areas, it has been said that in comparison with the 'territorial' loyalties of the Rek Dinka tribes, the Malwal and Abiem have 'clan' loyalties.

subtribally central descent groups. The Dinka masters of the fishing spear are not merely ritual agents for composing feuds when the parties to them both wish it; they do not, as is usual for the Nuer leopard-skin chiefs, stand outside the structure of agnatic groups with which the political groups are identified in their relations with each other. On the contrary, it is precisely those descent groups with religious functions which must be found among the several lineages with which political segments are identified, and they are found there in necessary association with descent groups of warriors for whose benefit they exist.

The complicated details of the actual associations of lineages in any Dinka tribe may be understood as developed around this principle of the dual association of priest and warrior, expressed in lineage form, and therefore having a degree of permanence. Yet, the influence in fact of any master of the fishing spear, or of any warrior, depends upon his reputation for strength and success. Since every tribe contains members of several different subclans of spearmasters, changes in the prestige and reputation of masters of the fishing spear can result in political cleavages and realignments, in the course of time, a fact which relates to the comparatively fluid associations of the Dinka made possible by their ecology. The extreme form of this is found in the case of an influential prophet, of whom there have been several in Dinkaland, and who is usually also a master of the fishing spear, but inspired additionally by a sky spirit. Such a man in the past has drawn his followers from widely separated areas of Dinkaland, from hostile tribes and foreign groups. It is said of the greatest of these prophets, Arianhdit, who died some years ago, that he was great enough to influence members of hostile tribes to compose their differences. No matter which descent group of spearmasters a master of the fishing spear may come from, he can, if he proves himself effective in his prayers, attract followers and impose some order in their dealings with each other. Thus, no matter which descent group of spearmasters may be traditionally associated with a particular political segment, it can, in time, be supplanted by another which has proved itself more effective. The most forceful spearmaster of a subtribe is the one who initiates and keeps open for a long time an age-set which the Dinka will afterwards associate with his name. In the records of age-sets which I was able to collect, it is clear that there have been occasions in the past when masters of the fishing spear from different clans have for long periods replaced each other in control of the subtribal age-sets, so that, at different times, the active men of a subtribe have identified themselves with masters of the fishing spear from different clans. The evidence indicates that Dinka age-sets were of military significance. The Dinka model of tribal segmentation in which one subtribe grows out of and separates from an earlier subtribe may be expressed in terms of the division of age-sets created by different masters of the fighting spear.[1]

I do not attempt to relate what I have called the associated lineage system of the Dinka to other political systems described in this book and elsewhere. Most readers will probably have the political system of the Nuer in mind when reading about the Dinka, and perhaps I can most profitably conclude by suggesting the lines on which these two peoples might be compared were longer and more detailed analysis possible.

(i) *Ecology*

Dinka political units are more mobile, and therefore more fluid in composition, than are those of the Nuer. For the Nuer, a cattle-camp is spoken of as 'the cattle-camp of such and such a village' (or larger local community). Among the Dinka, it tends to be rather the other way round, as the cattle-camp is composed of members from several local communities and a Dinka will tell one which local communities belong to which 'camp', in the sense of a political segment. Consequently, the political system of the Dinka is not based primarily upon the fixed spacial relations of clearly defined and isolated settled territories, but upon the relationships between relatively mobile groups of herdsmen, who have behind them old traditions of migration and separation from each other. The greater mobility of Dinka political groups follows from the fact that the Dinka have three patterns of distribution in each year—in settlements for the sowing and after the harvest, in wet-season camps during the rains, and in dry season camps. The Nuer have only two patterns of distribution—in the villages, where they are static, and in the dry season camps. Also, owing to the comparative nearness to each other of the wet and dry season pastures of

[1] P. P. Howell draws attention to this among the Ngok Dinka; see Howell 1951.

many Dinka tribes, and the wide distribution of sources of drinking water in the dry season, the Dinka do not need to acknowledge a kind of rule of law over such a wide territorial area as do the Nuer. It is significant that the largest tribes are those which dominate the best dry season pastures, and that the smallest tribes, less favourably placed, are often linked by many genealogical ties between their descent groups and are thus less exclusive than the largest tribes.

Finally, the wide distribution of water in the dry season and the availability of unflooded ground in the rains among the Dinka results in a measure of separation of the younger people from the older people for much of each year. The most effective fighting men, and the cattle which are the cause of most fighting, are thus often away from the settlements where the older people spend most of their time, and the current open age-set of a subtribe in effect forms its army. The age-sets are formed by masters of the fishing spear, who through them have a clearly defined political office unlike that of the Nuer leopard-skin chief.

(ii) *Descent groups*

Dinka descent groups of different origins traditionally associated with particular political groups are numerous in relation to the total population of those groups. Among the Nuer, there are comparatively few original 'aristocratic' clans, identified with tribes, and numerous small lineages of Dinka or other foreign descent. The Dinka have not thus had to absorb large numbers of strangers, unrelated among themselves, and the central descent groups of their political segments all have equal claims to be regarded as the original owners of the territories they now occupy. The genealogical pattern of a Dinka tribe, therefore, is not one of numerous small 'client' or attached lineages whose total interrelationship can be expressed only in terms of their common relationship to a single dominant agnatic group. It is a complex pattern of relationships between lineages of different descent associated in various ways from the earliest times. For this reason, the genealogical pattern of a Dinka tribe, even reduced to its simplest principles of the dual association of warrior and spearmaster descent groups, is more complex than that of a Nuer tribe. This is perhaps why the Dinka tend to discuss political interrelationships in a kinship idiom, in terms of several cognatic ties, and not simply like the Nuer in terms of one agnatic lineage system.

In this manner of tracing relationships, it is natural that great emphasis should be placed upon the female links between otherwise exclusive agnatic groups, all of which are seen by the Dinka to approximate to the link between maternal uncle, or grandfather, and his sister's or daughter's child. The genealogical pattern of segmental interrelationships of a Dinka tribe consists in its simplest form of a system of such female links between its associated lineages. The leadership of any group larger than the extended family is thus often spoken of in the idiom of the mother's brother/sister's son relationship, and not in terms of the agnation of the lineages of one particular descent group. Nuer also trace their relationship to their dominant clans by female links, but here the importance of the grafting is that it assimilates strangers, in political relations, to the total agnatic genealogy of the single dominant clan.

(iii) *Segmentation and size*

Many important questions under this heading have been lightly touched on, or not at all. Among the Dinka, it does seem that there is an optimum size for politically organized segments of any particular order, and that there is a relationship between size and degree of segmentation. Further investigation of the functional rather than the merely morphological aspects of political segmentation would require a more detailed comparative study of ecological conditions in different parts of Western Dinkaland than has here been made. Here it has been possible to indicate only that Dinka political segmentation, and descent group segmentation, have a functional aspect, and that from the Dinka point of view, the proliferation of descent groups and political groups by which some of their present dispositions and interrelations are explained depends upon the notion of an increasing population, for which, unfortunately, no reliable independent evidence exists.

ACKNOWLEDGMENT

I spent in all two years among the Dinka, in three field trips made between 1947 and 1951. Fieldwork was financed by the Sudan Government, and I hope to acknowledge more fully elsewhere the help and kindness of its officers. I also gratefully acknowledge generous initial assistance from Downing College, Cambridge.

BIBLIOGRAPHY

EVANS-PRITCHARD, E. E. 1940. *The Nuer*, Oxford.

HOWELL, P. P. 1951. 'Notes on the Ngok Dinka', *Sudan Notes and Records*, xxxii, 2, 240–93.

NEBEL, A. 1936. *Dinka Dictionary with Abridged Grammar*, Verona.

SELIGMAN, C. G. and B. Z. 1932. *Pagan Tribes of the Nilotic Sudan*, London.

STUBBS, J. M. and MORRISON, C. G. T. 1938. 'The Western Dinka, their land and agriculture', *Sudan Notes and Records*, xxi, 2, 251–65.

TITHERINGTON, G. W. 1927. 'The Raik Dinka of the Bahr-el-Ghazal Province', *Sudan Notes and Records*, 159–209.

TRUDINGER, R. 1944. *English-Dinka Dictionary*.

THE ABORIGINAL POLITICAL
STRUCTURE OF BWAMBA

Edward Winter

INTRODUCTION

THE area known as Bwamba lies in the extreme west of Uganda on the border of the Belgian Congo. It is a very small area comprising only 164 square miles and of this some 80 odd miles lie in the Bwamba forest, an eastern extension of the great Ituri Forest. Thus only about 84 square miles are available to the Amba. It is on the floor of the western Rift Valley and lies at altitudes varying from about 2400 feet to a little over 3000 feet. To the east Bwamba is bounded by the steep escarpment of the Rift which in this section is formed by the Ruwenzori Mountains, a high range some of whose peaks are perpetually snow covered. To the north the boundary coincides with the sharply demarcated point at which the rain forest is suddenly supplanted by the open grasslands known as the Semliki Flats which stretch down to the shores of Lake Albert. To the west the boundary of the inhabited area is formed by the closed sleeping-sickness area, the Bwamba Forest, beyond which runs the Semliki River, the international boundary, between Uganda and the Belgian Congo. To the south the international boundary, although clear-cut, is of little significance on other than political grounds. The boundary consists of a small stream, the Lamia, which is easily fordable at almost all points.

In 1948 the population of the area was approximately 30,000 people of whom the great majority were Amba. To the east the

point at which the Ruwenzori Mountains suddenly sweep up-
wards from the lowlands of Bwamba forms a sharp dividing line
between the area inhabited by the Amba and the territory of
the Konjo who form a relatively large and unacculturated tribe
inhabiting both the eastern and western slopes of the Ruwenzori. Beyond the Ruwenzori lie the Toro, an Interlacustrine
people. To the north of the Semliki Flats live small numbers of
purely pastoral Toro-speaking Hima. As has been noted above,
the Amba are now barred from direct access to any of their
trans-Semliki neighbours to the west by the Bwamba Forest.
However, beyond the Semliki live people who are very similar
to the Amba in their general culture. The country to the south
beyond the Lamia is inhabited by people who are also known as
Amba and who are identical to the people in the British administered area.

The people inhabiting Bwamba are short, stocky, forest
negroes who by their physical appearance and general culture
obviously deserve to be classified with the peoples inhabiting the
Ituri Forest of the Congo. The term 'Amba' is used by the
people themselves, their neighbours and by me to cover two
main groups, the Bulibuli and the Bwezi. The Bulibuli, who are
also known as the Amba proper, and the Bwezi speak two entirely different languages, the former having a Bantoid tongue
and the latter a Bantu language closely allied to the Nyoro-Toro
sub-group of Interlacustrine languages. However, beyond this
linguistic differentiation I was never able to discover even the
slightest cultural trait which might be used as a criterion for the
separation of these two groups. Also included under the term
Amba in the present context are two smaller linguistic groups,
the Vonoma and the Mvuba. The Vonoma speak a Bantu
language while the Mvuba speak a Sudanic language. In order
to complete the picture of linguistic confusion it might be
added that Swahili is the official lingua franca of the adjacent
area of the Belgian Congo and most of the people in Bwamba
are able to speak a certain amount of it. Further the language of
the courts and the government in general is Lutoro. The area is
also inhabited by a few small bands of pygmies who, however,
speak Kwamba, the Bantoid language of the Bulibuli. It should
be noted in regard to the two main linguistic groups that they
do not occupy separate areas within Bwamba. Each village

belongs to one or the other of the linguistic groups, but in many cases within a relatively short time a person may walk through a Bwezi village, then a Bulibuli village and then a Bwezi village once again.

The Amba are an agricultural people. Plantains traditionally have formed the staple item of the diet. Today sweet potatoes and cassava play major roles in the subsistence economy. The principal grain crop is rice which was introduced into the area about forty years ago. The Amba do not keep cattle because the country is unsuitable for them but certain numbers of goats and sheep are kept. In the last few decades cash crops have been introduced. Coffee is the principal crop, followed by cotton. In certain years considerable amounts of rice are exported. Land has always been plentiful and even today when the population is large in respect to the land base, and is undoubtedly increasing rapidly owing to natural causes and to immigration from the nearby areas of the Congo and from Toro, a good deal of land is still available. This seems to be chiefly due to the very small size of the gardens cultivated by the Amba, due in turn, it would appear, to the great fertility of the local soil (see Winter 1955).

In aboriginal days Bwamba consisted of a series of villages each of which acted as an independent political unit. Warfare between various villages was a constant feature of the local scene. There was, however, little or no warfare with the neighbouring Konjo, with whom there was surprisingly little contact despite their proximity. Bwamba was subjected from time to time to raids from the organized kingdoms to the east, Bunyoro and Toro. Against such raids the Amba were able to offer but little resistance due to the nature of their political system. Toro and Bunyoro did not attempt to conquer the area, but, at the turn of the century when European control over the Interlacustrine area had already been established, the Toro, perhaps realizing that it was their last chance for territorial expansion, announced that Bwamba was an integral part of their kingdom and set up an administration in the area with the consent of the British. The whole position was regularized in 1908 with the conclusion of the Anglo-Belgian border agreement. At this time Bwamba, hitherto an international no-man's land, became part of Uganda. The British then administered the area as part of

Toro, although Bwamba was not incorporated into Toro in a full legal sense until somewhat later. From that time onwards administrative progress was steady and at about the time of the First World War the area can be said to have been pacified. The twenties and thirties saw the introduction of cash crops. In 1938 a road linking Bwamba with Fort Portal and with the rest of Uganda was completed. Thus this previously rather inaccessible area was opened to the full impact of the modern world. Missionaries, both Catholic and C.M.S., have been active in the area for a great many years, although never on a full-time basis. At the present time a minority of the Amba are Christians. The number of converts is now increasing very rapidly and within a few years the Christians should outnumber the pagans.

THE ABORIGINAL POLITICAL STRUCTURE

(i) *The Village*

My first concern will be to describe the village and to attempt to explain its structure and the processes which operate within its context, because the village is the basic unit of the political system. The village, however, although it is the largest unified political entity within the society, is not a self-sufficient system of action, and a Bwamba village cannot be divorced from its larger setting. That is, we cannot imagine such a village being transferred to a remote island and continuing to operate indefinitely under the terms of its present organization. The basic reason for this is that the men of the village must obtain wives from the outside world if the village is to survive. Thus even the internal organization of the village can only be understood fully when the village is seen in terms of its interrelationships with the larger structure of which it is a part.

Each village occupies a clearly defined territory. In many cases the village area consists of a section of one of the ridges which run out from the base of the Ruwenzori towards the Semliki River with the streams or gullies on either side forming two of the boundaries. The houses and gardens of the villagers are dispersed within this area. In the past it would appear that in the majority of cases all of the houses were grouped together in one place, usually on the ridge top for purposes of defence. Today, these village groupings, characterized by the rigid alignment of the huts along either side of a wide street with an open-sided meeting hall in the centre, are seldom to be encountered. However, groups of ten or more houses are still quite a common feature of the landscape and form a very striking contrast to the Interlacustrine area to the east where the single homestead is the rule. Today the typical village consists of a small number of these clumps of houses which may be termed residential groups.

A village, which may number from fifty to four hundred or so inhabitants, does not consist of an *ad hoc* collection of people. Each village is organized around a maximal lineage, from which it takes its name.[1] Thus, Bundikaianja is the village inhabited by the members of the Bandikaianja maximal lineage and Bugarama is the village of the Bagarama maximal lineage.

What is termed the maximal lineage consists of all the descendants in the male line of a single eponymous ancestor. Thus, in the cases of the two maximal lineages mentioned above all of their living members claim to be descended from Kaianja and Ngarama respectively.

The Amba are forbidden to marry within their own maximal lineage. Therefore a man always marries a woman from another maximal lineage. The woman goes to live with her husband and in the normal case the latter lives with his father. It follows from this that maximal lineage and village are very closely interwoven. However, although it is permissible to speak of lineage villages, it must clearly be understood that even in the ideal case maximal lineage and village are never synonymous in terms of composition. Many members of any given maximal lineage, its adult married women, live in other villages. Correspondingly each village contains members of other maximal lineages, the women who are married to the men of the village. Ideally then a Bwamba village would be composed of all the adult men of the maximal lineage, their wives who belong to other maximal lineages, and their children who belong to the local lineage.

---

[1] I define a maximal lineage not as a lineage so many generations in depth or as the largest one all of whose members can actually trace descent from a common ancestor, but as the lineage about which a village is constructed. Thus the statement is tautological.

The Amba tend to speak as though villages always conform to this ideal pattern. In actual fact it is probable that no village corresponds exactly to this pattern. Every maximal lineage with which I have had any contact has had adult male members living outside its boundaries either in other villages in Bwamba, in the Congo, or in other parts of Uganda such as the area around Fort Portal or even Kampala. Again, almost all villages have living within their boundaries adult men of other maximal lineages. These additional people, who may be termed immigrants, almost invariably are relatives, either consanguineal or affinal, of the men of the local lineage. Very often such men are brothers-in-law or sisters' sons of the men of the local lineage. These immigrants constitute a floating population for it is seldom that such people spend their entire lives within the village, and it is very rare indeed to find men who are second generation immigrants. Each maximal lineage, although it complains bitterly when one of its own members moves to another village, is always very willing to have men from other villages join it. The basic reason for this would seem to be that in the past the addition of another able-bodied man made a considerable addition to the fighting force of the tiny community.

The lineage core in the form of its adult male members or at least a significant proportion of them gives continuity to the village. This lineage core is internally segmented. The genealogies of the Amba have a depth of from five to seven generations. It is possible therefore in certain cases to have as many as seven levels of lineage organization. In reality the number of levels rarely exceeds five. These tend to be minimal lineages formed by men and their sons, second generation lineages formed by the descendants of common grandfathers, lineages organized at the third or fourth generational level, that is lineages formed by reference to the great-grandfathers or great-great-grandfathers of present-day people and a further level organized in terms of ancestors who are said to have been the sons of the founder of the maximal lineage and the maximal lineage itself. Different maximal lineages do not have the same number of levels of organization, nor do two individuals who belong to the same maximal lineage necessarily belong to the same number of lineage groupings. The reason for this is that certain ancestors are structurally irrelevant. For instance a man with no brothers and only one son does not serve as a point of lineage bifurcation. Among the Amba only the maximal lineages and the lineages said to be formed by the sons of the founding ancestors are named units.

These levels of lineage organization structure the distribution of solidarity and power within the village. Thus, two members of a minimal lineage will support a third member against a man from another minimal lineage in a quarrel. However this latter individual may be joined with the first three men in a second generation lineage and all four of them will stand together against men of other second-generation lineages. The one exception to this very neat pattern occurs in the case of the old men who are supposed to remain neutral and to try and stop any disturbances in the maximal lineage as a whole and not to be carried away by sectional interests.

Clear-cut positions of authority are only to be found at low levels of organization. There is nothing comparable to the maximal lineage heads or village chiefs found in other societies. A father has institutionalized authority over his wives and children and, when his sons marry, over their wives and children. When he dies his authority is transferred to one of his sons, usually, although not necessarily, his eldest son. However, the authority exercised by the successor is seldom more than a pale reflection of that enjoyed by the father during the latter's lifetime. The position of the successor is not inherited. When the brothers die each of them has his own successor and there is no one who had rightful authority over the group composed of the grandsons of the original man.

The elders of the village do exercise authority of a limited and rather vague nature. The elders are able to expel people from the village, and they are responsible for the admission of immigrants to the village, but beyond this they have few executive prerogatives. The elders are most active in the field of judicial proceedings within the confines of the village.

Immigrants, because of their peripheral position, have but little power and influence. However, they often contribute to the power of certain men who gain influence beyond that which would seem to be their due in terms of the formal structure of the lineage. Sometimes a man who is the successor of his father and who has several much younger brothers and a number of sons may gain a good deal of power over village affairs by virtue of the size of the group which he heads. Such a man whom I call a residential leader may increase his power if he is joined by immigrants who swell the number of his supporters.

All of the land within the boundaries of the village is thought to belong to the maximal lineage as a whole. The individual has rights over land within the context of the village organization. The land in any given village falls into three categories, virgin land, land actually under cultivation, and resting land. The virgin land is seen as a repository of land for the future use of the community. No individual has rights over any particular bit of it, and all are free to use the products of the forest such as trees for building material and firewood, wild vegetables and fruits, etc. An individual can obtain rights to particular bits of this previously unused land by felling the trees and opening it for cultivation. Any member of the village is free to open any bit which he sees fit. He need not ask the permission of the community in general. The village organization only comes into operation in this sphere when two men want to open an identical piece of land at the same time, a very rare occurrence. Once a man has opened a piece of land it is his as against any other member of the village, irrespective of whether he is a member of the local lineage or an immigrant. When land goes out of cultivation after having been in use for three years or so, the man retains his rights over the land. However, with the passage of time, if the land is not put under cultivation once more, it reverts to its original status of virgin land. When a man dies his rights are transferred to his sons. Here the situation parallels that found between individuals and the village. In the beginning all of the sons have equal rights to all of it. However, once one brother cultivates a given plot that becomes his as against the other brothers. Coffee groves and banana plantations tend to follow the house property complex in that sons of a single mother inherit the groves tended by her during the lifetime of the father. Rights to land are continually being transferred. When a man wishes to use a bit of his neighbour's fallow land he asks him for it and if the latter has no immediate need of it he usually transfers his rights to the man requesting them.

Lineages of a greater depth consisting of a man and his sons do not have joint rights over land. The situation here is similar to that found in the distribution of authority. Of particular importance is the weak nature of the control exercised by the maximal lineage and village. The land tenure system tends to emphasize the importance of units of the smallest size as against the maximal lineage and village. The weak nature of the communal interest in land means that it serves only to a very minor extent as a focal point for feelings of joint interest and responsibility on the part of the village.

In any political unit a certain minimum degree of solidarity between its members is a prerequisite for its continued functioning. However, in a system such as that of the Amba in which authority is weakly institutionalized and found only at very low levels, the problems of solidarity become crucial. That is, the Amba system depends to a very small degree upon the use of force and other coercive measures and throws very great responsibility upon subjective feelings of loyalty, and motivations tending towards a willingness to subordinate personal interests to the well-being of the collectivity.

Ancestor cults are often given a prominent place in the discussion of solidarity within such units. The Amba practise an ancestor cult and it is undoubtedly true that ceremonies carried out in connection with it exert a strong cohesive influence because the lineage members realize that they share ancestors in common who are involved in their fate in this life. However, the Amba ancestors to whom sacrifices are made are ancestors who occupy significant positions in the lineage structure. While sacrifices are made to some, by no means they are made to all significant ancestors, and in particular in very few maximal lineages are sacrifices ever made to the ancestors credited with their foundation. Thus the ancestor cult tends to a certain degree to emphasize the independence of lineages of smaller span at the expense of their integration into a larger whole, the maximal lineage. Balancing this, however, are a series of non-ancestral gods in connection with which ceremonies are carried out by maximal lineages as total entities.

Witchcraft in the form of fears and accusations is probably the element in the system which is most destructive to intra-group solidarity. The Amba are witch-ridden, and witchcraft forms a constant topic of conversation. If witchcraft fears were directed outwards, that is, if people always felt that they were being bewitched by people of other villages and lineages, they could have a very strong integrative effect. Unfortunately, the majority of witchcraft accusations are made within the village community. No relationship is safe and brother accuses brother, father accuses son and son accuses father. Particularly striking is the concept of the village witch team. It is thought that in each village there is a group of witches who go about at night preying upon people, killing them and eating them. These witches, who may be of either sex and of any age, only attack people within their own villages. It is thought, though, that witches of various villages co-operate with each other. Thus if the group in village A kills a person in village A, the witches of village B may be invited to share in the ensuing feast. The witches of village B must at a later date reciprocate, attempting in so far as possible to provide a victim who matches the first one in all relevant characteristics, age, marital status, or degree of plumpness. On a supernatural level the activities of the village witch team are rather close inversions of the activities of the village war party and the operation of the blood feud. Witchcraft fears, since they are expressed openly, damage relationships in two ways for not only does the person who fears he is under attack conceive hatred for the person whom he believes to be causing his ills, but the person accused realizes the existence of this ill-will. These fears and accusations continually lower the morale of the village community. They become of critical importance when a person leaves the village and lives elsewhere in order to escape these difficulties.

The judicial system within the village on the other hand has an opposite influence. The judicial system like other sectors of Amba life is not rigidly organized. Two men who have a dispute merely seek out an elder who listens to their arguments and judges between them. In any serious case all the adult men of the community attend the hearing and all are allowed to take part although the older men have more influential voices. These village-wide hearings are of great importance for the airing of public opinion. The village as a whole does not accuse a person. Accusations are brought by a single person or a small group of them. The one exception to this occurs at the inquests which follow almost every death. On these occasions individuals are accused of having killed the dead person.

The village court has the power to expel a person from the community. However, for the most part its activities are confined to the levying of fines. These fines are usually paid to the person who is adjudged to have been injured, but in certain cases they are paid to the community as a whole. Thus, a man may be fined a goat which is then eaten by all the elders of the village.

It is quite clear from the procedure followed, the relative importance accorded to various cases, and the judgments given that the paramount aim of these proceedings is the restoration of breaches of solidarity. To put it briefly, when one man commits a wrong against another, what concerns the village is not so much the wrong itself as the ill-feelings which it has generated between the parties involved. Thus the principal goal is the restoration of good relations between the men concerned, rather than the administration of justice in some more abstract sense.

(ii) *Warfare and the Feud*

In the past the operation of the feud and the warfare to which it gave rise furnished the most important opportunities for the joint action of the maximal lineage and the village structured around it. Feuds were suppressed at about the time of the First World War, but even today people are often severely beaten and occasionally killed as a result of actions taken upon the basis of traditional feud patterns.

Warfare in Bwamba consisted almost exclusively of feuds. The one exception to this occurred when the villages in Bwamba were raided by armies from the Bunyoro-Toro area. One village attacked another because harm had been done to one of its members and it felt that it had to right this wrong. Offensive wars of conquest had no place in the Bwamba scheme of things. The basic reason for this is that warfare of such a type did not make sense in terms of the Bwamba political system, the world view connected with it and the physical setting of the political units. The village was seen by the Amba as essentially a kinship unit, more specifically, a lineage unit. A village could not increase its size and importance by conquering a neighbouring village because people cannot be made relatives by conquest. Kinship relations can only be formed through processes of marriage and birth. Again, the conquest of another village for the sake of its land was not a war aim since land was plentiful and no village cared to extend its boundaries merely for the sake of having more land. The taking of captives in order to use them as slaves was not practical. For the warring villages were often but a mile or two from one another and a slave, unless he were imprisoned, in which case he would have become an economic liability, could not have been held against his will. Booty did play a part in local wars and, if one village routed another, the victorious warriors did engage in pillage. However, the spoils of war thus obtained amounted to very little for the Amba had few grain stores which could be carried away and the principal items of wealth, goats and sheep, were usually hidden at the outset of battle and were seldom captured.

When a man was killed it was the duty of his maximal lineage to avenge his death and this could only be done by killing a man belonging to the maximal lineage of the murderer. If this was managed successfully the matter would usually end there. However, in the actual implementation of this ideal pattern all sorts of difficulties could arise. The avengers might kill two men in the battle and then the second lineage in its turn would feel that it had a death to avenge. Quite often the result of a war was not a clear-cut peace but rather a temporary cessation of hostilities due to the fact that the side which suffered the greater losses was afraid to continue the struggle. In such a case the defeated group would wait, perhaps for many years, until it felt it was strong enough to once more seek its revenge. Again, some slight incident between members of the two lineages might inflame the passions of the injured group to such a degree that they would be willing to take to the field again.

A striking characteristic of the Bwamba feud was the fact that the payment of blood-wealth was not institutionalized. I have heard of a couple of cases in which one lineage gave another two women to be married by men of the second lineage in payment for the death of a man in the second lineage. However, this procedure was very unusual and does not seem to have been an action which was even contemplated in the majority of cases. No payments in the form of livestock were ever made in the manner in which cattle were paid in so many African societies. Thus, there was no way in which a feud could be avoided once a man had been killed by a member of an unrelated lineage.

There were no age grades or warrior class among the Amba and all the able-bodied men of the village, lineage members and immigrants alike, were expected to join the village war party.

The feud pattern did not operate within the context of the village. No feud occurred if one member of a maximal lineage killed another. The presence within the village of immigrants who were members of other maximal lineages raised the possibility of feuds within the village but in fact these did not occur. If an immigrant killed a member of the local lineage he would automatically have been killed by the other members of the dead man's lineage and by the other immigrants. The only hope for such an individual was to flee immediately to the protection of the village inhabited by his own maximal lineage. On the other hand, should a member of the resident lineage kill an immigrant the only possible avengers of the latter's death would be the war party of the village of his maximal lineage.

In many cases one village seems to have attacked another on a moment's notice, a very simple matter given the usual proximity of the opposed villages. However, should the war become protracted beyond the first encounter, other people beyond the bounds of the two villages became involved. The identity of these allies will be made clear in a subsequent section.

(iii) *The Mother's Brother–Sister's Son Relationship*

Every individual in Bwamba is tied to a multitude of people in other villages and other maximal lineages by bonds of kinship. Indeed, it is seldom that two Amba, if they search long enough, fail to find some linkage, however remote, which will permit them to address one another by a kinship term. These kinship linkages which break down the isolation of the individual village and lineage, however important they may be for the operation of the total social system, are not of immediate concern in the present context. On the other hand, certain kinship ties, even though they are primarily relationships between individuals, have a significance for large-scale group relations. For example, in Europe marriages between royal houses have implications beyond the families immediately concerned.

The basic reason for the existence in Bwamba of the kinship ties which are of particular interest here, and in fact for all kinship ties which cross-cut maximal lineage affiliations, has already been mentioned. The maximal lineage about which the village is structured is an exogamous unit and thus the men of the lineage must obtain wives from other lineages. From one point of view the maximal lineage may be seen as a unit which is engaged in exchanging the women born to it for women of other lineages who can assume the roles of mothers of the next generation. This way of looking at the matter coincides rather closely with the way the Amba themselves consider the situation, for in the past marriage was regulated primarily by the exchange system, whereby a man desiring to marry a woman had to give the father or brother of the latter a woman of his own maximal lineage, almost invariably his sister or his daughter.

Marriage creates affinal ties between the members of the two lineages involved. However, these ties are very brittle due to the high rate of divorce in Bwamba society. When a child is born the situation becomes radically different. The men of the woman's lineage now have a consanguineal link with a member of the husband's lineage which can never be broken except by death. Thus by the process of birth, when the child is a boy, the mother's brother–sister's son relationship is brought into being.

Among the Amba the privileges and obligations allocated to the people occupying the positions of sister's son and mother's brother differ in kind. Thus, although the mother's brother may tease the boy, the latter cannot retaliate in kind, but he can take a certain amount of the older man's personal property without asking permission to do so. In so far as authority is involved in the relationship, it lies in the hands of the mother's brother. However, he is not supposed to act in an authoritarian manner, but rather as counsellor and helper to his sister's son. In spite of this last remark, in the days of warfare the sister's son was supposed to go to the aid of his mother's brother's maximal lineage when the latter was involved in war, while the mother's brothers owed no such obligation to the sister's son and his maximal lineage. On the other hand, should a man be killed, it was not the responsibility of his sister's sons either collectively or individually to initiate any action. They merely waited until the maximal lineage of the mother's brother formed an avenging war party and then joined it. The dead man's mother's brothers had a different responsibility. They might try to avenge the death themselves but their main responsibility was to see that the maximal lineage of which their sister's son was a member took appropriate action. That is, if a man of lineage A whose mother's brothers belonged to lineage B were killed by a man of lineage C the mother's brothers might attempt to kill the actual murderer (the actual person responsible for the killing, it should be noted, not just anyone in lineage C) immediately after the news was received. However, after this initial outburst their duty was to make certain that lineage A took the appropriate action, by threatening to attack them if they did not put the feud into operation.

The basis for the differential content of the roles of the mother's brother and the sister's son is to be found in the structural asymmetry of their positions brought about by the context of the Amba patrilineal system in which this relationship operates. A man is related by consanguineal ties to all of the men in his mother's paternal maximal lineage. By the rules of Amba kinship terminology, which is of an Omaha type, all of the men of his mother's generation and below it in her maximal lineage are called mother's brother. The men of the generation above her are called grandfather. This means that, even initially, the majority of men in the mother's lineage fall into the category of mother's brother and as time goes on the number of men entitled to be called grandfather decreases and finally disappears completely, leaving only mother's brothers. In contrast to this, the mother's brothers have consanguineal ties in their sister's son lineage only with him (and his full brothers). With other members of the latter's maximal lineage they have only affinal ties. A man's mother's brothers always form the core of a political unit, the village, and thus they are organized for collective action. His sister's sons on the other hand are individuals (or at the most a small number of full brothers) scattered among different maximal lineages and weakly related to each other. They do not form a permanent organized group. We may look at this from the point of view of a single maximal lineage. Let us say that a lineage has twenty pairs of adult brothers and sisters and that the twenty mothers of these sets of siblings belong to different maximal lineages. Let us further assume that the twenty sisters are married to men belonging to twenty different lineages and that they have children of their own. In this case there are twenty different sets of mother's brothers living in twenty different villages for each man has his own set of mother's brothers whom he does not share with his fellows in his own maximal lineage. In extra-lineage affairs therefore the mother's brothers act as differentiating foci of interest. In contrast to this the sons of the twenty married lineage women are sister's sons to all of the members of the lineage. Although these sister's sons are scattered among twenty different lineages these ties are shared by all the men of the lineage which we are using as our point of reference. Thus the men of our lineage share in common their obligations in regard to their sister's sons but they are divided by their obligations to their mother's brothers which pull them in different directions.

This structural exposition of the relationship between the mother's brother–sister's son tie in terms of its wider context permits us to see the logic of the differential content of the two roles. The sister's son goes to the aid of his mother's brothers when they are involved in a war because he is related to all of them, and as a group they form the core of the warmaking group, the village. Other members of his lineage do not accompany him since they do not share his obligations. The mother's brothers do not go to the aid of their sister's sons' maximal lineage when it is at war because they are not related to the group as a whole, only to one individual within it. When a man is killed, his sister's son is unable to take action because he is a lone person and his war group, his village, would not support him. Further, although he is only one of many sister's sons, he and they do not form a group accustomed to take collective action. The mother's brothers do form a group capable of taking concerted action. When their sister's son is killed they may try to avenge the death. However, in the ultimate analysis their responsibility is secondary to that of the man's own lineage. Further, in the normal course of things they may be far away from his village and may not receive the news. Thus the primary responsibility falls upon the man's own lineage. Yet, on the other hand, the sister's son among all the members of the man's own lineage is uniquely the concern of the mother's brothers. Therefore they hold his own lineage accountable for seeing that revenge is carried out.

At the present time the role of the mother's brothers' lineage and their power *vis-à-vis* their sister's sons' lineage is shown most clearly at death ceremonies. In Bwamba almost all deaths are attributed to witchcraft and after the burial an inquest which is often attended by hundreds of people is held in order to discover the identity of the witch. The man's own lineage is responsible for producing the name of the witch and the reasons for his guilt, but it is the mother's brothers' lineage which is primarily responsible for judging the truth of the matter. If the mother's brothers are not present the inquest cannot be held. It is remarkable on these occasions how quiet and diffident the dead man's lineage remains in the presence of the mother's brothers.

Usually the person who is suspected of having practised withcraft is a member of the dead man's village. Sometimes when the person accused is an old woman or a man of another lineage, she or he is driven from the village at once by the dead man's own lineage. However, if the man thought to be guilty is a member of the same lineage no action is taken by its members. At the present time, however, unless such a man is careful to absent himself from the inquest, he may receive a beating from the mother's brothers, and in the past it is said he was often killed by them.

The above statements lead to some further observations regarding the nature of the feud in Bwamba. To some extent the feud can be seen as a method whereby in a stateless society of the present type, murder can be punished in the absence of the executive and judicial institutions found in more highly organized political systems. However, it is better seen as a method whereby the small organized group, the village, maintains its integrity in the face of a potentially or actually hostile world. When a man is killed by a member of another village his own village can take up arms and by this action affirm its solidarity and its ability to withstand outside pressure and to protect its rights. When, however, the murder takes place inside the maximal lineage and thus inside the basic political unit, the village, the situation is quite different. The village is paralysed and unable to act. One man of the lineage has already been killed. The alternatives are to kill another man or to allow him to continue living and to remain a member of the community. To kill the murderer would only compound the village's loss and further weaken it in the face of the outside world. Thus the Amba lineages have chosen to allow the murderer to go free.

Nevertheless, the members of the lineage feel a very strong though hidden resentment against the guilty man. This emerges very clearly today in conversation with Amba concerning alleged witchcraft killings within the framework of the lineage. The result of the ambivalence caused by the inability to act, coupled with hidden resentment, is that when the mother's brothers who of course have nothing to lose by killing the guilty man try to do so, or when they accuse the lineage of inactivity, the dead man's own lineage feels ashamed before them and is unwilling to take any strong action to protect its own fellow member.

Thus we see that murder within the maximal lineage is the greatest crime which can occur within the Bwamba system. It so effectively breaches the framework of the group structure by demonstrating the ultimate in lack of solidarity between two members that the group is left helpless and confused. So great is the havoc brought to the structure of the maximal lineage and the village that spokesmen for justice can only come from the outside, from the lineage of the mother's brothers.

(iv) *Alliances between Villages based upon Lineage Ties*

The preceding section has focused upon power relations between villages and between individuals within them based upon asymmetrical kinship ties brought into being by inter-village marriage. We now turn to relations of solidarity between villages as total entities.

The maximal lineage does not stand alone. Every maximal lineage is part of a larger grouping which may be termed a clan. A clan, which is a named unit, consists of several maximal lineages. The members of a clan feel themselves to be related to one another. In the usual case, although not always, the members of a clan are said to be descended from a common eponymous ancestor, and the founding ancestors of the constituent maximal lineages are said to have been his sons.

The clan, however, does not always have political relevance. The unit which does have political implications is what I term the exogamous group. This unit consists of a number of maximal lineages belonging to the same clan among whose members intermarriage is forbidden. In some cases this unit is coterminous with the clan, but in other cases a clan may contain as many as four exogamous groups. Maximal lineages belonging to the same exogamous group, and thus the villages structured around them were obliged to aid one another in war. Such villages did not make war against each other for the feud was outlawed within the group. Between maximal lineages belonging to the same clan but to different exogamous groups no such obligations existed. They intermarried with one another and they often fought against each other, for if a member of one such maximal lineage killed a member of the other the feud pattern was put into operation in the same manner as it would have been had the two lineages been completely unrelated.

The above system of alliances between villages is readily understandable in terms of lineage principles. A departure from the logic of the lineage system occurs, though, in the system of linked lineages. Each maximal lineage is linked to at least one and in a few cases to two or three maximal lineages belonging to other clans and exogamous groups.[1] Between such linked maximal lineages there is a joking relationship and marriage and the feud are prohibited. These linked lineages were also obliged to aid one another in war.

These linkages do not extend to exogamous groups as wholes. Thus a lineage which is linked to another maximal lineage in this manner is not tied by any bonds to the other lineages in the latter's exogamous group. All this may be made clear by a hypothetical example. A, B and C are maximal lineages forming an exogamous group. A is linked with G, and G belongs to an exogamous group consisting of itself, H, and I. B is linked with M. which in turn belongs to an exogamous group composed of M, N and O. C is linked with X which belongs to the exogamous group, X, Y and Z. Should A become involved in a war with another village the other lineages in its exogamous group, B and C, should come to its aid. G, its linked lineage, should also aid it. However, lineages H and I are under no such obligation; nor are lineages M, N, O, X, Y or Z. However, these other lineages could become involved if called to the aid of lineages to which they owe obligations. Thus lineage H and I

[1] The parallel with the interconnections between Talis and Namoos among the Tallensi is very striking. It may be that this device, which has very important implications for the organization of the total power system, is a common feature of systems similar to those of the Tallensi and the Amba. See Fortes 1945.

might join the war begun by A, not in order to aid A itself, but in order to aid lineage G which belongs to the same exogamous group, and so with the other lineages. Thus a war between two lineages could set off a chain reaction. However, this reaction is self-limiting because sooner or later a point would be reached at which certain lineages would owe obligations to both sides. However, wars seem seldom to have reached these dimensions and for the most part they appear to have been confined to the villages originally involved, the lineages of their own exogamous group, and the linked lineages of the two principal opponents.

This system of linked lineages is related to the major linguistic division in the society, that between the Bulibuli and the Bwezi. Any given maximal lineage is either a Bulibuli or a Bwezi lineage. All of the other maximal lineages in its exogamous group and the clan, for that matter, belong to the same linguistic group. In the normal case lineages which are linked in this manner belong to different linguistic groups. That is, each Bwezi lineage is linked to a Bulibuli lineage. This pattern is modified by the presence in the system of two minor linguistic groups, the Vonoma and the Mvuba. Lineages belonging to these two groups do not figure on either side of the major linguistic dichotomy in any consistent manner. Thus a Vonoma maximal lineage may belong either to an exogamous group composed primarily of Bwezi lineages or to one composed primarily of Bulibuli lineages. If its exogamous group is a Bwezi one then its linked lineage will be a Bulibuli one; if its exogamous group is Bulibuli then its linked lineage will be Bwezi. Similarly with the Mvuba.

The pygmies are also drawn into this political system. Pygmy bands are tied to specific maximal lineages and here again the system of alliance is stated in terms of exogamy between the pygmy band and the Amba maximal lineage in question, even though in actual fact there is but little intermarriage between pygmies and Amba in any case.

(v) *The System as a Whole*

At this point we can note and comment upon the main features of the political system of aboriginal Bwamba. The basic political units are the villages. The village is organized about a core consisting of the men of a maximal lineage, and although immigrants may be joined to this core, the integration of the village and its ability to maintain its integrity in the face of its social environment depend, in the ultimate analysis, upon feelings of solidarity between the adult male members of the localized maximal lineage.

Although the village is the largest unilateral unit of power in the system, and is the war-making group, it does not stand alone but is allied to other villages by means of ties with the maximal lineages about which these villages are structured. If only the system of alliances on the basis of exogamous groups within the clans were utilized, the system would be one of groups of allies organized as autonomous power groups. However, the mechanism of linked lineages binds the whole society together in a completely interwoven mesh analagous to the situation found in every society when the kinship system is described from the point of view of ego. Each maximal lineage serves as a focal point for a unique concentration of power for every maximal lineage has a different set of ties.

It is of interest to note the way in which the achievements and limitations of the Bwamba political system are connected with the dominance accorded to kinship and more specifically lineage principles. The basic premise of the system is that one's close relatives in lineage terms are those to whom the individual owes loyalty and from whom the individual can expect aid and protection against a potentially hostile world. Together with this is the equally important premise that intermarriage with one's close lineage relatives is not allowed. Thus we get the following equations:

	Close lineage relationship
equals	Mutual aid
equals	Absence of the feud
and equals	Prohibition of intermarriage
while	Distant lineage relationship or absence of relationship
equals	Neutrality at best and potential opposition and war
equals	Willingness to implement the feud
and equals	Ability to intermarry.

In the past a maximal lineage's strength and potentialities for survival were seen to depend upon: (A) its internal strength in terms of the number of warriors which it could muster and the degree of solidarity between these men and (B) the number and strength of its allies. This view of the situation implied two major aims for the foreign policy of the village: (A) to obtain as many wives as possible, for this was the method by which the population could be increased and (B) to get as many allies as possible.

For the individual lineage and village these aims were to a certain point not too incompatible but in the ultimate analysis for the society as a whole they were contradictory and posed a basic dilemma. To put the matter in extreme terms, if all the lineages in Bwamba had become allied with one another, each lineage and village would have been very strong and would in any case have had nothing to fear since all its potential enemies would have become friends and protectors. However, this would have meant that no marriages could have taken place within the society. On the other hand, if the men of the maximal lineage were able to marry the daughters of all the other maximal lineage in Bwamba they would have had no allies. When we push the basic premises to their logical conclusion we see the fundamental structural reason why the system had certain inherent limitations, and we see why, for example, we could never expect to find all of the Amba forming a unitary political unit with peace and the settlement of disputes by judicial processes reigning throughout. At the very heart of the system, with its rigid adherence to a lineage ideology, lay a fundamental contradiction which, unless new political principles were introduced, doomed the society to continual internal warfare and bloodshed, no matter how much individuals within the society might wish the situation to be otherwise.

Towards the end of the last century there seems to have been an attempt to unify Bwamba by the introduction of a new political philosophy. Whether this new movement sprang completely from the ambitions of a few individuals, whether it was response to an insight into the internal limitations of the traditional system, or whether it was due to the realization of the weakness of the Amba in the face of raids from the organized kingdoms to the east, is not known. What happened is that one of the lineages in Bwamba began to claim that it was a branch of the Babito, the royal clan of Bunyoro and Toro and that one of its members was entitled to be recognized as King of Bwamba. Whether or not this movement would have succeeded will never be known, for soon after its inception the aboriginal political system of Bwamba was forcibly absorbed into that of the Kingdom of Toro and into the Uganda Protectorate as a whole.

THE ABORIGINAL SYSTEM UNDER CONTEMPORARY CONDITIONS

The kingdom of Toro is organized along the same general lines as the other Interlacustrine kingdoms of which the best known is Buganda. The capital of the kingdom is located at Fort Portal where the King, the Prime Minister and other officials reside. Port Portal is also the headquarters of the Protectorate district of Toro, the boundaries of which coincide with those of the kingdom. Toro as a whole is divided into seven large administrative areas called sazas which may be translated as counties. One of these sazas is known as Bwamba but, in addition to the area under consideration here, the administrative county of the same name includes the area inhabited by the Konjo on the western slopes of the Ruwenzori as well as the open grasslands which stretch from the edge of the Bwamba forest to the shores of Lake Albert and which are inhabited by cattle-keeping Hima. Under the county chief are five sub-county chiefs, three of whom rule the area inhabited by the Amba. Each of the sub-county chiefs has a small number of parish chiefs under him and each of these latter in turn is aided by one or two assistants. In recent years this autocratic system has been modified by the organization of a series of councils which are now to be found at all levels from the parish up to the kingdom as a whole.

There is no official relationship between the aboriginal system and the present one. For administrative purposes the village system does not exist. There are several reasons why this situation came into being originally and why it continues to exist today. For one thing, the minute size of the villages means that a recognition of them would entail the creation of a large number of posts. The administration has tended continually to decrease rather than increase the number of chiefs. The main reason for this has been financial. By cutting down the number of posts it has been possible to raise the salaries attached to the remaining positions and this has been desired in order to attract better people to this type of work particularly at the lower levels. The result, therefore, is that the smallest unit of modern administration contains several villages. Then there is the fact that the absence of authority figured within the villages made it difficult to graft the old system onto the new one whose principal feature is the clear-cut delegation of authority within a hierarchical pyramid. Another reason is to be found in the fact that all of the higher posts, the county and sub-county chieftainships, have been held almost without exception by Toro, who have had for the most part no clear grasp of the nature of the traditional system of the Amba.

Although the new regime does not take any official cognizance of the traditional system it has not destroyed the old village organization. In many spheres of activity the village has been interfered with only to a very small extent. On the other hand, the government has of necessity profoundly affected its operation and has stripped the village of many of its old prerogatives. Again, in still other spheres the government deals with the individual in ways which formerly were of no concern to the village.

The most important way in which the government has interfered with the operation of the traditional system has been by suppressing the feud and inter-village warfare and by appropriating the use of force to itself. This has undoubtedly weakened the level of solidarity within the village by making individuals within the village less dependent upon one another, for now the individual's safety is protected not by the village but by the far more efficient government.

An example of the way in which the traditional system has continued to operate is to be found in the judicial system within the village. Disputes between fellow villagers are almost always settled in the old manner. It is considered very bad form for one member of a village to accuse another in the government courts. In addition to this, however, there are other reasons for the viability of the village judicial system. For one thing, cases, such as a quarrel between a husband and wife, which would be considered far too petty a matter to bother with in the government courts, are willingly listened to within the village. Again the villagers are very interested in cases which usually are not admissible to the government courts. Witchcraft cases, for instance, are only heard in the courts of the chiefs when certain rather rigid requirements in terms of evidence are available, but cases which do not meet these requirements form the staple item of intra-village disputes. Finally, the differing procedures and aims of the two systems cause people to prefer to have their cases heard within the community. As has been noted previously, the main purpose of the village judicial system is the restoration of inter-personal relations which have been damaged in one way or another. The government courts administer justice based on other premises. Thus, if a man in a village steals something from one of his neighbours and the case is taken to the court of one of the chiefs, the latter is concerned only with the question of whether or not the man actually committed the theft. If he did, he is sent to jail. No attention is paid to the relationship between the thief and his victim.

The government now makes demands upon individuals which were formerly unknown. The best example of this is the annual tax which every adult able-bodied man is required to pay. This demand is quite outside the sphere of interests of the village organization *per se* although, of course, it is of great interest to the individuals within the village.

The government treats individuals as individuals and not as representatives of particular groups such as lineages or villages. In the case of the poll tax mentioned above, it is only the individual who is concerned, not the community as a whole. If a man fails to pay the tax when it is due, the penalties which follow fall upon him alone. They are not imposed upon his village as a whole or upon other individuals within it. The most striking example of this characteristic of the new political order occurs in the case of murder. Today the murderer alone stands trial and suffers the consequences of his act, unlike in the past when another member of his village might have been killed in retaliation by the victim's relatives.

The great advantages of the new system which are readily admitted by the Amba lie in the field of inter-village relationships. Warfare has been suppressed and, although a few older men complain that this is a great pity, most people appreciate their delivery from the constant fear of sudden attack and the great freedom which they now have in moving about the area without fear of being molested. The new courts are also able to handle disputes between individuals belonging to different villages in an efficient and just manner impossible in the past.

A very important feature of the present political organization is its ability to change institutional patterns. An example of this occurs in the field of marriage. For the last few years exchange marriage has been banned and the payment of bridewealth has been made the only legal method by which marriage can be arranged. Although a certain number of exchange marriages continue to be made and although a certain number of people are very much against this particular ruling, there is no doubt that the vast majority of people favour the bridewealth system. In the past an alteration of this type would have been very difficult to bring about even if most people had favoured it due to the lack of social machinery for effecting such changes.

BWAMBA POLITICAL STRUCTURE AND NON-CENTRALIZED AFRICAN POLITICAL SYSTEMS

The Bwamba political system may be classified among those non-centralized African political systems which are structured largely in terms of patrilineages. As yet the number of published studies which give adequate descriptions of such systems is relatively small. I think it best therefore, in this concluding section, to confine myself to noting certain contrasts which I believe to be of importance which emerge from a comparison of the political system of the Amba with that of the Nuer. The classic example of a lineage-organized society is, of course, presented by that of the Nuer, but further than this, there are very striking differences between it and the present system, differences which are so great that for the time being at least I think we may consider them as polar types within a common category. I shall confine my remarks to the overall significance of the lineage for the structuring of the political organization and leave aside such interesting and important considerations as the incidence and nature of positions of authority.

In both societies the village is the basic political unit and in both cases the lineage organization is crucial for the understanding of its organization. However, the role played by the lineage differs markedly in the two cases. Among the Amba lineage and village are almost synonymous in the sense that in the ideal case the population of the village consists of all the adult male members of a maximal lineage plus their dependants. In a Nuer village the connection between lineage and village is far looser.[1] The village is expected to contain members of various unrelated lineages. The adult male members of the community are bound to each other by a complicated network of kinship ties. These ties are given coherence and direction by the mechanism of the dominant lineage, the lineage about which the village may be said to be grouped and which operates in such a manner as to fit the village into larger and more inclusive political segments, sub-sections of the tribe and the tribe itself.

The above remarks lead to a further contrast between the two societies. Among the Nuer, lineages can be divided into two categories, aristocratic or dominant lineages which have implications for the large-scale political structure and commoner or non-dominant lineages which do not have such implications. Amba lineages cannot be categorized in this manner. All maximal lineages occupy equal status and perform similar roles in the political organization.

In neither case does the basic unit, the village, stand alone. Amba villages and Nuer villages alike are bound into larger power organizations. Yet the nature of this integration is very different in the two cases. The Nuer village forms merely the smallest building block in the pyramid form of the tribal structure. Thus several villages are grouped into a tertiary section, two or more tertiary sections are combined into secondary sections which in their turn are combined into primary sections. The primary sections together form a tribe. These levels of political organization are paralleled and given coherence by similar levels of organization within the dominant lineage or

[1] For the purposes of this discussion I have ignored the complications introduced into the Nuer system by the existence of dry season camps. Although this feature would deserve comment in a more extended paper, I do not think it affects the present analysis to any great extent.

clan. Among the Amba the situation is quite different. Political organization only exists at one level above that of the village, that of inter-village alliances. Villages so allied need not be, and very often are not, territorially adjacent. This point may be summarized by the statement that above the village level the Amba system *is not* a segmentary one whereas the Nuer super-village or tribal system *is* segmentary. This distinction is consistent with the fact that while lineage segmentation within the dominant lineage is to be found within the Nuer village, nevertheless lineage segmentation is primarily of importance *above* this level. Segmentation of Amba lineages on the other hand is primarily of significance *within* the village.[1]

When we consider the manner in which the villages are integrated into larger fields of political power in the two cases in conjunction with the contrast presented by the rigid connection between lineage structure and political groupings in Bwamba in comparison with the much looser connection of the Nuer lineages with the political system certain further implications in terms of the varying operation and varying potentialities of the two systems emerge. These further implications involve a discussion of the blood feud and exogamy.

In both societies the lineages are exogamous and they are the units entrusted with the operation of the feud pattern. In neither case does the feud operate within the lineage. The structural similarity found at this level leads, however, to very different results in the two cases because of the position of the lineage in the total structure.

Among the Amba the village and, from the point of view of any given village, the allied group of villages ideally are exogamous groups. In Nuer society no political group from the tribe to the village is even ideally an exogamous group. This is so because at all levels the political segments are structured in terms of dominant lineages, and the presence of members of other lineages with which intermarriage can take place is assumed. In fact, although I do not recall that Evans-Pritchard discusses the question, one imagines that the vast majority of

[1] It is due to these empirical differences in the structure of the two societies, as well as to theoretical reasons, that what I call a maximal lineage is more comparable to what Evans-Pritchard terms a minimal lineage than it is to a maximal lineage in his terminology. Concerning this point see the diagram in Evans-Pritchard 1940a: 248.

marriages in Nuerland take place between members of the same tribe and quite probably most of them occur between men and women belonging to much smaller political segments. In short, therefore, the weaker relationship between lineage and political groups among the Nuer avoids the complications introduced into the Amba system by the involvement of exogamy in the basic structure and operation of the political groupings. It would seem that it is largely due to this fact that the Nuer system offers much greater scope for the integration of large numbers of people into political units with at least some minimal degree of cohesion. It is significant here, I think, that while the largest number of people in Bwamba who could be said to have any degree of political integration, the group of allied villages when viewed from the standpoint of any particular village, would seem never to have comprised more than 2000 people, whereas, among the Nuer, some tribes are estimated to contain as many as thirty or forty-five thousand people (Evans-Pritchard 1940b : 278).

Since in the ideal case all the men who inhabit a Bwamba village belong to a single lineage and all of the men living in allied villages are members of related lineages the operation of the feud is ruled out between members of the same unit in the political system. In Nuerland this is not so. Since political segments of any order, including the villages, contain members of different lineages it is always possible for a feud to break out between members of these groups, for it is the lineage and not the political unit which is responsible for the prosecution of the feud. In other words, whereas among the Amba the feud always operates against members of *outside* political units, among the Nuer there is always the possibility that a feud may break out *within* a segment of any given order. The implications of the possibility for the cohesion and stability of Nuer social structure have been pointed out by Evans-Pritchard, who has said when speaking of the village, '. . . when a homicide occurs within a village general opinion demands an early settlement since it is obvious to every one that were vengeance allowed corporate life would be impossible'. (1940b: 292.)

Thus it is consistent with the differing constitutions of the two societies that we find institutions and roles such as blood payment and leopard-skin chiefs among the Nuer while we do not find analogous mechanisms among the Amba. For the Nuer the absence of such mechanisms would mean chaos. Among the Amba the internal stability of the political unit is not only not menaced by the feud but is actually strengthened by it. Therefore, such institutions are not found. Further than this they would have no meaning in the context of the only units in which they could be instituted, namely, the villages, and the groups of allied villages.

The Nuer system seems to have much greater potentialities for the development of more centralized forms. Indeed there seems to be no inherent reasons why all of the Nuer should not be subsumed under one tribal entity in Evans-Pritchard's sense rather than be divided as at present into a number of tribes. At a guess I should think that the reasons for the non-unification of the whole society along these lines may be sought in situational factors such as the enormous area occupied by the Nuer, the relatively large population or perhaps in the social structure itself in the weak development of authority figures. In view of the ability of the Nuer system to integrate territorial segments into larger wholes and the similarity of this pyramidal organization to that of centralized states, I do not consider it surprising that certain of the Nilotic groups, for all of whom a common basic structure has been postulated (Butt 1952: 178–181), have developed more centralized forms of political organization. No violence is done to the fundamental principles of the system when such centralization takes place.

By contrast the Amba system seems to have reached the end of a blind alley. It seemed unable to develop further without the introduction of radical new principles of organization whether these were developed internally or imposed from without. This is due to the fundamental dilemma brought about by the rigid adherence to lineage ideology which equates the abolition of the feud and alliance against outside foes with the erection of exogamic barriers.

In conclusion I again emphasize that the significant variations which emerge from a comparative analysis of the Bwamba system which may tentatively be termed a lineage village system with that of the Nuer or dominant lineage system have only the status of suggestions. Further research and comparative work should furnish the basis for the erection of more carefully formulated hypotheses. Of other societies for which we have adequate reports those of the Tallensi and the Konkomba, particularly the latter, seem to fall closest to the Bwamba end of the scale. However, the position is complicated by the absence of clear-cut territorial groups among the Tallensi and the existence of such mechanisms as the Great Festival and by the fact that the Konkomba seem to have formulated an alliance system without necessarily involving the principle of exogamy.

ACKNOWLEDGMENT

The fieldwork upon which this essay is based was carried out between June 1950 and June 1952. It was made possible by a Colonial Social Science Research Council grant.

BIBLIOGRAPHY

BUTT, A. 1952. *The Nilotes of the Anglo-Egyptian Sudan and Uganda*, London.
EVANS-PRITCHARD, E. E. 1940a. *The Nuer*, Oxford.
—— 1940b. 'The Nuer of the Southern Sudan', in Fortes, M. and Evans-Pritchard, E. E., *African Political Systems*, Oxford.
FORTES, M. 1945. *The Dynamics of Clanship among the Tallensi*, Oxford.
WINTER, E. H. 1955. *Bwamba Economy*, Kampala.

THE TERRITORIAL PATTERN
AND LINEAGE SYSTEM
OF KONKOMBA

David Tait

CLAN AND DISTRICT

IN this paper I discuss the pattern of territorial aggregation among Konkomba and the structure of the social units that occupy a territorial unit (Tait 1953). The paper falls into two principal sections: first comes an account of the units I call clan and district; secondly comes an analysis of the clan.

The Konkomba live in Northern Togoland in both French and British Mandated Territories. The total population is about 45,000. They have, for some four hundred years, occupied the Oti Plain, a region that suffers an alternation of severe flooding and considerable desiccation. They are grain farmers, their principal crop being sorghum or millet, but they also grow yams. The grain is grown on farms close to the compounds that straggle along ridges in the plain; the yams are grown farther out in the bush. The Konkomba also keep cattle but they pay little enough attention to them: they are herded by small boys and girls between the ages of about 10 and 14. Marriage payments are made in corn and services, not in cattle, though cattle are sometimes used to 'buy' wives from the Kabire, their neighbours to the east.

The Konkomba people is made up of a number of tribes, which may be distinguished in the following ways: they occupy territorial units, in that the tribal territory is the totality of the districts occupied by clans of one tribe; they have different face marks; clans of one tribe may stand in ritual relations to each other; clans of one tribe accept the rite of 'They bury the fight' through which feud between clans can be ended; and finally, clans of the same tribe assist each other in inter-tribal warfare. It is in inter-tribal warfare that one sees fusion of segments on the widest scale known to Konkomba. The tribe is the largest unit of common values and though the tribe is not a corporate body, there is a strong sense of tribal loyalty. At the other end of the scale is found what I call a lineage. The major lineage, the largest segment of the Konkomba system in which descent from one common ancestor is asserted to be known and is genealogically demonstrated, is itself a segmented structure. Major lineages are the units with which all the larger structures may be said to be built up, since from lineages clans are formed and from clans tribes are formed.

Between the major lineage and the tribe is found that unit of a structure which I call a clan; this is the unit which occupies the territory I call a district. I use the term district to denote a continuous territory and the hamlets in which live the inhabitants of that territory. Nevertheless, there is no Konkomba term translatable by 'district'. Konkomba speak of 'this land' (*keteng ke*) in contexts in which the phrase refers to the total area over which the speakers hold farming, hunting and other land rights. But there is no precise term for it in the form of an abstract noun.[1] Each such territory has its own proper name: for example, Kitiak or Kumwatiak. The occupants also have what may be called a clan name. It may be a name given to the clan without reference to the district or it may be derived from the name of the district. The name 'Benangmam', the name of the people of Kitiak, means 'they eat meat', though no account is given of how or why they got this name. Or the clan-name may be of the form Bemwatiak, that is the people of Kumwatiak, possibly, 'the people of the river place'. Just as there is no term for 'district' equally there is no term that is applied to and

[1] Froechlich 1949 says that there is a term for what I call a district, namely '*letingbale*'. I have never encountered this word. I have put it to a number of Elders, who found no difficulty in understanding it, but they all denied that they used it. One suggested that it might be a word of the Bemokpem tribe, the speaker being of the Betshabob. If one ignores the class prefix *le-*, which would look odd in any word referring to *ke-teng*, 'land', it looks like the Dagbane word *tengbale*.

only to the clan. The term '*onibaa*', literally 'one man', is applied in its strictest usage to the members of one major lineage. The clan, however, may be composed of up to six major lineages and this group of lineages is also spoken of as *onibaa*, even though no genealogical demonstration of common descent between the lineages is given. There is, or remains, only a belief in common descent from a now unknown ancestor.

Despite the absence of specialized terms in Konkomba for what I call district and clan, I will seek to show that these two units are the most important ones in the Konkomba political system and that they do in fact operate in that system, the former as the largest precisely known territorial unit and the latter as the largest precisely known structural unit. In what follows when I speak of a district, a precisely knowable group of real or putative agnatic kinsmen is implied as the occupants of the territory: when I speak of a clan, a precisely knowable stretch of territory occupied by the clan is implied.

Within each district there are stretches of farming land known by terms which denote the type of farm worked on them. The stretches of land which intervene between the cultivated areas are not suitable for cultivation because of laterite outcrops or wet season floods and swamps. A district therefore comprises both land suited to two major types of farm and also land which cannot be cultivated; it may include lakes and always includes water sources; it may include a stretch of river. From this land and the waters found on it the inhabitants of the district draw all their food supplies except salt and tobacco. Some raise small cash crops. From its trees they get wood for fires, dug-out canoes, and building poles. The district is often all but self-supporting. That it is not self-supporting is shown by the incidence of small markets which are not reached by travelling traders and which are attended by only a few and probably contiguous clans.

A district is occupied by a clan whose members live in one or more hamlets within its boundaries. The number of hamlets in a district varies from the one of Waju to the eight of Saboba. The number of compounds in a hamlet may be as few as one single compound; these arise when one man decides to build his house apart from his neighbours or by the removal of all inhabitants but one household. Such hamlets do not long remain in that stage of growth or disappearance. The largest hamlets

169

encountered at present include some twenty to thirty compounds. In the recent past larger hamlets existed at Kedzabo, Saambwer and Saboha, all of which districts have suffered severe depopulation and especially at Kedzabo, where the empty and ruined compounds outnumber the occupied ones.

All hamlets are named and the name of one of the hamlets may be the district name—for example, Kitiak, Kpeo or Saangul. Of these only some are held to be meaningful; Kitiak is said to mean 'the place of the stones'. Kitiak is therefore a toponym which refers to the beach of rolled pebbles found at the eastern extremity of the hamlet. Others are of the form Udzado or Gbiedo; these are anthroponyms and the suffix '-do' may be here translated as 'house' in the sense of a descent line.

Whatever may be the distribution of hamlets and population within the district there are three forms of district organization. There are, first, districts in which all male inhabitants and all unmarried female inhabitants belong to one unitary agnatic kin-group which claims descent from one man; secondly, there are districts in which two or more such groups each claim descent from one man: thirdly, there are districts in which the two differently descended groups are assigned different political and ritual roles in the district organization. I call the first type unitary, the second compound and the third, which is a special kind of compound clan, contrapuntal. The contraposition of major lineages is discussed below. At present, contraposition of lineages may be said to be the division of political and ritual rules between two major lineages of one clan.

There are some clans which have two, three, four and perhaps up to six major lineages, though the most common type of clan so far as is known is a dual clan, that is, one with two major lineages to a clan.

I now describe a number of districts. The district of Waju is a small one containing but one hamlet of four compounds, the heads of which claim descent from a common great-grandfather. Because of this they say 'We are the descendants of one man'. The district contains its own shrines of which there are several though the most important one is the land shrine 'Ntengbe'.[1] In

[1] Professor Fortes has pointed out to me that this word is of the same form as that for a land shrine in Talne. In Talne the word is *tengaan*, which is made up of *teng* = land and *gaan* = skin. Similarly with *ntengbe*. The word *ke-teng* (= *land*) is infixed into *m-be* (= *skin*).

the regions in which Konkomba have been settled since the Dagomba invasions the land shrine *ntengbe* is the *sine qua non* of a district; that is, in those regions included in the term *Kekpokpam*, Konkombaland. In the regions of northern Krachi and elsewhere, regions into which many Konkomba are now moving, the significance of this shrine disappears. To the possession of a land shrine other criteria will be added later, but that a district is centred on a land shrine is invariable in Konkombaland. It is at this shrine that the principal rites of the year are done when 'They pour to the land'.

The Elder (*onekpel*) of Waju also serves as its priest (*otindaa*). The term *onekpel* is applied to the most senior man of the kin group which occupies a district or to the senior man of one of its subdivisions. Of the Elder it is said 'O *dzo behib*', 'he holds the people'. The term '*otindaa*' has two applications: first, as the form of the word shows, he is the 'landowner'; of him in this case, it is said, 'O *dzo benib, o dzo keteng mu*', 'he holds people, he holds the land too'. In a contrapuntally organized clan the two kin groups are known as '*onekpelanib*' and '*otindanib*', the Elder's People and the Landowner's People, of whom the latter are thought of as the earlier settlers in the district. In another sense *otindaa* means 'one who was sent by the land'. He or she is therefore one who stands in a special relation to the land, and to the Land Shrine, and may be called on to cut the throat of a fowl or animal sacrificed to the Land Shrine. There was (1951) no *otindaa* in either sense in Waju and the Elder therefore led all sacrifices himself.

Waju is also an exogamous unit.

It has its own farm and bush lands which run down to the Oti river and therefore Waju contains a stretch of river and has fishing rights in it.

Another district of similar size and order to Waju is Kugar. Of Kugar nothing need be said except that it is, like Waju, an offshoot of the district of Nalog. Of these three districts the Elders say 'We are the descendants of one man'. Since Nalog describes itself as *onibaa* and the other two are offshoots from it, it follows *a fortiori* that the later districts are descended from some remote apical ancestor of the earlier clan. This statement summarizes an historical process of settlement, population increase and division of a larger group to form three groups of like

171

order. But the use of the term *onibaa* does not, as used in this extended sense, imply the reciprocal rights and duties which hold between members of one autonomous clan and district. The implied relation of common descent cannot be established genealogically. Nalog is itself a clan composed of two major lineages. It is not an exogamous unit.

The three districts of Waju, Kugar and Nalog describe themselves, not as Betshabob, a tribal designation, but as Benalog. This usage expresses their common derivation from Nalogni, a district of the Betshabob tribe. The district of Nalogni, itself a unitary one, has other offshoots of which one, Kutsha, lies to the north of Nalogni at a distance of about twenty miles and another, Tama, lies far to the east of the Oti. Yet others are in process of formation down the Kulpene valley and in northern Krachi. Between the long-established, distant offshoots of Nalogni and their parent clan all regular and formal communication has now ceased; there is merely the assertion of common descent. This is not the case between Nalogni and Nalog for they are bound by a ritual link. This link is an extension of a ritual link between the component lineages of a clan. Its formal expression is the sending of cloths to lay over the body of a dead Elder during burial by the Elder of one linked district to the other. It is similar to the ritual link between districts which are *mantotib* to each other, a linkage that involves reciprocal help on all ritual occasions. The link between parent and filial district seems to have no name in Konkomba though the persons who bear the cloths to the burial are sometimes referred to as *mantotib*. Nalog and Waju, Nalog and Kugar are similarly linked in this reciprocal ritual assistance. But the original link between Nalogni and Nalog is non-transitive in that the tie does not pass from a district which is the offshoot of a first district to a third which is the offshoot of the second. Nalogni and Kutsha are not so linked as are Nalogni and Nalog. The reason appears to be simply one of distance.

The relation between Nalogni and Nalog is asserted to hold between all Nalog and all Nalogni: between, that is, all the major lineages of either clan.

It must be emphasized that a new or filial clan and district has its own shrines distinct from those of the parental district. Of these the essential one is the Land Shrine. When a man or group of men wish to go and settle in a stretch of unoccupied bush they consult a diviner who discovers for them, first, whether or not it is advisable for them to move and, secondly, (if it is advisable) the shrines, commonly groves of trees, in the fresh land they propose to occupy. Thus is established a new relation from the beginning between a group of kinsmen and a territory. This does not necessitate the cutting of all links with the shrines of the parental district; these links die out in time. But it does imply the immediate carrying out of separate sowing rites and land rites. The first and major step to district autonomy has been taken for with that step a new clan and a new district has come into being.

Yet not all persons moving out of their parental district move into unowned bush. It may be unoccupied in that no one lives and farms there. Konkomba, however, though they claim to be the original occupants of much land now held by Dagomba, do not claim it as their land. Consequently, when a Konkomba moves to the Kulpene river south of Saambu in the Dagomba Chiefdom of Miong, he does not consult a diviner since 'keteng je Bedagbamja' 'the land is for the Dagomba'. He does not seek a land shrine. It is only within Konkombaland proper that the question of new shrines arises. This land is, in general, 'land for Konkomba', but the particular Konkomba who intend to use empty land must discover and sacrifice to the shrines on it. When a man or group of kinsmen move into an area in Konkombaland already occupied by other Konkomba, then it is with and only with the agreement of the existing occupants who already have the necessary shrines. This may be the origin of contrapuntal clans though only one instance of this kind of accretion was discovered.

Nalogni, the centre of dispersion of these clans discussed above, is itself a unitary clan though a large one with three minor lineages. It has its own land and shrines: it is an exogamous unit.

Sobib is an example of a triple district. It consists of three segments in three hamlets. The Sobibtib no longer have any tradition of whence they came but offshoots have gone out to settle at Natsha, only a few miles away, and at Kamwadzar, a place far distant to the east of the Oti, a place with which no close ritual connection is maintained.

The three segments of this clan may inter-marry and examples of these marriages were found. They have one common land shrine and the senior of the lineage Elders is also the clan Elder and Land Priest.

I have indicated something of clan fission and the way in which clan fission gives rise to new clans and new districts. There is no seniority, ritual or other, accorded to the first of a series of scattered, related clans. This follows from the non-transitivity of the ritual link between a parent clan and its offshoot and the autonomy of the new Land Shrine in each new district. The link between parent and offshoot clan is reciprocal and involves neither clan in a similar link with other districts. But the relationship between parent and filial clan is also symmetrical except for rare occasions. It sometimes happens, however, that a diviner will find that either a group or an individual should go to one of the shrines owned by their clan's parental clan to make a special sacrifice. This may be taken as a sign of juniority in the filial clan in a ritual context. But this juniority has never been used in Konkomba society as an organizing principle such that political consequences followed and larger units than the clan were built up. Any two clans whether in a parental/filial relationship to each other or of common descent from one parent clan are always independent units.

It was once stated by a clan Elder that the game caught in the great ritual hunts that are carried out every three years would go to the senior clan Elder of a group of clans of common descent. For example, that the game would go to the senior Elder of the clans of Waju, Nalog and Nalogni: not to the senior clan's Elder, but to the senior Elder. I never saw this done nor did the many Elders to whom I put the point confirm it. Were it so, however, the individuality of the clans of common descent might be less than I take it to be.

An example of a contrapuntal clan is found in the district of Kitiak, occupied by the Benangmam. The district comprises two hamlets, the larger being Kitiak proper and the second a single compound. The clan has two contraposed major lineages to both of which the name Benangmam is applied, and they describe themselves as 'the children of one man' even though each group traces its descent to a different apical ancestor. The two contraposed groups are known as the 'Land Owner's

People' and the 'Elder's People'. The clan has five shrines in the district of which the major one is a Land Shrine. The clan is exogamous.

The principal hamlet is a fairly compact one, but is divided into four sections on principles of descent. I will speak of the Land Owner's People as a whole as Kotodo and of its sub-divisions as Fanindo and Dzangendo (see Figure 1). All these terms are derived from the names of ancestors, of whom Koto is the apical ancestor of the major lineage of the Land Owner's People and Ngmangea is the apical ancestor of the contraposed major lineage, the Elder's People; I will speak of them as Ngmangeado and of the sub-divisions as Natiado and Kugbedo. The compounds of these divisions are to be distinguished by their territorial distribution (see Figure 2). These two divisions give each other ritual assistance in the principal rites of the district and at burials, but there are occasions on which they are ritually distinguished.

Kitiak is an example of a closeknit, compact hamlet since the compounds all lie near together except the one owned by Ngkwo; that one demonstrates the first step towards the formation of a new hamlet within the district. The clan has farm lands of both kinds, bush lands and river rights. It also has three lakes.

Several offshoots of Kitiak have come into being; most of these still exist but one, which lay adjacent to the hamlet of Kitiak and which was formerly occupied by a now-lost major lineage of the Benangmam clan, is now occupied by a segment of the neighbouring Bekumbwam clan.

To summarize so far: a district is a territorial unit occupied by one or more descent groups which together form a clan. Some of these districts are contrapuntally organized, in that they are occupied by two descent groups each claiming a single apical ancestor; that is, each is a major lineage and there is division of ritual and political roles between the two groups. When the district is occupied by a single major lineage it is always an exogamous unit; when the district is occupied by more than one major lineage then it is not an exogamous unit but usually is so if the major lineages are contraposed. The major lineage is invariably exogamous.

The district can be defined as a territorial unit containing a land shrine and inhabited by a clan. The district is the largest

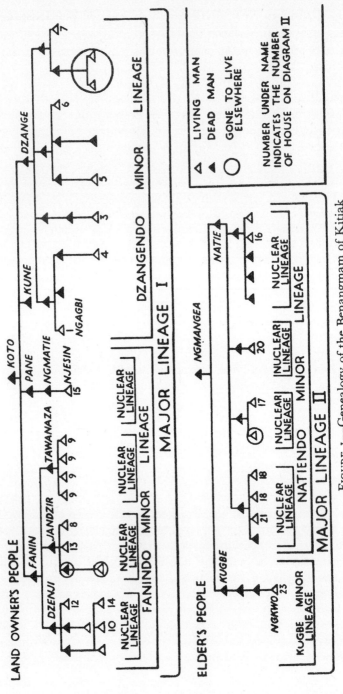

FIGURE 1—Genealogy of the Benangmam of Kitiak
Only names mentioned in the text are given

demarcated territorial unit of Konkomba organization and the clan occupying it is the largest unit of Konkomba political structure.

The examples I have given of clan and district are all examples of the simpler forms of the clan. Each kind of clan varies somewhat in form and complexity of structure but for the purposes of this essay the three kinds I describe may be regarded as the norms about which the variant forms range. Were I, however, concerned with the dynamics of lineage growth and segmentation the three forms would have to be regarded as stages in a process of growth or rather, dual and contrapuntal clans would have to be regarded as alternative processes of growth from unitary clans.

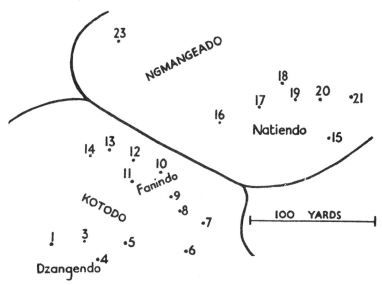

FIGURE 2—Ground Plan of the Hamlet of Kitiak

The variation about these norms may be briefly indicated. The unitary clan is one that has only one major lineage, the major lineage being defined in terms of lineage depth. The major lineage varies in its own internal segmentation and lineages are found with two, three and perhaps four minor lineages. The dual clan seems to be by far the most common of Konkomba clans at present though this may not always have been the case. There are two known clans that possess three major lineages, two that have four and one that may have six. These larger and more complexly segmented clans all lie off the flood plain on the low hills to the west of the plain in places where larger populations than those normally found can be aggregated. But these clans differ from the dual and contrapuntal clans only in the number of major lineages they possess and they involve no principle of organization not found in the simpler forms of clan.

The contrapuntal clans also vary. Contraposition of major lineages is rare in Konkomba—I know of only six such clans (about 5% of those known). In one and one only do the component major lineages claim to be of different tribes. In all the others the component major lineages are of the same tribe. Of the remaining five three are exogamous units and two are not. The two that are not exogamous units are so, I believe, because they too represent a stage of growth beyond that of simple contraposition; the breakdown of exogamy between the Owner of the Land's People and the Elder's People is due, in part, to a wide dispersal of their segments in unusually large districts.

I have said that there is no precise Konkomba term translatable by 'district' and no term translatable by 'clan' which has no other usage. Nonetheless, the reality of these two units of organization, the land unit and the social unit, is demonstrable in all activities. Their reality is also apparent in Konkomba myths and consequently in Konkomba thought about themselves.

There appear to be few migration myths among Konkomba. Most Konkomba songs and stories are ephemeral and for the greater part they deal with recent events and are consequently topical. Such migration myths as are found are also explanations of the totomic tabus of the clan that tells the myth. On the other hand not all clans observe such tabus. So far I know of only seven clans that do observe them: the Benangmam tabu (*kwo*) the leopard; the Bwakwintib tabu the crocodile as do the Kpaltib; the Sobibtib tabu the cobra; and the Bekumbwam tabu the wolf. Totemic avoidances are more generally found linked with the beliefs of those who 'hold spirits' and with those 'sent by' a shrine. Totemic avoidances do not seem to occur at the tribal level.

Such myths as have been noted all refer to the time of the Dagomba invasion when some Konkomba were driven from their former territories. The retreating Kpaltib were, they say, taken over the Oti by a crocodile that swam with them on its back and when the pursuing Dagomba saw the Konkomba on the opposite bank they plunged into the river only to drown. The leopard of Kitiak brushed with his tail the path along which the Benangmam fled and so obliterated their tracks to prevent the Dagomba from pursuing.

Such myths refer to the clan and district and express clan unity.

The autonomy of clan and district can be seen in all activities of Konkomba life. Indeed, it is sometimes difficult to discover the smaller segments of the clan since Konkomba speak of it as a whole rather than of its segments. Konkomba always speak of fighting as though it concerned whole clans from the beginning. In actual fights, however, it is plainly to be seen that they begin between individuals or lineage segments and only gradually are other segments of a clan involved. Again, if one asks a man where his wife came from, he will first give either the name of her clan or the name of her district (if she is of his tribe; if she is of another tribe he gives the tribal name) for it is only when other marriages are to be arranged that more precise genealogical connections need to be traced.

Both these examples concern inter-clan and inter-district relations. Yet, within the clan and district, the same tendency to think of the whole as indivisible is sometimes apparent. The senior Elder of the lineage Elders of a clan regards all clan members as his people and it is only in contexts of particular activities that degrees of responsibility and privilege can be observed and recorded. In discussing affairs outside the actual context of work or rite, the senior Elder of a clan asserts his undivided authority without contradiction.

I seek therefore to do two things in describing farm, market, ritual and other activities. First, to demonstrate the autonomy of the clan and district as a unit of the Konkomba political system; secondly, to show that this autonomy is a fusion of parts. It is this fusion of lineage segments into a clan by means of territorial, ritual, legal and agnatic ties which creates the political system of Konkomba.

179

I show Konkomba at work on their farms, going to market, performing rites and dealing with socially disapproved acts. All the activities and events discussed take place within the territorial boundaries of the district and within the social framework of the clan.

First, I take some aspects of farm work and land tenure. Each head of a household, which may be an elementary, a polygynous or an extended family, has his own lands for compound farms and for bush farms. When a man marries he will continue to live in his father's house and, as his own family grows by the births of children and by the addition of a second wife, he acquires lands of his own, first in the bush and later on the compound farms. On the death of a household head some of his elder sons may already be farming on their own and his younger sons may still be farming the compound farms of their father but working bush farms for themselves. If the younger sons are of suitable age and married they will receive a share sufficient to their needs on their dead father's compound lands. This share is allotted to them by their lineage Elder. The sons will not necessarily share all their dead father's land. Ownership is vested in the lineage and the distribution of land for use is vested in the lineage Elder. On the death of a household head his household begins to break up and his wives are inherited within his minor lineage, taking their young children with them. Consequently, on the death of the head of a large household there is a considerable redistribution of people and of compound land. It is the duty of the lineage head to redistribute such land equitably; should there be land left free after such a redistribution the lineage Elder will himself retain it and use it, perhaps, until such time as other lineage members require it.

But any man may cultivate as much land in the bush as he is able to. Unmarried girls may have ground-nut farms there that are cultivated for them by their lovers. It is only compound land that is closely controlled. On this land individuals have rights of inheritance to a suitable share of their father's land even after a period of years. For example, a man died leaving two young sons. His lands were worked by the lineage Elder's household until first one and then the other was old enough to require land. All the lands of this man who died some thirty years ago have in recent years been given over to his sons.

Further, when men move out of Konkombaland their land is used by the lineage Elder and held by him, as it were in trust, for the young men who have not as yet got their own households.

Since land is given over to sons as a father ages or to sons on the death of the father, should they be of suitable age at his death, particular pieces of land tend to pass from father to son. Konkomba are not fully aware of how strictly land passes down a descent line and assert that the Elder always inherits from a dead person. Diviners condemn the modern practice of inheritance by the younger brother, which, they claim, shows a decrease in the authority of the Elder. However, the strong tendency of the territorial groupings of the compounds to show close agreement with subdivisions of the main kin groups of a district demonstrates further the line of inheritance of land, at least at present and in the recent past. Though this division of land is seen at its strictest between the Elder's People and the Owner of the Land's people, and each of these is a major lineage each is itself segmented into two or three minor lineages and it is the minor lineages which are the effective units in which the land passes. For example, in Kitiak one man has no compound land. He belongs to the Fanindo subdivision, a division in which all compound land is in use; but land was made available to a younger man who belongs to Dzangendo in which subdivision there was unused land which could not pass to someone outside that subdivision.

Lineage growth and segmentation and the appearance of new hamlets within a district or of new hamlets which begin a new district go together, but not *pari passu*. If compound land is sufficient to provide farms for all, then, though the lineage segments, the hamlet does not divide. This is the case in the Kitiak district. Conversely, in the Saboba district lineage segmentation and hamlet formation have kept more equal step, and this is the case in many districts.

In reciprocal assistance in compound farming, that is in sorghum or millet farming, the divisions or minor lineages of a clan are again seen at work. The reciprocal assistance is given when a man invites a work party (*o gba ngkpawin*) for which those who respond are paid in beer at the end of the day. The invitations are sent, not to individuals, but to the heads of compounds, who assign members of their households to this or that work. This giving of assistance is reciprocal in that, should members of a household fail to co-operate, then when the head of that household in turn invites assistance few respond. In clans composed of contraposed lineages or in compound clans members of one major lineage attend the work parties only of Elders of the other major lineage; they do not attend those of more junior men. They attend the work parties of junior men of their own major lineage only.

Women do not go to sow at work parties outside their own major lineage and married women do not sow for men of a minor lineage other than that into which they are married.

When a minor lineage is also a separate hamlet the position is simplified: there is then a tendency for people to attend work parties only in their own minor lineage, though members from all minor lineages attend the work party of the clan Elder.

Another example of the clan and its divisions at work is the late dry season hunt which follows the making of poison and arrows. This hunt may be referred to as *leluu* from '*bi nga leluu*' 'they make quiver'. This hunt is carried out every two or three years and is done by each clan separately. Among the Betshabob tribe only the people of Kitiak district carried out this hunt in 1951.

The Kitiak hunt begins on Kakã, the day of the Saboba market, and ends on Sakpa: that is, it begins on a day when there are some limitations on farm work and ends on a day of *lekwobil*, a day on which no farm work may be done, a day of rest. On the day of the hunt no-one goes to market. Six groups of hunters were formed as follows (see Figure 1): two from Fanindo, two from Dzangendo and two from Ngmangeado. The first four are of the Land Owner's People and the last two are the Elder's People. The grouping follows the contrapuntal division of the clan and within each major lineage further division takes place according to the segmentation into minor lineages.

Before the hunt began I had been assured that such hunts could go anywhere and that hunters do not remain only within the boundaries of their own district. The only time that this hunt crossed a boundary it was into the lands of a neighbouring clan; the actual area entered once belonged to Kitiak but was ceded some time in the past to a section of the people of Saboba. No other clans' lands were entered.

The hunt ended with a triumphal march round the hamlet, finally to encircle the house of the Elder of each major lineage three times before entering it to give the bag to the Elder. This he then divided. He gave a share first to the Elder of the other minor lineage, a share large enough for that Elder to share with his own people, the remainder he divided among the compound heads of his own minor lineage.

In this hunt the divisions of a clan come together in a common activity. Throughout the hunt the divisions maintain their identity and at the end of the hunt they separate to present the game to the heads of the major lineages involved. In this form of ritual hunt each of the major and minor divisions of the clan keeps its own place in the line.

In seeking to demonstrate the autonomy of clan and district I now briefly describe the organization of Konkomba markets. No market could exist solely for the use of members of a single group the size of Konkomba clans. Markets are therefore part of inter-clan, inter-tribal and inter-national relations. But, since markets are controlled by one clan, by the clan on whose land the market is held, market control is a pointer towards clan and district organization.

In Eastern Dagomba there are six principal markets, each one of which is the central market of a cycle of six markets. The seven-day Muslim week has not yet affected the market cycle. One of these markets is held in the district of Saboba and is known as Kakã. Though it is regarded as the market of the Betshabob tribe by other Konkomba, Konkomba of many tribes attend it, as do Kabire, Tshakosi and a number of Yoruba and Dagomba traders.

Kakã, like all Konkomba markets, was once wholly, and remains partly, under the control of the clan on whose land it is held. Each market is a shrine, which bears the same name as the market, to which sacrifices are made every three years and as occasion may demand. The market itself is a group of kapoks and baobabs, and one ancient baobab is the shrine; among its exposed roots are stones on which the sacrifices are offered.

The Market Elder, 'Onjandaa', is at present a lineage Elder of one of the segments of the Bekumbwam, the clan that occupies

Saboba. In contrapuntally organized clans there are always some shrines at which the Elder of the Elder's People carries out the sacrifices and not the Land Priest. Thus the market at Saboba is not controlled by the 'Owners of the Land' but by their contraposed group. As far as memory goes the Eldership has run in the lineage segment in which it now runs. The Market Elder attends every market and collects tax in kind. This customary tax is still paid despite the imposition of the Native Authority tax.

The sanction that the Market Elder may invoke to control the market is his ritual control of the shrine. In the trees are swarms of bees and it is believed that an unconfessed thief would be stung to death by them. If a thief were to confess he would buy a guinea fowl which the Market Elder would sacrifice on the shrine Kakã.

Thus markets too show the clan and its segments at work since control of markets is vested not merely in a clan but in one particular lineage of a clan.

In ritual activities also the clan and district is a unit, the largest ritual unit known to Konkomba. It is true that clans participate in each other's rites and that representatives of several clans will gather to sacrifice to the land of a clan carrying out the rite of 'They pour to the land'. At such a rite, however, the sacrifices are made to the land of one clan and of one clan only at a time. There are no tribal rites. There is no wider fusion of ritual segments than the segments of one clan and, though these segments may be joined by representatives of other clans, these men come from clans which stand in special and dyadic relations to the clan that carries out the rite.

Take, for example, the celebration of a rite of purification in the unitary clan of the Nalogtib. A child died after a short illness and was buried with little ceremony but in the presence of the Elder of the clan and the Elder of its father's minor lineage. Four days later a rite was performed to drive the sickness out of the clan. It was carried out by the Elder of the Clan, the Elder of the minor lineage of the dead child and other senior men of that minor lineage including the father. The third minor lineage was not represented but during the rite the apical ancestor of that minor segment was invoked. The rite itself was a lustration.

On another occasion in the same clan a rite was carried out to prepare the way for a major rite. Before carrying such a series of rites as the New Food Rites, Konkomba consult a diviner to find out whether or not there is some ritual impediment to the carrying out of the rite. The diviner is consulted on behalf of the whole clan. On this occasion the diviner found that a girl of the clan was ritually unprepared and that certain rites should be carried out for her. Her spirit wanted a fowl and a ring. Since she was pregnant at the time the full rites could not be carried out so a provisional sacrifice was made for her. The diviner found that the Elder of her minor lineage was to provide the fowl; that the Elder of the clan (who is, *a fortiori*, an Elder of a minor lineage) was to pour the libation; and that a senior man, not the Elder, of the third minor lineage was to perform the sacrifice. Thus all three segments of the clan came together in this rite and it was one that cleared the way for the carrying out of 'New Food Rites' which are carried out in the compounds by household heads.

Similarly in the district of Kitiak when a special sacrifice was carried out to the land. A diviner had found that the land wanted a white sheep. To carry out this rite there came together in the Land Shrine the following persons: two men of Dzangendo (see Figure 1) of whom one is the Owner of the Land; two men of Fanindo; and two men of Ngmangeado. The Owners of the Land are thus represented in both minor segments but the second minor lineage of Ngmangeado is not represented. The reason is that there is no very senior man living there at present.

In the rites described the district and clan can be seen to be a ritual unit or whole, but it is a whole consisting of parts which can, on occasion, work by themselves.

THE CLAN AND DISTRICT AS UNITS OF SOCIAL CONTROL

We now come to what is perhaps the most important phase of the demonstration of district and clan autonomy, namely the district as an area and the clan as an entity in a system of social control. It might be held, *a priori*, that in such a society as this, that if the clan and district is the major ritual unit then it will also be the major unit of social control. It is the case that these two concepts—ritual unity and legal unity—do, in this society, go *pari passu*. The more closely two men are united in ritual ties, and this closeness follows, in the main, from closeness of agnatic kinship, then the more surely operate the sanctions on good behaviour between them. Within the clan and district there are divisions which are localized lineage segments and as structural distance between segments increases so does the force of the application of moral control diminish.

The principle stated by Fortes (1945), that the unit of moral control is the group of men that sacrifice together, is true also of Konkomba society. But it is here less firmly stated and I never saw it invoked; none the less, should one clansman offend against his fellow clansman, the offence can be expiated or eradicated by sacrificing together.

The clan in its territorial setting of the district centred on a Land Shrine is a morally conscious body. Within the bounds of a district there is a sense of moral obligation towards one's fellow clansmen, an obligation that decreases with an increase in structural distance. But there is also a consciousness of moral obligation towards the clan as a whole and towards the district as a whole. This is best seen in inter-clan disputes when whole clans may be involved in warfare or brawl. In warfare a man may be obliged to aid any man of his clan; in a fight over fishing or hunting rights a man may be called on to defend any part of his clan's district against encroachment.

I do not here discuss 'law' because Konkomba have no legal institutions, in that there are no patterns for formal legislation nor for judicial decisions, nor are there law enforcement officers of any kind. Law, in the sense of 'social control through the systematic application of the force of politically organized society' (Radcliffe-Brown 1933), does not exist in Konkomba-land. This assertion is no less true at the clan and district level than it is at the tribal level. Where does there exist a Council of Elders in the sense of a coming together of a group of senior men to hear both sides of a case and to reach a decision on it? When Konkomba call upon Elders in a dispute it is in order that the Elder of one disputant can put his case to the Elder of the other disputant. Each Elder takes up and argues the case of his own follower and together they may reach agreement. But this is neither arbitration nor decision by a judicial body, nor can the original disputants be compelled by force to accept any agreement of their Elders.

Evans-Pritchard (1940) speaks of law as 'a moral obligation to settle disputes by conventional methods and not in the sense of legal procedure or legal institutions. We speak only of civil law for there do not seem to be any actions considered injurious to the whole community and punished by it'. In a similar sense the term 'law' could be applied to Konkomba practice, yet it seems appropriate and useful to reserve the term to the stricter usage of Radcliffe-Brown and Seagle (1941), usages in which law is prescriptive as well as normative and is publicly sanctioned. Yet, as among the Nuer so among Konkomba, there seem to be no public delicts and even witchcraft is, except for repeated offences, a private delict.

Wilson (1938) speaks of law as 'that customary force which is kept in being by the inherent necessities of systematic co-operation among its members'. In this he seems to be expressing an idea similar to Evans-Pritchard's 'moral obligation'. Wilson goes on to say 'a breach of law is a course of action, on the part of some individual or minority group, which is inconsistent with the normal and accepted form of co-operative action and which would therefore, if unchecked, make continued relationship between law-breakers and other members of their community impossible'. This point goes near to the facts of the Konkomba situation. One may perhaps say that some acts by individuals and groups impede communication within the society and disrupt the steady running of the parts. When such acts occur, then countervailing action may be taken to restore communication. Or it may be that it will be left to God to intervene, for when Konkomba say 'God will not agree' they imply that a religious sanction operates to adjust imbalance.

What Evans-Pritchard emphasizes is a positive obligation to behave according to standards. What Wilson emphasizes in the second quotation is action taken by society after a breach of customary standards. The existence both of such standards and of sanctions on breach of them, are, of course, found in Konkomba society. But the standards were at no time laid down by a legislature, are not interpreted by a judiciary and are not enforced by an executive. Therefore, if the term 'law' is to be used only in the strict sense of Radcliffe-Brown's definition some new term should be found to cover the quasi-legal or para-legal methods of peoples like Konkomba. I will speak of jural activities. This is a term used by Fortes; he says that jural relations involve lineage segments: 'What we find . . . is that all jural relations involve a configuration of rights on the one side and a configuration of responsibilities on the other, both corresponding to the range of lineage segments involved. And no jural transaction is complete until the whole configuration of rights and responsibilities, on both sides, is brought into action (1945: 230).

By the term 'jural' I seek rather to emphasize the quasi-legal executive activities; those acts on the part of individuals, as in retaliation, or of groups, as in ostracism, which are acts on the part of those offended against an offender, acts of retribution which are approved by Konkomba society as a whole. An offender who calls out against him the anger of his society has failed to attain the required standards of behaviour and in retributive acts or jural acts by individuals or groups against an offender the moral support of the society is always with the offended persons. A jural act in this sense is a punitive act which has the moral backing of the society.

This definition must also include the action of the Elder in situations of breach of custom. The Elder's role is never punitive or retaliatory, as I see it, for he does no more than exert his ritual power and his moral authority to insist, for example in a case of theft, on restitution by the thief. In brawls he commands obedience because brawling is an offence against the land and the Elder who stands in ritual relations to the land as its Guardian. The Elder is the oldest man of the clan, the closest to the land and to the ancestors and is the repository of custom. His authority is moral and ritual, he is most learned in the mores of his clan and his role is primarily to remind his people of their moral obligations to their clansfolk, to recall them to proper standards of behaviour. Though he has no power to punish by force, still, to run counter to his commands is itself sacrilege. It may be added that when sanctions are enforced against an offender they have always the backing of the Elder.

Some examples of jural acts will include the action taken after a homicide, in quarrels and brawls, destruction of crops and theft.

No instance of homicide is known in which one man killed another man of his own clan. On two occasions there were quarrels which almost led to homicide. The first of these is readily dismissed since the would-be killer was a trypanosomiasis case, who fired arrows at and wounded one of his brothers. He is not held responsible for his actions.

In the second case two men of the same minor lineage quarrelled. Their lineage is that in which a market eldership runs. One of the men had stood by and said nothing when a visitor to the market came carrying his bow and arrows. Such weapons were never permitted inside a market and it is the duty of all men of the lineage to help the Market Elder to maintain order in the market. But when the first man was reproved by the second he became angry and not only insulted his accuser but insulted his father, the Market Elder, also. The two men then fought but were separated. The second man then went and fetched his arrows saying, 'Nnekwe and I are going to kill each other'. This is a challenge, not a threat. But their kinsmen prevented any further fighting and later Nnekwe went and complained to the police and had the other arrested; he was later sentenced to three months' imprisonment.

The sympathies of their clansmen were wholly with the man sent to prison. Nnekwe was first ostracized and, after earlier accusations of sorcery against him were renewed, he was driven out of his hamlet and he built himself a new homestead outside the hamlet in which he had formerly lived, though still within his natal district.

It seems likely that homicide between close agnates is almost impossible. The supernatural sanction is very strong and the necessary conditions for murder do not occur, for a brawl between kinsmen leads to the intervention of their kin to prevent bloodshed, whereas a brawl between men of different clans leads to a swift line-up of opposing sides.

There is no ritual purification for one who kills his brother. Should any man do so the religious sanction would operate to eliminate the fratricide and so restore communication within the clan.

The method of settling in a rite a quarrel between men who

'sacrifice together' appears to be seldom invoked. It was not invoked on this occasion, possibly because Nnekwe was held to be in the wrong and he was punished by ostracism. The quarrel was not composed ritually. I never, in fact, saw it done though Konkomba say that disputes between agnates can be ended in a shared sacrifice to the land their quarrel polluted.

Quarrels between clansmen, especially young clan-fellows, are not uncommon but they may not occur within the hearing of an Elder, in whose presence voices may not be raised, and they die rapidly away on the arrival of an Elder or even of a senior man.

Though many quarrels occur within a district none are over women, for the incest rules and the system of joking relationships operate to evade friction over women, since it is jealousy of husbands for wives and not jealousy of lovers for their mistresses that leads to fights. Further, within the district and hamlet, the presence and active intervention of kinsmen-neighbours operate to hold quarrels within bounds.

Women too quarrel in the compounds and in their anger reach out for branches of brushwood as weapons. But I have never seen these weapons used and the quarrel usually dies away under the pressure of neighbours, of elderly women and, in the last resort, of the compound owner.

Destruction of crops is never deliberately done by one man against another, but a man's livestock may damage corn since cows may wander from the paths or pigs may root among it. On one occasion a man shot his clansman's pig which he found in his corn. The men were of the same minor lineage. The owner had no redress against the killer of his pig and could only cut his losses by selling the meat.

The conjunction of cattle-keeping with corn-growing on compound farms often leads to friction. The cattle are herded on open land by small boys and girls. The cattle have to be brought back to the compounds at night where they are stalled. The boys drive the cattle at great speed along the paths which lead back through the corn to the compounds, but in the early growing season before the shoots are tall cattle often stray from the path. Once a man severely beat his neighbour's son for letting a cow stray on to his corn; he chased the boy through the corn lashing him as they ran. The Elder came along and called on the man to stop it and pointed out that, if the boy had offended, it was the father who should punish him; no one else had the right to do so. Such an instance shows the power of the Elder to intervene in a dispute; not to impose a solution, but to insist that things be done in the proper way. It also shows him protecting a weaker person against a stronger. The Elder did not decide the boy's punishment, but asserted that, if punishment were required, it should be given by the proper person, the boy's father.

Theft is exceedingly rare in Konkombaland. Money was little known until recently, though the practice has always been for men to bury money for safe keeping if considerable sums were held. A man returned from a visit to find that some money he had buried had disappeared. He believed that it was stolen and he accused the young men of his own minor lineage. It was not a specific accusation but a general one, so all the young men accused went together to a diviner who was to be asked to divine which of them had taken the money. The diviner said that there were too many people and refused to start until some of them had been eliminated. The accuser explained all this to an Elder, who was not at all sympathetic and who made it plain that he, in common with the young men, thought that the accuser had simply forgotten where he had buried the money. It is noteworthy that the accusation was made only against men younger than the accuser.

There is, in any case, very little private property among Konkomba. The young men of a hamlet, or rather of a lineage of major or minor span, sleep in a room in the compound of the Elder, but they keep only bows and arrows or other weapons and some clothing in this room. No one would take another man's bow and arrows for these are sacred objects. Garments are by no means private property and a pair of shorts will pass round all those whom they more or less fit. But the cotton cloths now sold by travelling Yoruba, or bought in the south by young men who go to work on the farms there, are very highly prized and do not pass from hand to hand. These and other precious things, including money, are kept in the mother's room, or the room of the woman to whom an orphaned child is assigned. Apart from the woman herself only her children will enter the room; not even her husband does so during her absence unless it be the room of his senior wife in which ritual objects are kept. Thus, only the woman herself and men and women who stand to each other in the closest of all Konkomba relationships, that of *naabo*, literally 'mother's child', to each other may enter the room.

Again, it may be argued from the precautions taken that theft is something to be guarded against. On the other hand there is no privacy in Konkomba life; one is hardly ever alone. These precautions may then be an expression of a desire to have a place of one's own, rather than as precautions against loss.

I have given an account of the types of Konkomba clans— the unitary, the compound and the special form of the compound clan, the contrapuntal. Though there are slight variations of custom all clans may be classified as one or other of these three types.

A district comprises a territory on which lie shrines and of these the most important is the Land Shrine. The unitary clan and district is one composed of one major lineage. The compound clan is one composed of two or more major lineages which together occupy one district. The contrapuntal clan is one composed of two major lineages to which are assigned different ritual roles, together occupying one district. The major lineage is always an exogamous unit: the unitary clan is therefore also an exogamous unit. Dual clans are seldom exogamous units while the contrapuntal clans are usually exogamous. I believe contraposition and the prohibition on marriage between major lineages to go together and that the absence of contraposition and the permission of marriages between major lineages of a clan to go together. They are alternative processes in lineage fission. When a unitary clan of one minor lineage grows and segments to form two lineages of like order, then if the two lineages are together in one hamlet they will go into contraposition and the two new major lineages remain an exogamous unit. But if the two new lineages are separated into quite distinct hamlets within the district and are separated from each other on the ground, then the lineages do not go into contraposition and in time marriages will be permitted between the two major lineages. Contraposition and exogamy are principles of organization which are applied to lineage organization only in special circumstances and at certain stages of lineage growth and segmentation.

The district is an economic unit in the sense that it can be all but self-supporting; yet it is a divisible unit especially in the compound districts.

The clan and district is a ritual unit though districts also come together to share in each other's rites. But it is a divisible ritual unit since subdivisions of the clan carry out separate rites.

It is an autonomous unit of social control in that there is no supra-Elder authority to impose a solution on recalcitrants of a district. Within the district there is no organized force which can be employed to ensure acquiescence; there is no coercion other than the ritual and moral power of the Elder and the diffuse sanctions of kinsmen's disapproval, though this latter may on occasion extend to physical restraint.

The organized clan and district, with its ritual and moral head the Elder, is the political unit of Konkombaland. The district is the largest unit within which arbitration is the rule.

The district is a territorial unit occupied by a clan. The association between the clan and the land is close and the highest values expressed in the rites of the clan are those of fertility of land and of the group. The clan and the land are a duality; both can be seen and delimited. But each has its unseen, its religious aspect: for the living group of kin the unseen, dead ancestors are recalled in the ancestor cult and in their function of providing points of reference about which the lineage structure is articulated. For the land, the unseen, the religious aspect is expressed in the land cult and in the sacrifices at the land shrine. But the land is not only the provider of food, it is patrimonial land since it was this land that the ancestors walked and in it they lie buried. These two cults are in the end unified, in the final conception of the supreme deity.

The lineage too has its mystical aspect and this aspect is symbolized in two ritual symbols. I speak of ritual symbols since *Dzambuna*, the symbol of the major lineage, and *igi*, the symbol of the minor lineage, can only be defined in description. The former is a crocodile's head encased in pulped roots which stands on a turtle shell. The latter is a horn containing the charred roots of plants and to which feathers from former sacrifices are bound.

Dzambuna is not spoken of as a *'luwaa'*, a shrine; nor is it on the other hand a medicine, *'njog'*. Yet both have protective powers used by men of the lineage that owns them. The homocide, when he has killed his man, goes straight to the room in which the *igi* stands and lies beside it. He keeps it beside him for three nights as a protective against the ghost of the man he has killed. The ritual protection of the *igi* is also invoked during the Second Burial rites of lineage and clan Elders. The *igi* symbol is found in the possession of all Elders of minor lineages and consequently of all Elders of major lineages as well.

Dzambuna has no such obvious uses as has the *igi*, though it is sometimes said that a man who kills another man kills a fowl to it. Sacrifice, of a very simple sort, is made to it during the new food rites. *Dzambuna* is always found in the compound of an Elder of a major lineage.

We may say, therefore, that each order of segmentation has its own ritual symbol and that with order of segmentation there goes also a ritual hierarchy. In the compounds the heads of households sacrifice on the wall of the room of the senior wife or at the door which gives entry to the compound. The minor lineage has its *igi*: the major lineage has its *Dzambuna*: and the clan has its Land Shrine.

THE STRUCTURE OF THE LINEAGE

A lineage is a genealogical structure and between any two members of a lineage of any span and generation depth kinship can be stated in precise terms. This is not to say that the relationships so stated are statements of historically accurate descent: it is only within the units of the lower orders of segmentation and narrowest span that actual relations of descent are accurately known.

The Konkomba major lineage is commonly segmented into two or three minor lineages and the minor lineages are segmented into a number of nuclear lineages. Below that level we find the families of living compound heads. Each lineage is an agnatic descent group and until the highest level of segmentation is reached two or more lineages make up a lineage of wider span and greater time depth in the genealogical structure.

Starting with the lower orders of segmentation, the nuclear

lineage may be defined as the group of agnatic kin descended from an apical ancestor who is the father or grandfather of living compound heads. The minor lineage is a group of agnatic kin descended from an apical ancestor two to four generations back from the living compound heads. The major lineage is a group of agnatic kin descended from an apical ancestor three to five generations back from the living compound heads. For two major lineages of one clan no common ancestor is known. In describing the lineage in this way one adopts the point of view of the mature men of the society, the men who have married and established their own compounds, who are heads of families and are all of ages over forty. From this point of view the lineage stretches back through time as a ladder of generations ascending to the remote, apical ancestor who is the founder of the major lineage.

Clans are localized genealogical structures and each order of segmentation of a clan contains localized structures which together make up the localized structure of wider span and higher order of segmentation. The localization of a clan is precise and is exactly known. One clan occupies one district which is focused on one Land Shrine. The lower levels of segmentation are not so precisely localized as are the clan and major lineage. One hamlet and its surrounding compound farms is usually one minor lineage and the compounds of men of one nuclear lineage are often contiguous.

Konkomba do not often speak at any length about their lineages. The clan seldom numbers more than about three hundred souls and relations between members of one clan are face-to-face relations. Konkomba never come together in large numbers to discuss common problems. The largest meetings of people are in markets or at Second Burials—but these are not corporate groups. The largest gathering of Elders is at the ceremony of divining the cause of death of an Elder, when perhaps thirty Elders and senior men meet. These are occasions of more discussion and argument than occur for any other reason. The rite to purify the land also draws together groups of ten to fifteen Elders and senior men and it is on this occasion that the names of the apical ancestors of major and minor lineages are called and these dead are invoked to aid the living. Even on these occasions names are not invoked in orderly sequence and sometimes names occur that cannot be fitted into any genealogy.

Over against the identity of status of men who are *onibaa* stand contrasted those men of whom it is said '*Bi je bibaba*', 'They are by themselves'. There are thus two categories into which men are classified: from the point of view of men of one minor lineage, men of another lineage of the same major lineage are *bibaba*; men of the same two minor lineages are *onibaa* as against men of a second major lineage of the same clan who are *bibaba*. The term *bibaba* can, according to context, indicate men of a different minor lineage, major lineage, clan or tribe from that of the speaker. The term '*Benatshom*' is one used by an Elder when speaking of men of his segment and can be used by the Elder of a minor lineage, a major lineage or a clan.

It is only in response to pressure that difference of descent is invoked. It is clear that between men of different clans there is no agnation, while between men of clans as small as those of Konkomba, difference of descent within the clan is easily knowable and is known to the mature person. A major lineage Elder distributing the game after a hunt is in no doubt about who should get a share since there are only two or three men who are eligible and they get a share of such a size that, when all Elders divide the meat amongst their compound heads, the compound heads have a share proportionate to the size of their families. That is to say that the Elder divides the meat with full and detailed knowledge of the households of its final recipients. An Elder of a major lineage so distributing meat, if asked why he gives shares to the Elder of a minor lineage, replies '*O mu dzo wa nib*', 'He too holds his people'.

That is to say that sub-groups of agnatic kin are known within the larger grouping of the clan and major lineage. They are in fact differentiated by difference of descent, but since lineages do not spread widely in space, differentiation of descent does not reach far back through time.

There are no specialists in genealogies among Konkomba: no one learns genealogies by a deliberate effort of study. Children hear the names of the nearer ancestors—their grandfathers—invoked in the rites in the compounds, but do not enter the shrines in which are performed the major rites of the annual cycle; nor should they be near when the Elders purify the land.

Some post-adolescent men always attend a sacrifice in a shrine, for theirs is the work of leading the sacrificial animal, of killing and later skinning it and of cutting it up. But not all men go along to these rites; only two or three go to carry out their part and they are taken at random. Yet here is one situation in which the names of remoter ancestors are learned. As men grow older they begin to attend occasional rites such as a sacrifice to the land done on the advice of a diviner, even though they have no duties in the rite. An Elder going to a rite always takes someone along with him 'to help him' and his companion is generally his successor-designate in the office. It is in ritual contexts, then, that names of remoter ancestors are invoked and consequently may be learned by young and by mature men.

These names can also be learned from the names of hamlets. Many hamlets are known by the name of the apical ancestor of the segment that occupies it and all can be referred to by such an eponym.

Konkomba acquire their knowledge of the remoter ancestors haphazardly and not by the discipline of learning a genealogy. Children grow up in hamlets under their Elder. The authority of the Elder is an ever-present fact; their fathers consult the Elder about their personal affairs while the children are there to see and to hear all that goes on. No unit is so large that the Elder cannot know every child nor that every child does not know the Elder. To any child the Elder is '*n te*', my father; any child of the lineage is '*m bo*', my child, to the Elder. From this it follows that no child is ever in doubt where he belongs in the groupings of his clan: conversely, there is no doubt about who is the Elder responsible for any child or man.

The validation of inter-lineage relations in kinship terms is seldom invoked in other than ritual contexts. Yet it is there ready to be invoked when occasion demands. The founding ancestor is recalled in the simplest of myths and the time between him and the fathers and grandfathers of living men is filled in with other named ancestors whose names not only complete a time scale but also diversify the groupings descended from the founding ancestor. Though seldom invoked, the genealogy is always there ready to be invoked; it is a mnemonic device by which present practice can be explained in terms of descent.

The genealogy given in Figure 1 is that of the Benangmam clan of Kitiak and is composed of two contraposed major lineages. The Owner of the Land's People are those descended from Koto; the Elder's People are those descended from Ngmangea. Koto is described as 'the man who first came here' while Ngmangea is described as 'he who helped Koto'. The Benangmam, in such a context as explaining their genealogies to me, tend to regard Koto as the ancestor who first settled in their present place after the Dagomba had invaded what is now Eastern Dagomba and expelled many Konkomba. The Benangmam claim to have come from the region that is now Yendi; other clans claim to have come from further west. At other times their accounts of their movements seem to indicate that they came from east of the Oti river to their present site on its western bank. However this may be, in their thought Koto settled in Kitiak a very long time ago and he is, however vaguely, connected with their expulsion by the Dagomba. This, if accurate, would place Koto in the early seventeenth or late sixteenth century.

To Koto are ascribed four 'sons'—Fanin, Pane, Kune and Dzange. The status of Dzange is dubious. He was first described as a 'brother' to Koto. When I pointed out that this meant that only one generation lay between Ngagbi, the present Owner of the Land and the people who first came to Kitiak, it was first suggested that Dzange was a small boy when Koto was old and secondly that he was Koto's son. That is to say that by juggling the relationships between persons named in a genealogy any doubtful point can be explained.

Fanin is ascribed three sons and the line descended from Pane is, in practice, assimilated to that of Fanin. Pane has one living grandson, Njesin, who is spoken about and treated as a member of Fanindo.

Kune is ascribed no sons at all. There are two possible explanations of this: either his 'sons' have been assimilated to the line of Fanin or Dzange, or his 'sons' left their native district to found a new district elsewhere. The former seems to be the more likely explanation since his is a name recalled by elderly men and one which has to be fitted into a genealogy somewhere. The effective segmentation of the major lineage is into two minor segments, Dzangendo and Fanindo, each with its own Elder of whom the senior is the Owner of the Land of the major lineage and clan.

The minor segments are in turn segmented into nuclear lineages. Fanindo has four effective nuclear lineages: Dzenjido, Jandzirdo, Tawando and Ngmatiedo. The apical ancestors of these segments are either the fathers or the grandfathers of the living compound heads. Dzangendo had six segments of which one has died out without male issue and one has been lost by fission to found a new district elsewhere.

The contraposed major lineage of the Elder's People has as its apical ancestor Ngmangea. To Ngmangea are ascribed two sons, Kugbe and Natie, each of whom is an apical ancestor for the minor lineage descended from him. The minor segment of Kugbedo has only one household, that of Ngkwo, to represent it at present since it has lost many members by fission. It is perhaps helped to survive as a separate segment by its territorial separation from the rest of Ngmangeado; it survives as a segment co-ordinate with that of Natie. Each minor lineage includes nuclear segments; Kugbedo has only one while Natiedo has four.

In view of the definition of lineage that I have given above, what I now call a nuclear lineage is not, perhaps, strictly to be called a lineage though it is a segment of a supraordinate minor lineage and it is a localized descent group. But nuclear lineages are short-lived segments and their functions are not primarily political. They are in fact outgrowths of a unit which may be called the 'extended house' (Konkomba use the word '*do*', a word that has several usages). The extended house is a group descended from a common grandfather, counting through both males and females. This unit has, so to speak, an agnatic core that is localized in the hamlet of the founding grandfather. The nuclear lineage is an extension of this agnatic core and is a short-lived segment that is interstitial between the enduring minor lineage and the transient extended house.

From the plan that accompanies the genealogy (Figure 2) it will be seen that the hamlet of Kitiak is a compact hamlet except for the compound of Ngkwo. Both the major lineages are localized in one settlement and the minor lineages are also clearly localized units. The nuclear lineages are not so clearly localized as are the supraordinate segments.

Both these examples are simple examples of the Konkomba system of segmentation. The clan is a contrapuntal one and the two major lineages are, in practice, segmented into two minor segments. The only problem is the difference in generation depth of some of the nuclear lineages. Yet this can be explained, at least in part, in the following way. It is impossible to collect genealogies except in the presence of an Elder. Though the Elder may not himself always speak no other will speak of the ancestors unless he is present. Thus, to give a genealogy the entire hamlet turns out to join in the game, so that where fairly young or young men do not recall their grandfather's names the old men do. The nuclear lineage tends to lengthen when the living representatives are elderly and old men. Further, I take a lengthening of the nuclear lineages to be an indication of segmentation to come and the shortening of nuclear lineages to be an indication of recent segmentation.

The nuclear lineages and the extended houses operate in the system of proscribed marriages and the marriage rules may relate, *inter alia*, to the nuclear lineages of the father's mother and the mother's mother. This is the farthest extension back through the generations of proscribed marriages. Now a girl's marriage is fixed at her birth; there can be no doubt about her mother's mother's or her father's mother's kin. A man's first marriage is arranged when he is about twenty and a second sometime later at perhaps the age of thirty; a third may be made later still. The first marriage is always and a second is possibly arranged by the father or *pater* of a youth. It is, consequently, the older men who must know the kinship relations of the young men to see that the rules are not broken. Apart from this every man knows his mother's and father's maternal kin since he may have duties towards them.

The economic, ritual and jural activities described in the previous section illustrate the relations between the localized segments of clans and lineages described in the present section. The territorial groupings are also kin groupings and each local group is either a clan or a segment of a clan.

CONCLUSION

To what extent can the Konkomba system of segmentation be described as a lineage system? Fortes and Evans-Pritchard (1940: 6) defined a lineage system as 'a segmentary system of permanent, unilateral descent groups' which 'establishes corporate units with political functions'.

I do not believe the Konkomba major lineage to be a permanent structure, though Konkomba believe it to be so; yet it is certainly long-enduring. The clan is a segmented structure and each segment of the clan is itself segmented. Each segment is localized and gives rise to corporate groups. It may, however, be thought that the segments of the clan are without political functions. It is true that the clan is the major political unit in the political system that spreads throughout, not only Konkombaland, but over the Oti plain to include the Basare, Kabire and Gurma. None the less, there are degrees of political control and political responsibility within the clan. Fighting does not, at once, involve members of a whole clan but begins between members of a smaller segment and spreads, gradually to involve wider and wider spans and in the end to involve the whole clan. It is possible, in the past, when many clans were larger than they are now, and in the larger and most complexly segmented of clans today, that not all major lineages of a clan would in the end be involved in warfare on behalf of one of its component major lineages. The point cannot now be settled. Yet in all present clans there are degrees of control within the clan and degrees of responsibility without it.

The segmentation of the clan is seen in territorial distribution, in economic activities, in jural activities and in ritual activities. The orders of segmentation also give rise to a ritual hierarchy. We may speak of this lineage system as a segmentary system of long-enduring, unilateral descent groups which establishes corporate units with political functions.

BIBLIOGRAPHY

Evans-Pritchard, E. E. 1940. *The Nuer*, Oxford.

Fortes, M. 1945. *The Dynamics of Clanship among the Tallensi*, Oxford.

Fortes, M., and Evans-Pritchard, E. E. 1940. *African Political Systems*, Oxford.

FROECHLICH, O. 1949. 'Les Konkomba du Nord-Togo', *Bulletin IFAN*, xi; 3–4.

RADCLIFFE-BROWN, A. R. 1933. 'Primitive Law', reprinted in *Structure and Function in Primitive Society*, London, 1952.

SEAGLE, W. 1941. *The Quest for Law*, New York.

TAIT, D. 1953. 'The political system of Konkomba', *Africa*, xxiii, 3, 213–223.

WILSON, G. 1938. *Land Rights of Individuals among the Nyakyusa*, Rhodes-Livingstone Papers.

THE POLITICAL SYSTEM OF
THE LUGBARA OF THE
NILE-CONGO DIVIDE

John Middleton

INTRODUCTION

THE Lugbara number 242,000 people, 183,000 in Uganda and 58,000 in the Belgian Congo. They are members of the Eastern Sudanic-speaking group of peoples, who extend over the area of the Nile-Congo divide from the Azande in the north-west to the Lugbara and Madi in the south-east. Little is known of other peoples of this cluster[1]; most are politically uncentralized and small in numbers, and they were all, except for the Lugbara, seriously affected by the Arab slavers of the last century. In the indigenous organization of the Lugbara there were no chiefs: these were created by the Belgian administration in 1900. They are generally in charge of groupings larger than any of traditional political significance. It is clear from Government reports that it is only since the mid-1920s that in fact the indigenous system has been at all seriously affected by administration. Feud and war were common until that time, and most old men can remember in detail the days before the Europeans, other than an occasional traveller, entered their country.

The Lugbara live along the line of the Nile-Congo divide where this forms the international boundary between Uganda and the Congo. The country consists of open, almost treeless

[1] They are described in Tucker 1940, and Baxter and Butt 1953.

203

rolling plains between 4000 and 5000 feet above sea level, with two mountain massifs, Eti and Liru, rising in the centre. There are many permanent streams and rivers and a well-distributed rainfall of some fifty inches a year; the soil can at present maintain a population of over 200 to the square mile in the heart of the country. The people are sedentary cultivators, with eleusine and sorghums as staples; they have cattle and other livestock, but there is no transhumance. With little ecological variation, economic specialization or internal trade, and with a high density of population and the small-scale nature of their social organization, there is little direct contact between local groups over large distances, although there seems always to have been a good deal of individual movement between local groups. Great distances are visible in clear weather across the open plateau and the visibility of the two great mountain massifs and the territories of other groups, which may be well beyond the range of direct social relations of any given group, is of significance in their conceptualization of their society. The mountains feature in all Lugbara myths and genealogical traditions and provide important foci of unity. There is considerable cultural and dialectal variation in Lugbara, but the large areas characterized by peculiarities of culture—dialect, tattoo marks, granary types and so on—have no political significance. In spite of these differences, which are often as great as those between themselves and neighbouring peoples, Lugbara recognize themselves to be one people, although they rarely know where are the boundaries of their country.

THE LOCAL GROUP

The smallest residential grouping is that living in the hut, *jo*, the elementary family of husband, wife and children. The hut is the home of a single wife. Lugbara are polygynous, but 64% of married men have only one wife. The home of a married man—whether one hut or several—is the *aku*, or compound, also used in a general sense to mean 'home'. Although the compound is very frequently territorially distinct, being separated by fields from neighbouring compounds, it is in most contexts considered as merely a component unit of the basic political group, which occupies the settlement of a family cluster. This is the smallest group which bears a clan name[1] and which is a single unit in other than purely domestic relations. It is characterized by its having a head, the *'Ba wara*, 'Big Man', to whom I refer as an Elder. The role of an elder is overtly primarily a ritual one and his status is expressed by his custodianship of special shrines to which only he has access. These I call Lineage Shrines, and they are distinct from the ordinary ghost shrines found in every adult man's homestead. The lineage shrines are placed outside the compounds in the bush and are for distant ghosts, usually the ancestors of major lineages and clans.

The composition of the family cluster varies considerably, according to the stage reached in its cycle of development. It may include more than one joint family, in which case the head of each may well consider that he should be an independent elder: it is then likely to segment at the death of the incumbent elder of the cluster. Or it may consist of only one or two compound or elementary families.

A family cluster is based upon an agnatic lineage of three or four generations, and is known by the clan name of its core lineage. It consists of between fifteen and fifty persons—usually some dozen adult men and their families. The elder has his status by virtue of his genealogical seniority in the lineage. The cluster may include attached personnel, the commonest being sisters' sons or daughters' husbands of a senior member. Nowadays most of the attached kinsmen come to find land; in the past they came also as a consequence of warfare or famine. They are under the domestic authority of the elder, the sanctions for which are primarily ritual. An elder may invoke the ghosts of his agnatic ancestors against his own agnates and their wives in the group, and against a sister's or daughter's child. A sister's or daughter's husband is not under this ancestral authority, but their children are; Lugbara say that therefore the individual families concerned are so, being represented, as it were, by the child.

There may also be persons known as *atibo*, whom I call Clients, non-kin who attach themselves to a member of the host

---

[1] A clan-name is one of several hundred specific names given to clans and lineages. It is typically that of the group of the ancestress by whom the clan or lineage is differentiated from co-ordinate segments. There are about two hundred such names in Lugbara.

group. Clients are people who have fled from their own homes elsewhere in time of famine or warfare, who have been expelled for persistent witchcraft or other offences, or who were in the past war-captives. They are given wives, without bridewealth, and so acquire social status and rights to settle and farm. Clients are not under the ritual authority of the host elder unless they marry a daughter of his group; it is said that a man can fight his own clients, as non-kin, or may expel them, and will have the support of his own kin in doing so.

The minimal lineage holds its livestock as a group, in that its elder has overall control over its use, and he allocates rights of use in its territory and rights in its other resources—including lineage daughters, for whom he has ultimate responsibility. A minimal lineage is a corporate group with a territory, *angu*, 'place'. Its territory belongs to it in the sense that it is occupied and used by it at the present time. So long as a lineage has a piece of land as its own the actual site may be changed in the course of expansion and migration. There has always been considerable fluidity of territorial groupings, which were until very recently continually changing their relative positions under a slow process of migration-drift from the north or north-west. This can be seen from the distribution of burial trees. When an elder dies a barkcloth tree is planted on his grave and named after him. These trees are a prominent feature of the landscape, and there are comparatively few groups whose ancestors' trees are on the land they occupy today, except in the long- and densely-settled northern part of Lugbaraland. Land is not allocated to a minimal lineage or family cluster by any higher authority, either on grounds of clanship or territorial affiliation, for there are none other than those created by the government and these do not concern themselves with land except in cases of open dispute. True, the government has now fixed inter-group boundaries, but this is felt by Lugbara to be wrong and to interfere with the rights of family clusters one against the other. Its territory is a necessary attribute of a family cluster; that is to say, rights over a stretch of land must be vested in its senior member for his group to be regarded as an autonomous unit. A landless family cluster would be a paradox, but it must acquire its land by force of numbers and maintain it by the same means against the demands of others.

The family cluster is a unit in a wider territorial system. Wider groups of this system are also associated with territories, *angu*, but there are no senior functionaries to allocate rights in them; the family cluster is the largest productive unit with autonomy over its own land. Consistent with a high density of population and consequent sporadic and localized land shortage there is continual movement of individuals from one family cluster to another as tenants; there is also almost continual pressure of one family cluster against its neighbours and between its component segments. These factors, together with the lack of higher authority within the lineage and the lack of inherited attachment to a particular piece of land (seen in ritual or other terms), are consistent with, even if they do not cause, a high rate of segmentation at the minimal lineage level and much fusion of minimal lineages or lesser segments that are alone unable to maintain their rights over land *vis-à-vis* other groups that are increasing in size and strength. There is not space here to develop this theme, but it would seem that the Lugbara system is extremely fluid and in many ways unstable, with a comparatively high degree of economic and political autonomy of small local groups and a low degree of interdependence or any form of superior control. In northern Lugbara there are rainmakers and other functionaries, but they are of little significance in this respect: I discuss them below.

GROUPINGS WIDER THAN THE FAMILY CLUSTER

Relations between family clusters—or between minimal lineages on which they are based—are not controlled by elders. These relations are mainly those of competition for land, of intermarriage and of ritual collaboration, and they are sanctioned by fighting, certain ritual processes and by positive values of clanship and neighbourhood. They are distinct from interpersonal relations between individual members of different family clusters. The family cluster is the nuclear group of Lugbara society and we may say that relations between these groups, as corporations, compose the political structure.

There are in Lugbara some sixty or more groups called *suru*, which average some 4000 people occupying a territory of on the

average twenty-five square miles. I call them Tribes. The tribe
is the largest unit within which it is said that disputes should
ultimately be settled by discussion. Fighting may break out
within the tribe but it should give way to discussion and there
are institutionalized means to achieve this. Fighting between
tribes cannot so be settled—or at least there is no machinery to
ensure such settlement—and there may be a permanent state of
hostility between them. For this reason I refer to inter-group
fighting within the tribe as feud and to that between tribes as
warfare. Formerly a tribe formed a territorially distinct unit. In
the centre were the settlements, surrounded by farms and
grazing areas which formed a no-man's-land between it and
neighbouring tribes. Today in most areas the population has
increased and settlement is almost continuous, and inter-tribal
boundaries are not always obvious to the casual observer.

Tribes are divided into smaller territorial sections, also called
suru. There are usually three levels of segmentation within the
tribe, which may be referred to as major, minor and minimal
sections, the last being coterminous with the family cluster.
There may, however, be only two levels and there are often
four or five in any given tribe.

A territorial section is associated with an agnatic descent
group, by reference to which the cluster of people on the ground,
the section, sees its position relative to others within a single
system. Membership of a local group is by kinship or a fiction
of kinship, and the term suru refers to both section and descent
group. Relations of either sort may be expressed by Lugbara in
terms of the other and all are conceived and validated in terms
of descent. Lugbara conceive of their generic unity in terms of
blood; they are 'one people, all one blood' which came from
God the Creator. Of descent groups it is said 'people are with
different bodies, though all one blood'.

Lugbara say that they are descended from two hero-ancestors
Jaki and Dribidu, who entered the country from the north and
begat sons by many women whom they found on their arrival
in the region.[1] These sons were the founders of what I call
'clans' and for which Lugbara also use the term suru. Clans are
genealogically equal in that they are all descended from the

[1] See Middleton 1953 for a brief account of the Heroes.

sixty or so original brothers, the sons of the two heroes. They are dispersed from the original clan-homes. Lugbara see their social organization as one of descent groups of varying genealogical depth, continually proliferating and merging, which originated in the original families of the clan founders. A family cluster increases and segments and the new segments later segment in their turn; co-ordinate segments are ideally differentiated by maternal origin, although this may not always be so in historical fact. The present-day distribution of descent groups is said to have come about in this way.

A clan may have segmented into two or more sub-clans, also called *suru*, or it may merely have shed segments which moved off elsewhere from the main body. Either co-ordinate sub-clans of one clan or the main body of a clan that has merely shed splinter-segments form the agnatic cores of tribes: that is, the internal tribal organization is seen as one of local groups clustered round a central agnatic clan or sub-clan genealogy. Splinter-segments of a clan do not form cores of tribes but are merely attached groups in tribes associated with other clans. I refer to the descent group that provides the core of a tribe as the 'sub-clan', and use the term 'clan' for the scattered totality of members descended from a single son of one of the hero-ancestors. They may not compose a single group of any political significance, but in theory they may not intermarry and they form a single ritual congregation; however, even if the genealogical tie between them be remembered it is rarely reflected in behaviour, due to the difficulty of direct intercourse between groups separated by more than a few miles. Reckoned from the present-day generation sub-clans are not genealogically equal but vary from seven to twelve generations in depth. But it is axiomatic that they are so equal since they are defined by reference to their founders and not to subsequent genealogical tradition. That is, their equality is defined in mythological terms, by reference to the sons of the Heroes of myth. Lineages, the segments of sub-clans, are defined by the place of their apical ancestors in genealogies, and within the sub-clan the relative genealogical seniority of lineage founders is known.

Within a family cluster, as I have said, there may be attached personnel, most of whom are under the ritual authority of the elder. After a generation or two the personnel of these attached families may become numerous or short of land and they break away to become an accessory family cluster on their own, with their own elder and perhaps their own attached personnel. They then form an accessory minimal section within the same minor section as their original hosts, no longer under their domestic authority but still with strong ties. They continue to be known as 'sisters' sons' or 'sisters' husbands'—the original link is kept to refer to them as a category; that is, former 'sisters' husbands' do not become 'sisters' sons' as a group, although they become so as individuals after a generation. Clients, if they have not acquired kinship by marriage, remain 'our clients', but in most cases they intermarry and become 'sisters' sons'. A host group may also have segmented internally. Each new segment, host or accessory, has its own elder and is independent as far as its own internal affairs are concerned. Together they form a minor section, which has no single head with internal authority. The senior elder of the agnatic lineage which is the core of the section acts as the group's representative at the sacrifice of agnatically related lineages, but he has merely powers of representation and not of internal control.[1] The relationship of minor to major sections and major sections to tribes is analogous, although the process of segmentation is slower and so not open to observation in the same way. There is also a high rate of fusion of segments at the minimal and minor section level, as part of the overall process of segmentation, but fusion at the higher levels is rare. The senior elder of a major lineage acts as ritual representative of the associated section in the same way as that of a minor lineage, but there is no recognized representative elder of any wider segment.

The agnatic lineage is the core of the local group in the sense that accessory lineages are attached to it by virtue of a cognatic kinship tie; if clients, such a tie is assumed to develop in time. The head of a local group can therefore come only from the agnatic lineage, attached lineages not being equal in genealogical stature. Heads of co-ordinate segments of a lineage of

[1] That he does represent the whole section may be seen from the fact that on his return from a sacrifice he brings sacrificial meat which he distributes among the whole group, accessory as well as host segments. This re-affirms the close association of accessory and host lineages.

any span are also agnatically related, their genealogies composing that of the entire lineage. Above the major segment, however, at the sub-clan level, there are no lineage heads, and an accessory lineage is regarded as an 'equal' member of the local group and no specific cognatic tie is usually known to account for its presence; it is said merely that there must have been such a tie once but that it is now forgotten. The nature of the link between host and accessory lineage thus varies at these two different levels, that of major and lesser segment and that of sub-clan.

The core of each tribe is a sub-clan: people conceive the relations between different sections—ultimately of different family clusters—within a tribal territory in terms of a sub-clan genealogy, at the apex of which is the sub-clan or clan founder. On the whole, reference to a single agnatic sub-clan genealogy is sufficient to explain the relations between all groups of a tribe, with the exception of the few accessory groups that may have separated from their host groups several generations ago and then have dwindled in numbers. Above the level of the major segment fusion does not occur, or but rarely, and these segments exist in a genealogical vacuum, without reference to the sub-clan which provides the core of the tribe in whose territory they live. They are referred to as *sur̥u acep̥ir̥i*, 'groups which are left over' or 'remnant lineages'. Even so, in everyday matters they are generally subsumed under the section in whose territory they live.

The organization of a typical tribe, that of Vura in south-central Lugbara, is given in Figures 1, 2 and 3.

Any section, whether containing accessory segments or not, is referred to by the clan-name of the host lineage. In everyday reference they are not distinguished. Neither are they distinguished generically by Lugbara, who use the terms *sur̥u* and *ori'ba* to refer both to territorial section and its agnatic lineage core.

Ori'ba means literally 'ghost people' and refers to a group of people who have interest in common ghost shrines. Lugbara distinguished between ancestors, *a'bi̥*, and their ghosts, *ori*. All one's ancestors in any one line as far back as they are remembered are *a'bi̥*, the members of genealogies; but only those who are given individual shrines are *ori*. Thus not all a man's *a'bi̥* are his *ori* and not all dead people become *ori*, since to become one a man must leave living male descendants who will build shrines.[1] *Ori'ba* refers therefore to a ritual group, or more accurately to a group which conceives itself as a group primarily because it has common shrines, the ghosts for which they are built being shared by all members of the group. Although they also have other common ties—of residence, for example—it is felt by the

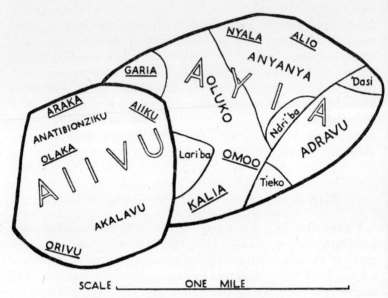

SCALE ————— ONE MILE —————

Names in outline and capitals = Host lineages.
Names underlined = Accessory lineages.
Names in lowercase letters = Remnant groups.

FIGURE I—Vura: diagram of constituent segments of Ezuko major section

people that such ties are common precisely because they share common ghosts. If they did not do so then they would not live together, is the theory. *Ori'ba* is used to refer to minimal and minor segments and to one's own major segment, but not to other major segments. Although wider groups may share common ancestry they share few common ghosts. Accessory groups within the minor section are considered to be still close enough

[1] Lugbara practise neither the levirate nor ghost marriage.

ritually to their host lineage to have an interest in their hosts' ghosts, although of course they also have their own agnatic ghosts; but they attend their hosts' sacrifices.

Surụ is a term which lacks the ritual content of the other. It can be used to refer to a category or type (e.g., of birds or trees) but its primary meaning is that of a social group. It can be used to refer to a unit of any size, from a family cluster (*surụ were were*, 'a little little *surụ*') to a tribe, clan or nation. It is typically used for the larger segments (major lineage and section, tribe, sub-clan and clan) since in situations in which they are significant the ritual content is usually absent. It is not always used for one's own major segment, since its internal structure is seen in terms of ghost-sanctioned relations based on interpersonal kinship; but other major segments are seen in purely political and non-ritual terms. At this level accessory segments no longer have interest in the ghosts of their host lineage: these will have 'forgotten' them.

THE RANGE OF SOCIAL RELATIONS

I have described the formal structure of territorial groups, each associated with an agnatic descent group. Lugbara rarely speak of the relations between these units in these terms, nor of a total, ideal social structure as I have described it. Rather the members of each family cluster conceive of a field of social relations of which they are in the centre and of which the units are neighbouring local groups. The major section is the main political group, in that relations within it are ultimately in terms of a common ritual field whereas relations with other co-ordinate groups are ultimately in terms of force. The use of the terms *surụ* and *ori'ba* is consistent with this distinction. Yet it is usually a minimal section, the family cluster, that acts as a single unit *vis-à-vis* other minimal sections. Marriage is primarily the affair of the family cluster and wider sections are drawn into hostile relations only if one of their members is killed in fighting as a representative of his group. It is unknown for such a victim to belong to another major section than that of the family cluster originally involved.

The range of the field of direct social relations of a single

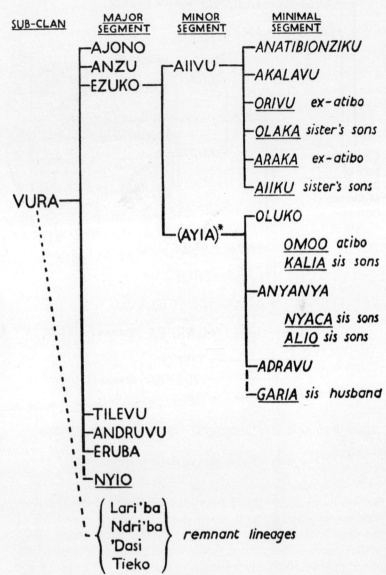

*The name AYIA is now being forgotten and its constituent segments are usually regarded as independent minor segments.

FIGURE 2—Vura: the interrelationships of component segments

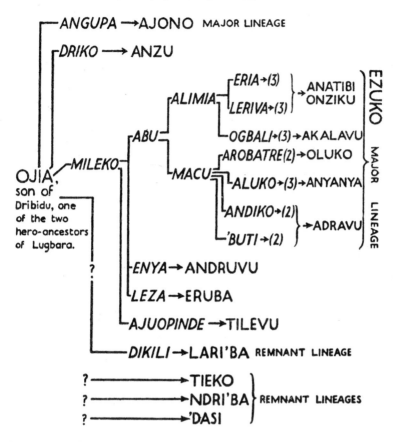

NUMBER IN BRACKETS INDICATES TOTAL OF GENERATIONS

FIGURE 3—Vura: part of skeleton genealogy

family cluster is very small. Everyday relations between individuals are mainly within a neighbourhood which may have at the most a radius of five or six miles in the more densely populated areas, although it is larger in the peripheral areas with a lower density. It rarely extends beyond the far limits of the immediately adjoining tribal territories. The widest economic unit is this vaguely defined neighbourhood, in which there is generally a small market for the exchange of surplus foodstuffs, especially maize used in the production of beer. It is within this neighbourhood—for which there is no specific terms in Lugbara —the composition of which varies for each section, that most intermarriage takes place. It is also the grouping within which most fighting occurs and within which most members of the group have their uterine and affinal kin. To express social relations in which he and his group are involved a Lugbara uses the concepts of *o'dįpį* and *jųrų*, which together comprise the whole field of direct social relations of any given group.

Jųrų are groups in a potentially hostile relationship and *o'dįpį* are those groups within a group's field of direct social relations which are not *jųrų*. *O'dįpį* refers basically to the agnatic descendants of a common ancestor, but non-agnatic kin may be subsumed under the term, since the ideal behaviour towards agnates may be extended to other kin in certain situations. A man's *o'dįpį* are often said to be the members of his sub-clan, but they are defined in many ways. They do not fight, or they do not intermarry, they call their girls 'sisters' and not 'girls',[1] they dance together at death dances or have the same ancestors, in any line. The range varies. In the context of fighting a lineage may regard another agnatically related lineage as its *o'dįpį* on one occasion and as *jųrų* on another. In intra-tribal fighting a lineage may fight another lineage of its sub-clan or even major lineage. That lineage is then *jųrų*, and also *arį'ba*, 'enemy' against whom one is actually fighting with weapons. In extra-tribal warfare the sometime 'enemy' may come to its assistance against more distant groups and then becomes *o'dįpį*.

The range of *o'dįpį* in the context of intermarriage is different. Usually a man may not marry into any agnatically related lineage of the same sub-clan; but often the exogamous group is smaller, only the major lineage. Neither may he marry into any accessory group within the same minor section but he may marry into accessory groups of the same tribe beyond that range. Thus accessory lineages of the same minor section are *o'dįpį* of the host lineages, although not agnatically related. They are not *o'dįpį* to one another but only to their hosts. With their hosts they have a uterine or affinal tie that prohibits intermarriage for two or three generations, according to the rules of

[1] *Ezo*, 'girl', plural *ezoanzi*, means an unmarried female with whom one may have sexual relations.

cognatic kinship. When the tie becomes distant or 'forgotten'—usually beyond the minor section—then they may intermarry with their host lineages. The range of exogamy varies from tribe to tribe, being wider the greater the proportion of accessory lineages and narrower the fewer such lineages in the tribe.[1]

There are thus two patterns of organization of *o'dįpį* and *jųrų* in the two contexts of fighting and exogamy. Both have the same rationale in terms of common descent. 'We marry our *jųrų*' and 'we fight our *jųrų*' are consistent axioms even though the *jųrų* may not be coterminous. Intermarriage is fraught with the possibility of strife: women are the most common cause of fighting in Lugbara. And fighting is of necessity the only sanction between groups negotiating marriage and in the later relationship of affines. For intermarriage to occur kin relationship must not exist or must at least be regarded as irrelevant. A group must be able to fight the people whom its members marry. The reverse proposition is, however, quite different. The principal sanction for relations between closely agnatically related groups is in the ghost cult. At a distance, beyond the major lineage, the sanction based on the ghosts becomes weak and that based on organized force is important. Thus beyond the major lineage agnatically related groups are *o'dįpį* in the context of exogamy but may be *jųrų* in that of fighting. The terms refer, of course, only to groups and categories of persons. Relations expressed in these terms are political relations. They are conceived ultimately in terms of force in that *jųrų* are essentially groups of different ritual fields and so any ritual sanction for their relationship is lacking.

The field of direct social relations of each family cluster is unique: in its centre is the cluster itself. Its field of relations is composed of the totality of those groups which are its *o'dįpį* and *jųrų*, in all situations. *Jųrų* do not extend to the edges of Lugbara society. They consist of those groups with which one marries or fights, and include only those groups in a fairly direct relationship. This does not mean only face to face relations but includes such groups as maternal kin of maternal kin, with whom some

---

[1] For example, the sub-clan is the exogamous unit in Vura, a tribe with many accessory groups within its boundaries. Maraca, on the other hand, a tribe in the densely populated northern part of Lugbara, has few accessory groups and the one tribe consists of three exogamous units, even though all recognize the same sub-clan founder and so admit common agnatic relationship.

sort of tie is recognized and expressed in occasional visiting, and the *o'dįpį* of a group with which one is in a state of feud, if they are involved as well. A circle cannot be drawn on a map to de-limit a group's field of direct social relations; it can only be vaguely delimited. Nevertheless any group can point out this field, referring to other groups actually visible on the open Lugbara plateau.[1]

The field of social relations is seen also in terms of genealogy. A man knows something of the genealogies of the groups that compose it, certainly the names of the founding ancestors of sub-clans that comprise his *o'dįpį* and some of those of his *jųrų*. He is unlikely to know anything of the genealogies of lineages of sub-clans other than his own, beyond the names of their founders. Lineages are recognized by Lugbara to be impermanent units in a system that is always in a state of flux, relations between units of which are expressed in terms of kinship ties between the apical ancestors of the segments. Although lineage re-alignment is recognized it is axiomatic that clans and sub-clans do not change in this way but are everlasting units in a system that covers all Lugbara. Although the processes of lineage segmenta-tion and of clan segmentation are ultimately of the same order, Lugbara cannot admit the latter without destroying the con-ception they have of their society as a single social system. Clans and sub-clans are defined mythically, in terms of their founders, the sons of the hero-ancestors. Sub-clans are equal in status and their later genealogical history is irrelevant to their nature as sub-clans. The number of generations between present-day members of a lineage and the sub-clan founder is irrelevant since sub-clan founders are seen only in relation to one another and their fathers. Any inconsistency in later genealogical depth is not apparent to Lugbara since no one knows enough of the genealogies of clans other than his own to compare them in this respect. He can compare only the genealogies of lineages of his own sub-clan, which change with the vicissitudes of lineage seg-mentation and so show no inconsistencies. The number of generations varies according to the size of the group, the wider the span of the group on the ground the more generations there being in its founder's genealogy.

[1] See Middleton 1953 for a description of Lugbara notions as to the character-istics of *jųrų* and people beyond them.

THE OPERATION OF THE SYSTEM

Relations beyond the family cluster are outside the control of the elder, who is concerned primarily with the ordering of relations within this group, which are seen in terms of personal kinship. He will, however, initiate hostile or other action against other groups, and he may decide to try to bring hostile relations to an end. Social activities—those of fighting, intermarriage and ritual collaboration—and the relations of which they are part between family clusters are expressed as relations between lineages and sub-clans, of varying span or level of segmentation. This level, in any particular situation, need not be the same in every part of Lugbara, nor may it be the same even within the same tribe; and it may vary, of course, over time in a given tribe. As I have said, Lugbara discuss these relations in terms of the concepts *o'd̨p̨* and *j̨ur̨u*, by which deviations from an ideal pattern of relations can be accepted.

In the traditional system relations between groups beyond immediate neighbours are in terms of fighting.[1] The nature of fighting, and the means to end it and the type of reparation to settle the dispute vary with the social distance between the parties, expressed in lineage distance. Fighting, *a'd̨*, occurs between groups which do not share the same or sufficiently closely related ghosts. Although they may have common ancestry the ghosts in their shrines are said to be too far back to affect their living descendants by bringing sickness if they quarrel among themselves. This is not to say that they may not have shrines to the same ghosts, nor that they may not send representatives to one another's sacrifices, nor that common ancestry may not be invoked to validate other relations than those of fighting between them.

Political relations are essentially local relations, and in Lugbara the local group and the descent group are not coincident, although closely associated. Relations between the former are

---

[1] Inter-group fighting no longer occurs: it may break out but is quickly suppressed by the Government-appointed chiefs. The last feud of which I have knowledge and which lasted for several weeks took place in the late 1920s. But Lugbara still discuss intergroup relations largely in terms of fighting, and compensation and reparation for injuries are still much as they ever were but are exacted by the courts instead of by self-help. I use the present tense in discussing fighting.

seen in terms of those between the latter. Reversion to the use of
weapons is the antithesis of kinship, and also that of close
neighbourly relations, which are to a large extent modelled on
those of kinship. The closer the kin or neighbours the more destructive the use of force; relations between them are instead
controlled to a large extent by other means, those to do with
various types of mystically caused sickness. This may be from
one of several processes: ghost invocation by the elders of family
clusters against their dependants; ghostly vengeance brought by
ghosts themselves without the intervention of living elders;
cursing between non-agnatic kin for breaches of personal kinship ties; witchcraft between neighbours; the public complaint
against a man that results in his becoming sick through 'the
words of people'; all these together form a single system of
mystical sanctions that maintain orderly relations between kin
and neighbours within the range of community based on the
minor or major segment. It is only above this range that
organized force is really important and that religious sanctions
play a lesser part. The bringing of sickness by the ghosts, with
or without the intervention of the elders, results in sacrifice to
the ghosts responsible. Ghosts bring sickness as a result of behaviour that is considered to be detrimental to social relations
within the kin group. Elders can invoke the ghosts against their
own dependants within the family cluster and ghosts may themselves bring sickness for misdemeanour both within the cluster
and on the part of elders one against the other within the major
lineage, the widest group with common ghosts. The significant
aspect of these processes in this context is that sickness is brought
for breaches of kin-group solidarity and that it is cured by
promise of sacrifice. At the sacrifice representatives of the major
lineage, and often of the whole sub-clan and even clan, gather
together to share the meat and to bless the victim to show that
they have no grudges in their hearts and that they consider the
wellbeing of the group to have been restored satisfactorily.

Groups that attend one another's sacrifices are *enyati* to one
another. *Enyati* means 'eaters together' and the essential part of
being members of a ritual congregation is the sharing of the
sacrificial meat according to the pattern of lineage segmentation. The group that gives the actual sacrifice and calls its
enyati is the minimal lineage headed by an elder. Such a group's

enyatị consist of its co-ordinate lineages in the minor lineage and of other minor lineages, as units, of the major lineage. The lineages act as units in that they each send only a single representative, the senior elder. It also calls the accessory lineages of its minor and often major section, so that all minimal lineages, host and accessory, of the widest segment called *ori'ba* attend. The emphasis is on ties of community, the section, rather than on agnatic ties only, since of course accessory lineages are of different agnatic ancestry. *Enyatị* come together as a community, in consequence of an offence against community relations. The community is based upon an agnatic lineage and so these offences are usually conceived in terms of offences against lineage values. Members of different local communities, even of different tribes since agnatically related lineages of other tribes may attend if within visiting distance, are members of the same ritual congregations. By attendance at sacrifices, which is compulsory, they meet not only to show their unity in terms of shared lineage values but also of shared community values, acceptance of which is incompatible with mutual hostility.

Force, socially approved and exercised according to certain accepted rules, is a sanction for relations between groups whose agnatic relationship is non-existent or too distant to be relevant in a given situation. The nature of fighting and the means by which it is controlled vary with the lineage distance between the groups. Whatever the actual level of segmentation of lineage concerned in any situation in any tribe, we may distinguish three levels of lineage relationship, each associated with certain activities and values. First is that of the minimal segment, the nuclear group, the family cluster and the elder. Above this is the level of, typically, the major segment, marked by being the limit of the use of interpersonal kinship terms, of true incest and fratricide, and which is the main political unit in the sense it is the feud unit, feud occurring between these units and rarely within them; and above this in turn, that of the tribe, the grouping based on the widest agnatic descent group that provides an organizing core to a local group, the unit within which there is accepted the necessity for discussion between quarrelling segments but beyond which this necessity is not accepted.

The major section marks the range of the recognition of personal kinship ties between members; within it incest is a sin and its occurrence is not humanly punished but the ghosts are left to send punishment by sickness if they so desire. It is the limit of what we may call ties of close neighbourhood and marks the range of most accusations of witchcraft: that is to say, within this range hostility takes the form of accusations of witchcraft rather than being actualized in fighting.

Within the major section fighting rarely occurs. Within the minor section fighting with weapons—arrows and spears—is a sin, and quarrels at this range are with fists or sticks only. They arise for personal reasons which do not affect the interests of a group *vis-à-vis* other groups and are soon stopped by onlookers. It is thought inconceivable that a man should deliberately and cold-bloodedly use weapons against a man of his own minor lineage, since they are close 'brothers'. When it does occur it seems always to be the result of drunkenness. It is a sin for which there is no response in terms of violence, no punishment or vengeance by the victim's family. There are no cleansing rites for a fratricide: he destroys the bonds of siblingship and they cannot be repaired. He inherits his victim's widows and gives a bull to the victim's mother's brother. The beast is not bloodwealth and is eaten and not placed in the herd. Beyond the minor lineage but within the major segment much the same applies, except that compensation is payable for homicide—it is, however, extremely rare. The killer does not inherit his victim's widows, since the ties of brotherhood between them are weaker. This range is at the borderline between interpersonal and intergroup relations and it would seem that the response to homicide depends largely upon the closeness of the bond between the individuals concerned and on the recentness of segmentation of their respective lineages. We may say that if compensation for homicide is paid then the offence is a crime; if not, it is a sin. The change in category occurs between minor and major segment.

A group fights with weapons against those other groups which in this situation it calls *jụrụ*: this is *a'dị*, intergroup fighting as opposed to individual duelling. *Jụrụ* in this context are usually beyond the minor lineage, certainly beyond the major lineage, and include both host and accessory lineages. Within the major lineage it is rare for fighting to start with weapons. But retaliation for homicide is considered permissible and right if the killer and his victim are of different minor lineages. Or the killer may give compensation of two bulls and two cows to his victim's sons 'to get wives with', and another bull to the mother's brother also. Beyond the major lineage no bloodwealth is payable but retaliation will be made. The situation is now of a different order. The hostilities are between *suru* and not between *orĭ'ba* and the ritual content of the relationship is absent. A man who kills another outside his own major lineage formally and cere-moniously rejoices and is ritually cleansed 'to drive away the blood'. If this is not done he will die of sickness due to his victim's anger, since at this range compensation is not paid.

Within the tribe prolonged or widespread fighting may result in disruption of everyday social relations and is also in contra-diction to ideal ties of clanship, and it is recognized that this fighting should be settled by discussion. It continues until each side grows tired of killing and peace is then made by the senior elders of the major lineages concerned and as many elders closely related to the parties as can be found. The elders are all linked by the tie of their having custodianship of their respec-tive lineage shrines, which emphasizes that their relationship is one of 'brothers', even if genealogically they are of different generation. They are all elders of extant family clusters and so equal in that sense. There is no set mechanism for them to talk peacefully. The senior elders of the major lineages involved use their powers to persuade the parties to cease fighting, but they can do very little until the parties have each considered that further fighting is wasteful of their men and they are ready to welcome the end of hostilities. They then decide not to take weapons with them to the fields in the daytime. That is, fighting is usually brought to a close when it begins to interfere with farming activities. A group will not attack unarmed men of its own or even neighbouring tribes, although of course unarmed strangers are fair game. The elders may jointly curse the parties if they continue to fight. A boundary is drawn between them over which armed men cannot cross until the affair is settled by discussion, in which elders not immediately involved take no part. The curse involves the ghosts, in that they are asked to bring sickness to anyone who disobeys. The ghosts are those of the ancestors of a single sub-clan and so may be expected to have a common interest in ensuring peace among their descendants.

Payment of compensation is made within the tribe but not beyond it.

If, however, the fighting groups belong to different tribes this does not occur and they continue to fight until the matter has been settled by intervention of a third party or forgotten after the original dispute has been closed by individual reparation by the original offenders. Violence between tribes is significant in certain situations only. Groups not directly involved carry on normal social intercourse, and since the groups are all very small in size a state of hostility does not affect intertribal relations to any great extent, once the initial fighting is over—usually a few days only. It is the minimal sections only which are primarily involved. Hostile groups may have members who are simultaneously uterine kin and enemies. In these situations *jµrµ* can include groups related to a family cluster as one of its member's wife's or mother's kin. Such people try not to be involved personally in the fighting, since it is a sin to kill a close kinsman. Their position is ambivalent and difficult, but they are able to maintain contact and act as go-betweens to bring fighting to a close, although there is no institutionalized way for them to do so. Women also may act as intermediaries.

In northern Lugbara the situation is rather different. There fighting within the tribe can be stopped by the rainmaker, *opiezo*. This functionary is unique to north Lugbara tribes, near the Kakwa and Madi, both of which have rainmakers. He is the senior member of the senior line of the senior major lineage of the sub-clan. Rainmakers of different tribes are 'like brothers' and have important ritual and rudimentary political powers. The rainmaker calls people together after a lull in the fighting, wearing a cattle-skin, and forbids further strife. His words carry the force of a curse and in some areas his person is a sanctuary for shelter of an evildoer, whose case can then be put to mediation by the rainmaker rather than be closed by the summary killing of the offender.

More widespread are functionaries called *'ba rµkµza*, 'men whose names are known'. They are men who are important because of their character, influence and usually their wealth; they attract dependants and are 'like the great trees in the forest' against which lesser trees lean for support. They may also curse combatants in the feud, act as sanctuary and as mediator. They may carry white staves as a mark of status. They are not attached to the lineage system and the status is not formally hereditary. Their distribution is more haphazard than that of rainmakers, but there are rarely more than one to a tribe. Some have a wide influence spreading over several tribes. Today much of their influence has been usurped by Government-appointed chiefs.

At one time prophets were important in Lugbara. They appeared first about 1895 and later about 1910. In both phases two Kakwa entered Lugbara bringing with them water with magical properties. They quickly gathered adherents who drank the water in order to ward off epidemic sickness. A cult sprang up, known as *Yakan* or *Dede*, its expressed aim being to 'bring fighting to an end' and to establish—or re-establish—the rule of peace and order. The two prophets travelled through north and central Lugbara setting up local leaders of the cult, who administered the water. It soon became the centre of anti-European sentiment, and its spread culminated in the *Yakan* revolt of 1919. It was believed that adherents were invincible to European bullets. After the defeat of the revolt the cult declined in importance. At its height its leaders, who were one to each tribe, seem largely to have superseded the rainmakers and 'men whose names are known'; in fact many of the latter and most of the Government-appointed chiefs joined the cult themselves. The distribution of its officers was closely related to the political structure, and from 1914 or so until 1919 it seems to have had an important political function.

THE·SYSTEM TODAY

Today intergroup fighting is prevented by the Government, through its agents the chiefs. The Belgians began nominal administration in 1900 and appointed a few chiefs, principally as collectors of cattle for levy, from local men of wealth and prestige, many of whom were adherents of the *Yakan* cult. Since then more chiefs have been created and today there is a system of County and sub-County chiefdoms in both the Uganda and the Congo parts of the area. They are almost all much greater in size than any indigenous groupings. Beneath these chiefs are Parish headmen and Councillors. Generally the unit under a headman is either a tribe or a major section. Headmen's principal duties are to act as the means by which disputes are brought to chiefs' courts. They sift cases and act as canalizers of hostility that would traditionally have broken out between groups over such matters as bridewealth and land disputes. Formerly a man would have taken direct action against the other party to a dispute and would have been supported in any retaliatory action by his own group: there was then a state of intergroup fighting. The whole process was haphazard in outcome and slow—retaliation might not follow insult for weeks or months. Today the lower grade of officials, who are usually considered by the people to be of themselves (as opposed to the 'upstart' chiefs) and to be representatives of tribes and lesser sections, guide the retaliatory action of an individual direct to the original offender by taking the dispute to the chiefs' courts. The courts, under direct control of sub-chiefs and chiefs, arbitrate using Lugbara custom as a guide.[1] Compensation and reparation for traditional offences are judged by traditional standards and the chief's authority is a sanction for their being carried out. The important point is that the chiefs' courts are brought into the situation almost entirely in respect of cases which would formerly have led to the use of organized physical force, a'dí. These include cases over bridewealth, divorce, adultery, seduction, the theft of livestock, assault, damage to crops, and so on—and of course cases concerned only with modern administration such as tax evasion. The former are all disputes that arise between unrelated or only distantly related persons. The use of chiefs' courts is directly equivalent to the use of armed and organized violence between groups in the traditional system. Disputes that traditionally would not have been so settled rarely come to the chiefs' courts, and when they do public disapproval of their being so brought is often strong. As much use as ever seems to be made of the ghosts and other mystical means of bringing sickness to individuals who break or weaken orderly kinship and neighbourhood ties. The two sets of sanctions are kept distinct. In Lugbara the ghost cult and belief in the power of witches and the curses of kin have not been weakened by

1 Except for modern administrative offences for which there are officially defined punishments and for certain offences which can be tried only by District or higher courts; of these the most important is homicide.

modern structural changes, except that it is sometimes possible to circumvent their efficacy by the increased territorial-mobility. A young man can run away to southern Uganda as a labour migrant to escape the wrath of kin or ghosts. But his escape is only temporary: when he returns he enters into the system again and is liable to its sanctions.

CONCLUSION

In such a small-scale and fragmentary society such as the Lugbara it is impossible to isolate clearly a part of the total social system and call it 'political'. The way in which the use of organized and approved force shades off into the use of religious and other mystical sanctions is an indication of this. I have referred to the major section as the main political unit in that relations between it and other like segments are ultimately in terms of force; but inter-major segment relations cannot be understood without consideration of intra-major segment relations, which might strictly be called 'non-political'. I prefer to consider all intergroup relations, that is, relations between minimal segments or family clusters, as composing political relations.

The Lugbara political system, in this sense, has certain characteristics, as has total Lugbara society, which mark it off from others of not dissimilar type.

1. Lugbara areas have all a similar ecology, with wide cultural independence and variation and little social contact over a wide range. They are a sedentary people with in most areas a high density of population.

2. There is no political centralization. There is no wide-spread lineage system, although there is a widespread clan system—clans being units which are formally only large lineages—which is a means by which Lugbara conceive of themselves as a single society.

3. There is evidence in myth, genealogical tradition and the distribution of burial trees of a great deal of movement of territorial groups relative to one another, movement which still occurs. This is not transhumance but re-settlement of groups on new land. Land has no great social value, certainly no ritual value, despite the importance of the ghost cult. There were no

large-scale wars, only small-scale feuds which might result in territorial movement. But feud is an essential part of the political system.

4. The Lugbara political structure is characterized by highly independent and autonomous territorial groups which are conceived in terms of a segmentary agnatic lineage system. The independence of the wider groups, the tribes, is seen by the lack of any considerable intertribal links other than purely personal ties of mainly uterine kinship. Although it is known that there must be a remote genealogical connection between sub-clans and lineages of the same name, it is not recognized in institutionalized behaviour. There are no overlapping clan links of the type found in Tallensi, for example, although ritual congregations may include related lineages of different tribes if they are still living within easy walking distance.

5. Tribes, based on agnatic sub-clans, are the largest units that have political significance. Organized violence is the only sanction for intertribal relations. Since these small communities are more or less economically and ritually self-sufficient fighting does not seriously affect everyday relations, and is in any case limited to small segments of tribes.

6. Within the tribe unity is seen in terms of common descent from the sub-clan founder and of attachment to his descent line. The segmentary conception of society enables a balance to be maintained between constituent groups of the system (ultimately the countless family clusters, each with its elder); there are neither traditional chiefs nor any horizontal organization such as an age-set system cutting across these largely autonomous groups and wielding them into a whole. They are linked together by contiguity and by the relationship of the feud, which operates within a segmentary genealogical framework. Neighbouring groups are linked by the values and obligations of kinship; more remote groups are linked by the recognized antithesis of effective kinship, open violence. Violence is, however, disruptive, and the dogma of common descent provides a means of stopping fighting, by the curses of elders. And the fact that the agnatically related elders of a sub-clan meet together as members of common ritual congregations ensures that unsettled disputes and grudges within the sub-clan cannot persist for very long.

7. Rainmakers and 'men whose names are known' have rudimentary political authority. Like the Nuer leopard-skin chief they provide a mechanism for the peaceful settlement of disputes when the parties immediately involved are ready to do so. Neither are 'chiefs' in any real sense.

8. Within the major segment, more or less coterminous with the close community of everyday neighbourly life, relations are sanctioned by the ghost cult and other mystical sanctions. Minimal and minor sections, even though not agnatic but cognatic clusters, are single ritual units. Within the minimal segment the elder holds strong authority by his power to invoke the ghosts against his dependants. Leadership between these groups, between elders, is provided by the ritual seniority of the senior elder, expressed in his power of ritual representation—he has no other authority.

ACKNOWLEDGMENTS

Fieldwork research among the Lugbara was carried out for most of the period between December 1949 and March 1952, and was financed by grants from the Worshipful Company of Goldsmiths and the Colonial Social Science Research Council. Writing up of the material has been made possible by a grant from the Wenner-Gren Foundation for Anthropological Research, New York. I wish to express my gratitude to these bodies for their generosity and encouragement.

BIBLIOGRAPHY

BAXTER, P. T. W., and BUTT, A. 1953. *The Azande and related peoples of the Anglo-Egyptian Sudan and Belgian Congo*, London.

MIDDLETON, J. 1953. 'Some social aspects of Lugbara myth', *Africa*, xxiv, 3.

TUCKER, A. N. 1940. *The Eastern Sudanic Languages*, Oxford.

INDEX

INDEX

'Leopard-skin chief', 16, 131, 133, 164 229

Levirate, 212

Lineages, 3ff, 9, 11, 14f, 18, 20, 26; Amba, 140, 143, 149, 152f, 155ff, 162; Dinka, 105, 112f, 126, 128ff, 133; Konkomba, 22f, 168, 175, 179, 181f, 192ff, 199; Lugbara, 205f, 209ff, 216, 220f; Mandari, 73f, 85f, 90; Tiv, 37ff, 52, 62

Lineages and territorial organization, 5, 12, 14, 28; Amba, 140, 155f, 162; Dinka, 105ff, 111ff, 124ff, 128ff, 132ff; Lugbara, 208ff, 219, 228; Mandari, 93f; Tiv, 35, 40f, 42ff, 51, 64f

Lineage structures, 3ff, 7, 14, 16, 21ff, 27; Dinka, 126ff, 133; Konkomba, 168, 192, 194ff, 201; Lugbara, 208ff, 216, 218, 221f; Mandari, 74, 93; Tiv, 34f, 37, 42ff, 64ff

Lugbara, 1, 9, 11, 12, 13, 14, 15, 17, 18, 19, 20n, 24, 28, 71, 203–229

Luo, 68n, 102, 107, 108

Madi, 15, 18, 203, 224

Magic, 54, 62

Mandari, 1, 9, 11, 14, 15, 17n, 18, 67–96; Bora clan of, 11, 70, 72, 75f, 93, 95

Markets, Konkomba, 169, 179f, 183f, 195; Lugbara, 215; Tiv, 35, 49, 57, 59, 62ff, 65

Marriage, 6; Amba, 139f, 149, 154, 157, 161; Dinka, 112f, 118n; Konkomba, 167, 180, 200; Lugbara, 206f, 213, 216, 219; Mandari, 73, 76, 78, 82, 86f; Tiv, 33, 39, 65

Migration, 9, 12; Amba, 138; Dinka, 114f, 132; Lugbara, 206; Mandari, 69f; Tiv, 40, 46

Military organization, 47, 118, 132f

Mobility, 5, 12; Dinka, 114, 130, 132; Lugbara, 206, 227; Mandari, 73, 86f

Moots, Tiv, 54ff, 65

Mortuary rites, 84, 152

Moru, 67, 71, 78n, 94

Mythology, 16f, 26f; Konkomba, 178f; Lugbara, 204, 209, 218, 227; Mandari, 68ff, 75

Nilo-Hamites, 3, 67

Nilotes, 67, 92f, 97

Nuba, 10

Nuclear group, 8, 10, 14, 19, 25

Nuer, 9n, 12, 13, 14, 15, 16, 18, 20n, 24, 28, 93, 126, 129, 187, 229; and Dinka, 97, 99, 100, 101, 102, 103n, 104n, 106, 127ff, 132ff

Nyangwara, 67, 71, 92

Nyefu, 67n

Opposition, of groups, 2, 6f, 42f, 46f, 114

Pastoralism, 21n, 67, 69f, 98, 117, 128

Peacemaking, 9, 20, 22; Dinka, 116, 120f, 125n, 131; Lugbara, 223; Tiv, 39, 42, 46, 58, 62

Peace treaties, 47, 61f

Political systems, 1ff

Political units, 4, 7f, 14f, 21; Amba, 125, 155f; Dinka, 103f, 106, 113, 116ff, 126ff, 129; Konkomba, 177, 201; Lugbara, 204, 213, 221, 227; Mandari, 71ff, 95; Tiv, 38ff, 41ff, 64f

Polygyny, 111, 204

Population, 9, 18, 25; Amba, 136, 138; Dinka, 29n, 97, 99, 102f, 104, 121, 134; Konkomba, 167; Lugbara, 203, 227; Mandari, 68, 71; Tiv, 33, 134n

Property, 4, 19, 28, 191

Prophets, 18, 131, 225

Purification, ritual, 23, 184f, 189, 222f

Pygmies, 137, 155

Radcliffe-Brown, A. R., 21, 186

Rainmakers, 18, 70f, 83, 224f, 229

Religion, 22f; Dinka, 103, 131; Mandari, 71, 76, 79f, 83, 95; see also Cult, Ritual, Sacrifice

Residence at marriage, 25, 73

Ritual, 6, 13, 22ff; Dinka, 118f; Konkomba, 171, 179f, 184ff, 193, 195f; Lugbara, 207, 217; Mandari, 70f, 78, 83, 88; —collaboration, 15, 27, 219ff, 228, see also Cult

Sacrifice, 22ff, 26; Amba, 144; Konkomba, 171, 173, 175, 183, 185f, 190; Lugbara, 210n, 220f

Sanctions, social, 16, 19, 25; Amba, 144; Konkomba, 186ff, 193; Lugbara, 205, 217, 220, 226, 228; Tiv, 57

INDEX

Sanctuary, 22, 224

Seagle, W., 187

'Section', Dinka, 103, 113, 122ff; Lugbara, 208

Segmentary systems, 7f, 12ff, 24ff

Segmentation, 4, 6f, 8n, 21, 25; Amba, 162f; Dinka, 104f, 112, 114f, 116ff, 123f, 128f, 132, 134; Konkomba, 172f, 177, 181, 186, 192, 194f, 200f; Lugbara, 207f, 218, 220, 228; Mandari, 74f, 78, 93; Tiv, 33, 38ff, 42ff, 50, 64f; orders of lineage, 38ff, 105, 195, 208

Seligman, C. G. and B. Z., 102, 118n

Sera, 67n, 68, 75, 92

Settlement pattern, 4; Amba, 139ff; Dinka, 98ff, 110, 115, 129; Lugbara, 204ff; Mandari, 68, 71f, 80, 89ff; Tiv, 34, 52ff; see also Territorial organization

Shilluk, 93

Shrines, 183, 205, 211, 219, 223; see also Cult, Ritual, Sacrifice

Slavery, 38, 45, 50f, 54, 108

Social control, 16, 20f, 48, 52ff, 185ff, 207, 221ff, 226; see also Law, Sanctions

Social relations, field of, 10, 164, 213ff, 221f

Society, concept of, 27, 92f, 106f, 114ff, 120ff, 127f, 132, 227f; range of, 27f, 134, 165

'Sons', in Dinka lineage structure, 120ff

Sorcery, 189

States, 2, 4, 15n, 19

'Strangers', absorption of, 15, 18; Amba, 141, 148; Dinka, 133f; Lugbara, 205, 210; Mandari, 72, 74, 76, 78, 80f, 85f; Tiv, 40, 42ff

Stratification, social, 51, 93, 105, 119, 130, 133

Subclan, Dinka, 105, 110, 112ff, 116, 121ff, 126, 129f; Lugbara, 209, 211, 216, 218, 220, 228

Subtribe, Dinka, 103f, 110, 116ff, 120f, 123, 126, 130

'Symbiosis', 18, 105, 119, 131, 133, 171

Tallensi, 9, 13, 17, 20n, 28, 154n, 166, 228

Territorial organization, 5, 15; Amba, 139ff; Dinka, 102ff, 109ff; 115ff, 121ff, 129f, 132f; Konkomba, 167f, 170ff, 177, 199; Lugbara, 204, 207ff, 228; Mandari, 71ff, 92ff; Tiv, 35, 40ff, 46, 51, 64f

Theft, 41, 50, 191

Tiv, 1, 9, 10, 12, 21n, 22, 24, 28, 33–66

Toro, 137, 138, 146, 158

Totemism, 4, 104, 121, 123, 178

Transhumance, 89ff, 99ff, 116f, 132f, 204, 227

Trees, burial, 206, 227; council, 81; market, 183

'Tribe', Dinka, 102, 104f, 109f, 113, 116ff, 120, 128; Konkomba, 167f; Lugbara, 207f, 211, 223f, 226, 228; Tiv, 35

'Tribal group', Dinka, 108ff, 128f

Tribute, Mandari, 82

Udam, 33, 46

Vengeance, 19, 117n, 147ff

Village, Amba, 138ff, 143ff, 148, 152f, 155ff, 158, 162

Warfare, 6, 16, 19ff; Amba, 138, 145ff, 151, 155, 157, 159f; Dinka, 118; Konkomba, 168, 186, 201; Lugbara, 203, 205f, 208, 216, 224, 228; Mandari, 80ff, 89, 94; Tiv, 41, 45ff, 58, 65; see also Feud, Fighting

Wealth, differences in, 4, 53f, 63, 82, 224, 229

Wilson, G., 187

Witchcraft, 20; Amba, 144, 152f, 160; Konkomba, 187; Lugbara, 206, 220, 222, 226; Mandari, 86f; Tiv, 22, 24, 52, 54ff, 59f

Yakan cult, Lugbara, 18, 225

Yakö, 3, 10

Yoruba, 4, 183, 191